ENCHANTING FAIRIES

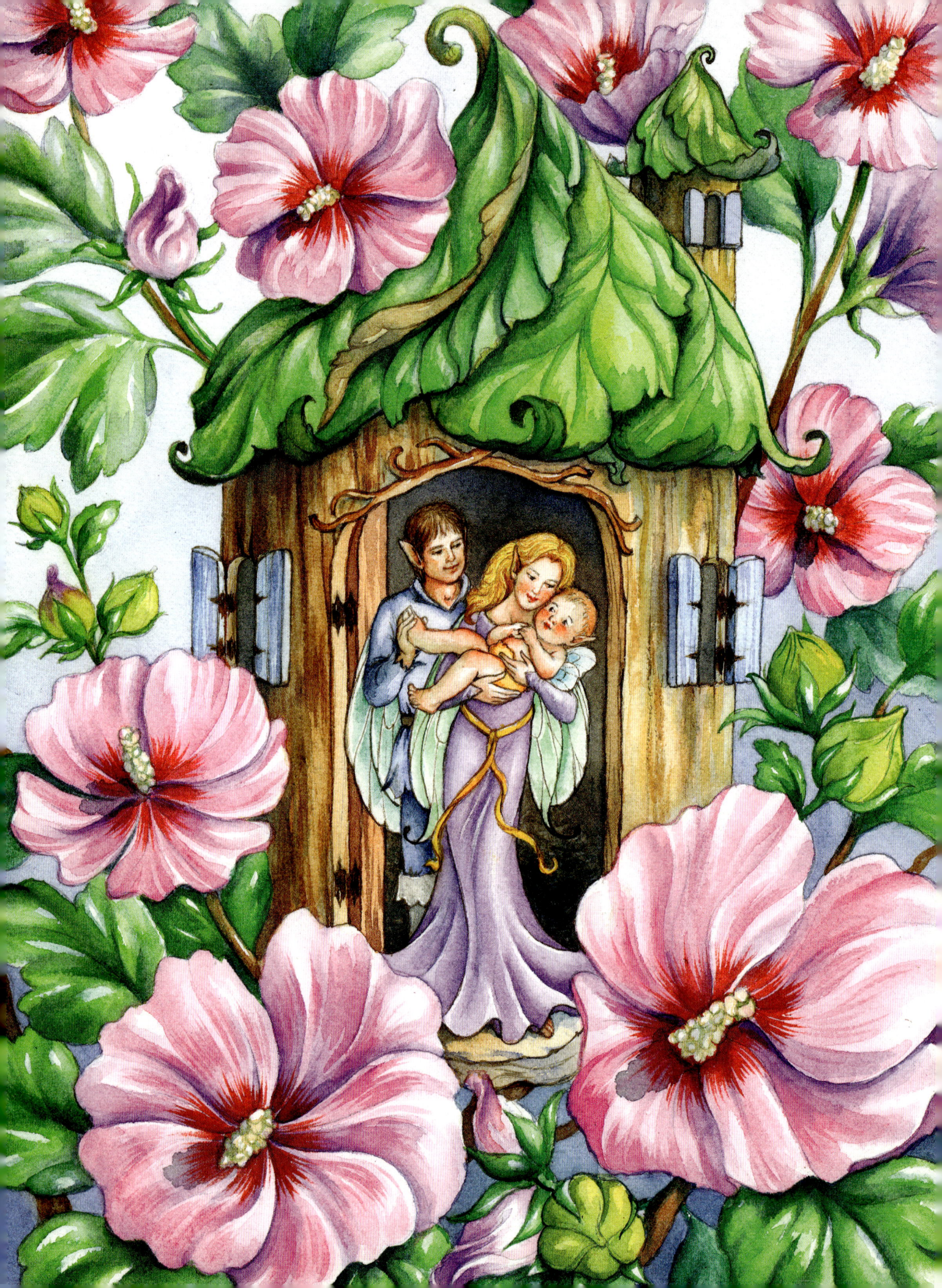

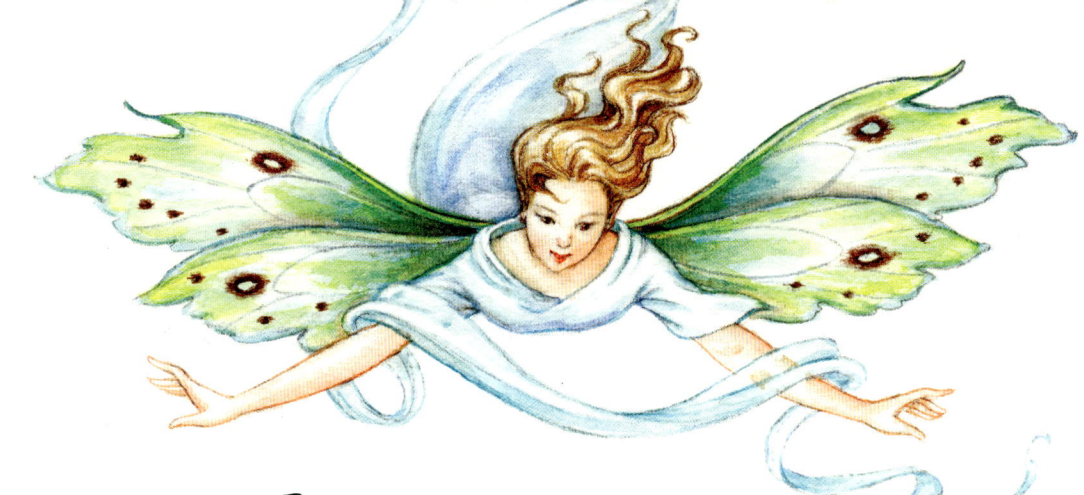

# Enchanting FAIRIES

## HOW TO PAINT CHARMING FAIRIES AND FLOWERS

BARBARA LANZA

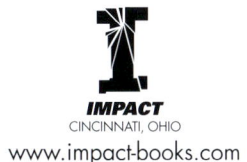

CINCINNATI, OHIO
www.impact-books.com

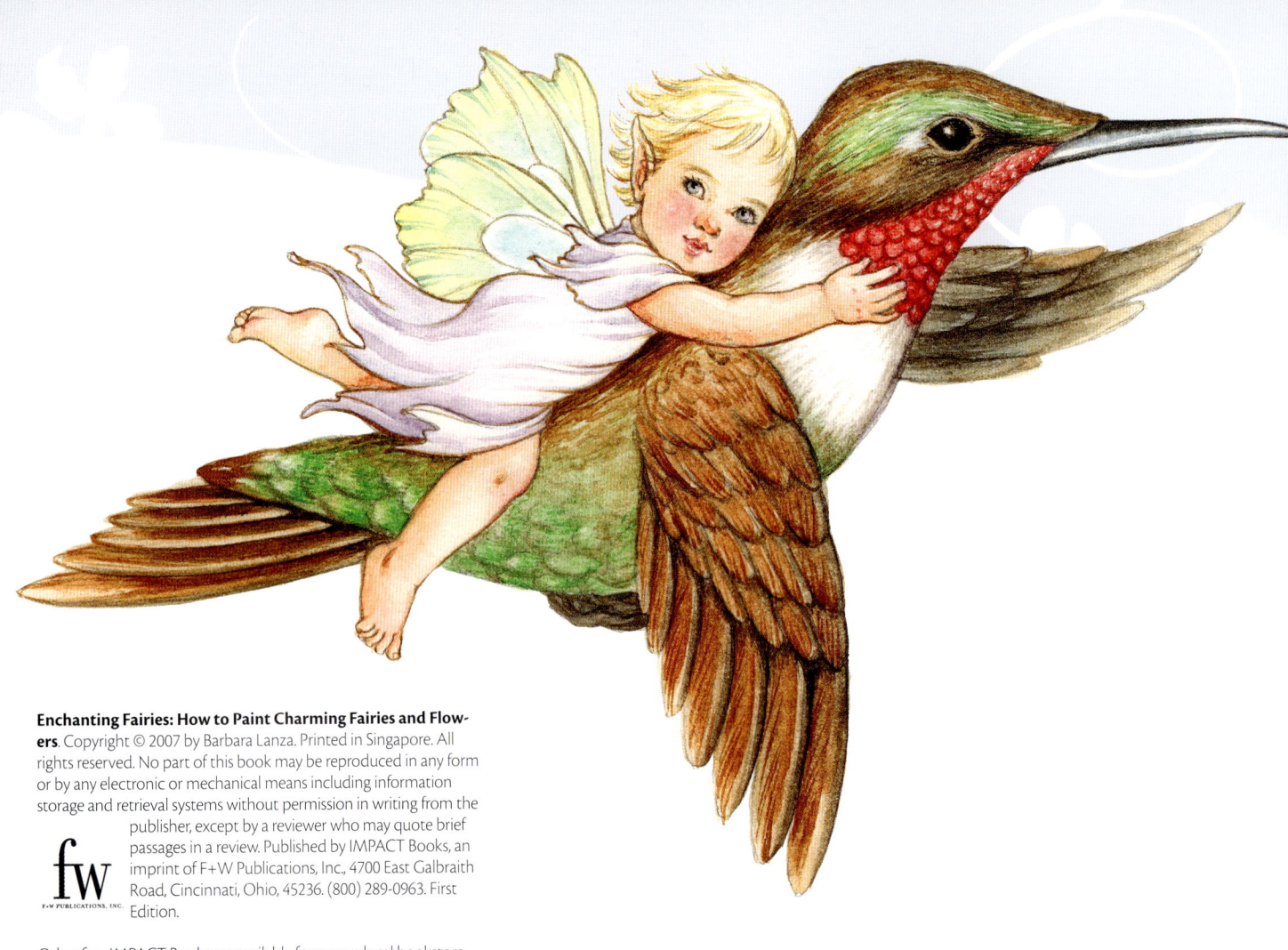

**Enchanting Fairies: How to Paint Charming Fairies and Flowers**. Copyright © 2007 by Barbara Lanza. Printed in Singapore. All rights reserved. No part of this book may be reproduced in any form or by any electronic or mechanical means including information storage and retrieval systems without permission in writing from the publisher, except by a reviewer who may quote brief passages in a review. Published by IMPACT Books, an imprint of F+W Publications, Inc., 4700 East Galbraith Road, Cincinnati, Ohio, 45236. (800) 289-0963. First Edition.

Other fine IMPACT Books are available from your local bookstore, art supply store or direct from the publisher.

11  10  09      5  4

DISTRIBUTED IN CANADA BY FRASER DIRECT
100 Armstrong Avenue
Georgetown, ON, Canada  L7G 5S4
Tel: (905) 877-4411

DISTRIBUTED IN THE U.K. AND EUROPE BY DAVID & CHARLES
Brunel House, Newton Abbot, Devon, TQ12 4PU, England
Tel: (+44) 1626 323200, Fax: (+44) 1626 323319
Email: postmaster@davidandcharles.co.uk

DISTRIBUTED IN AUSTRALIA BY CAPRICORN LINK
P.O. Box 704, S. Windsor NSW, 2756 Australia
Tel: (02) 4577-3555

**Library of Congress Cataloging in Publication Data**
Lanza, Barbara.
 Enchanting fairies : how to paint charming fairies and flowers / Barbara Lanza. -- 1st ed.
    p. cm.
 Includes index.
 ISBN-13: 978-1-58180-956-5 (pbk : alk. paper)
 ISBN-10: 1-58180-956-5 (pbk : alk. paper)
 1. Fairies in art. 2. Flowers in art. 3. Painting--Technique. I. Title.
 ND1460.F32L36 2007
 751.42'247--dc22                                             2007001672

Edited by Kelly C. Messerly and Amanda Wheeler
Designed by Wendy Dunning
Page layout by Terri Woesner
Production coordinated by Matt Wagner

### METRIC CONVERSION CHART

| To convert | to | multiply by |
|---|---|---|
| Inches | Centimeters | 2.54 |
| Centimeters | Inches | 0.4 |
| Feet | Centimeters | 30.5 |
| Centimeters | Feet | 0.03 |
| Yards | Meters | 0.9 |
| Meters | Yards | 1.1 |

## About the Author

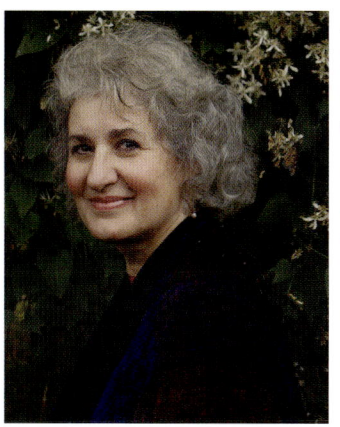

Barbara Lanza has been imagining fairy worlds since she was a child on the resort island of Wildwood, New Jersey. Encouraged to develop her artistic talent, she graduated from the Philadelphia College of Art, then moved to New York City. There, she began her career as a fashion illustrator, moving gradually into the fields of children's book illustration, collectible, doll, stationery and textile design.

Using graceful drawing and charming imagery, Lanza has illustrated children's books of everyday family life, holiday activities of forest animals, and classic fairytales for Little Golden Books, Scholastic/Cartwheel and Viking. These themes were blended into a picture book she wrote and illustrated entitled *Time To Fly, A Fairy Lane Book*. It is published by Moo Press, a division of Keene Publishing.

Along with her children Emily and Dan, Barbara and Jerry Kalogeratos live with a dog and two cats in Orange County, New York.

## Dedication

This book is dedicated to the best teachers of my life, Lena Lanza, my mother, who carried the books I've illustrated in her purse, and my father, Edward Lanza, who instilled in me a love of nature.

## Acknowledgments

A shower of fragrant petals on the following:

Jane Maday, you are as generous as you are talented. Thank you for the recommendation.

Pam Wissman, thank you for your conviction that my approach to painting fairies would be helpful to other artists. This book could not have happened without you.

Kelly Messerly, your fairylike voice lifted me out of moments of doubt and frustration, and your keen guidance and expertise kept me on course—no easy feat. I am so grateful.

Ruth Preston and Wendy Dunning, thank you for pulling it all together and making the pages flow.

Jerry Kalogeratos, thank you for your love and support, and for using your expertise in taking the photographs for this page and the materials pages.

And Emily, Dan and Ashley, thank you for posing patiently.

# TABLE OF CONTENTS

*Introduction*   9

SECTION 1
## Fairy Faces & Figures   22

SECTION 2
## Fairy Types   44

SECTION 3
## The Realm of Fairies   110

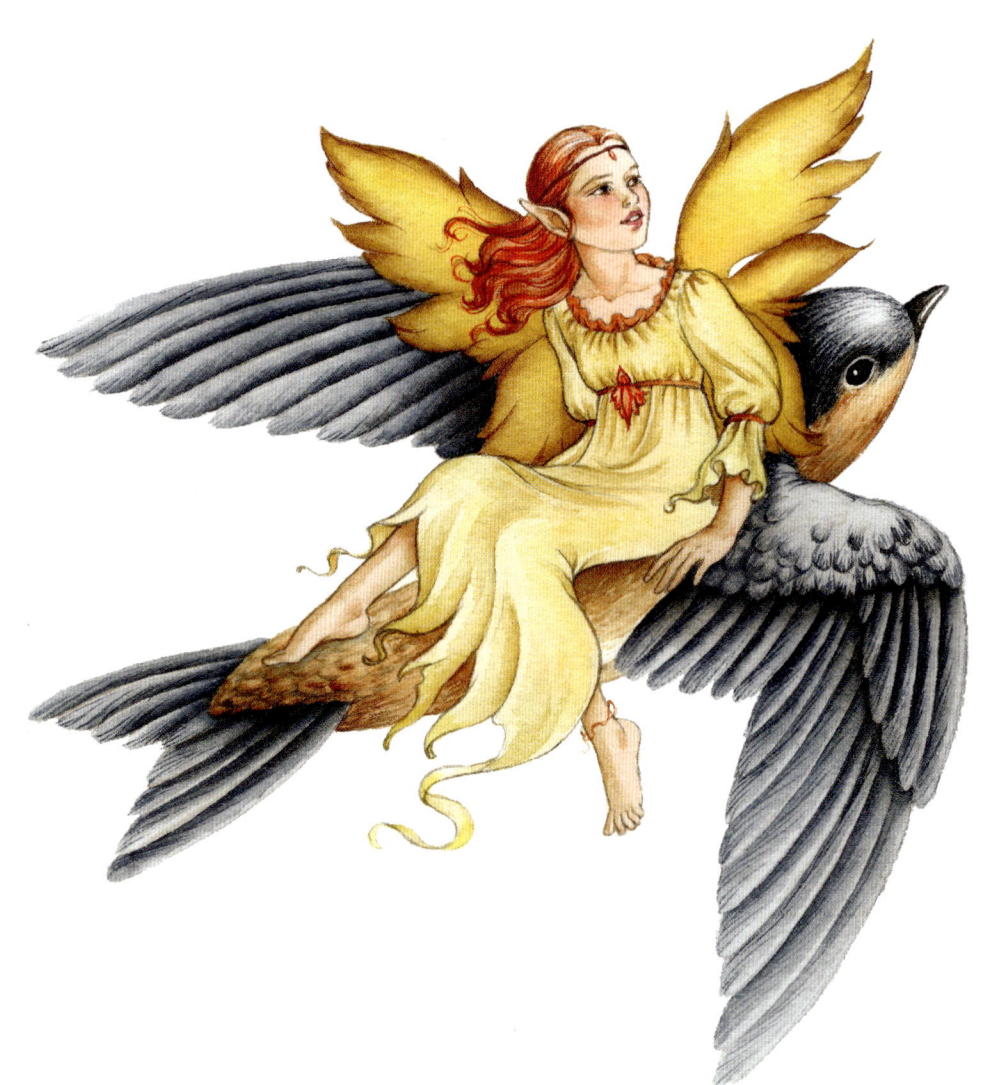

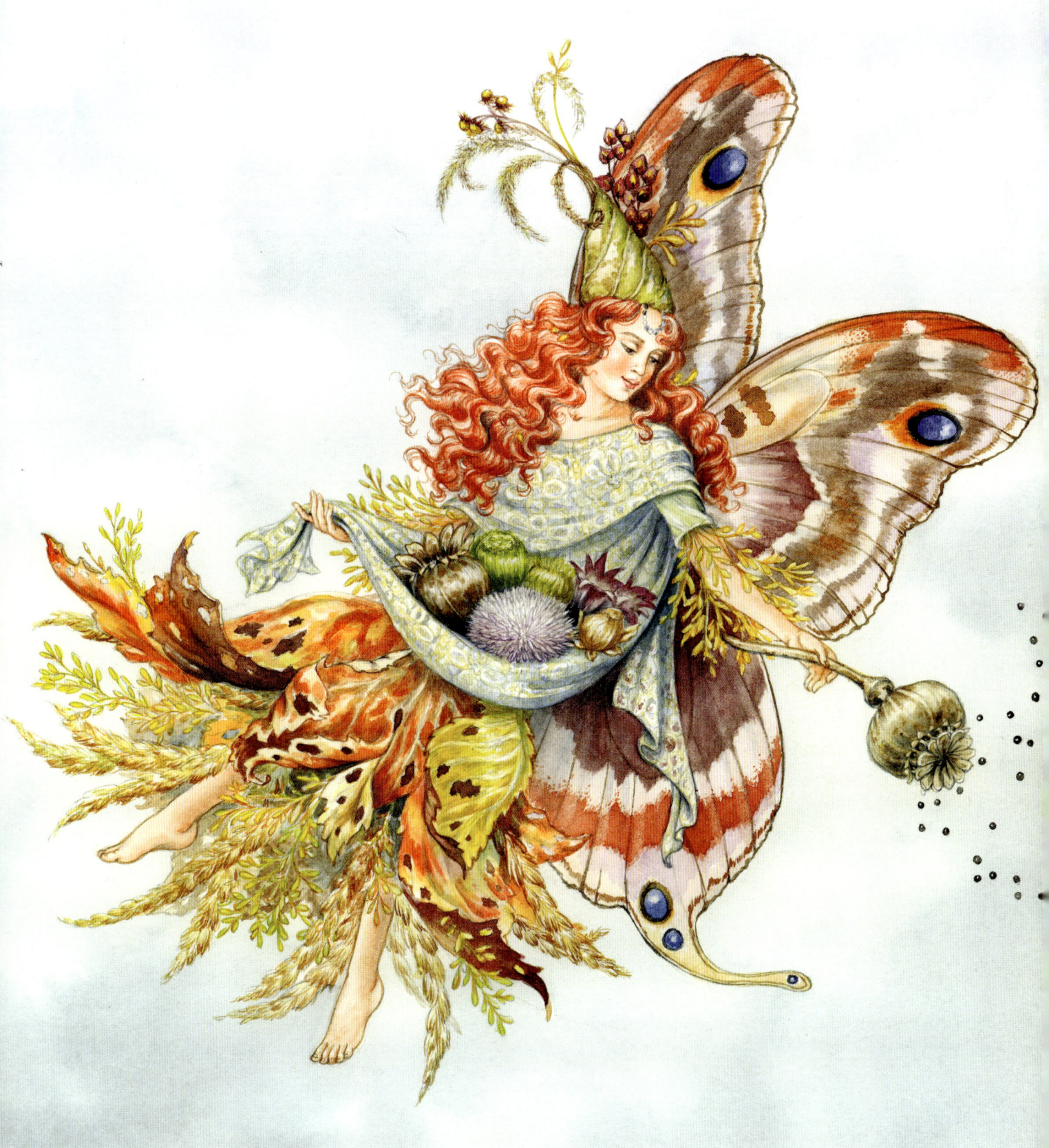

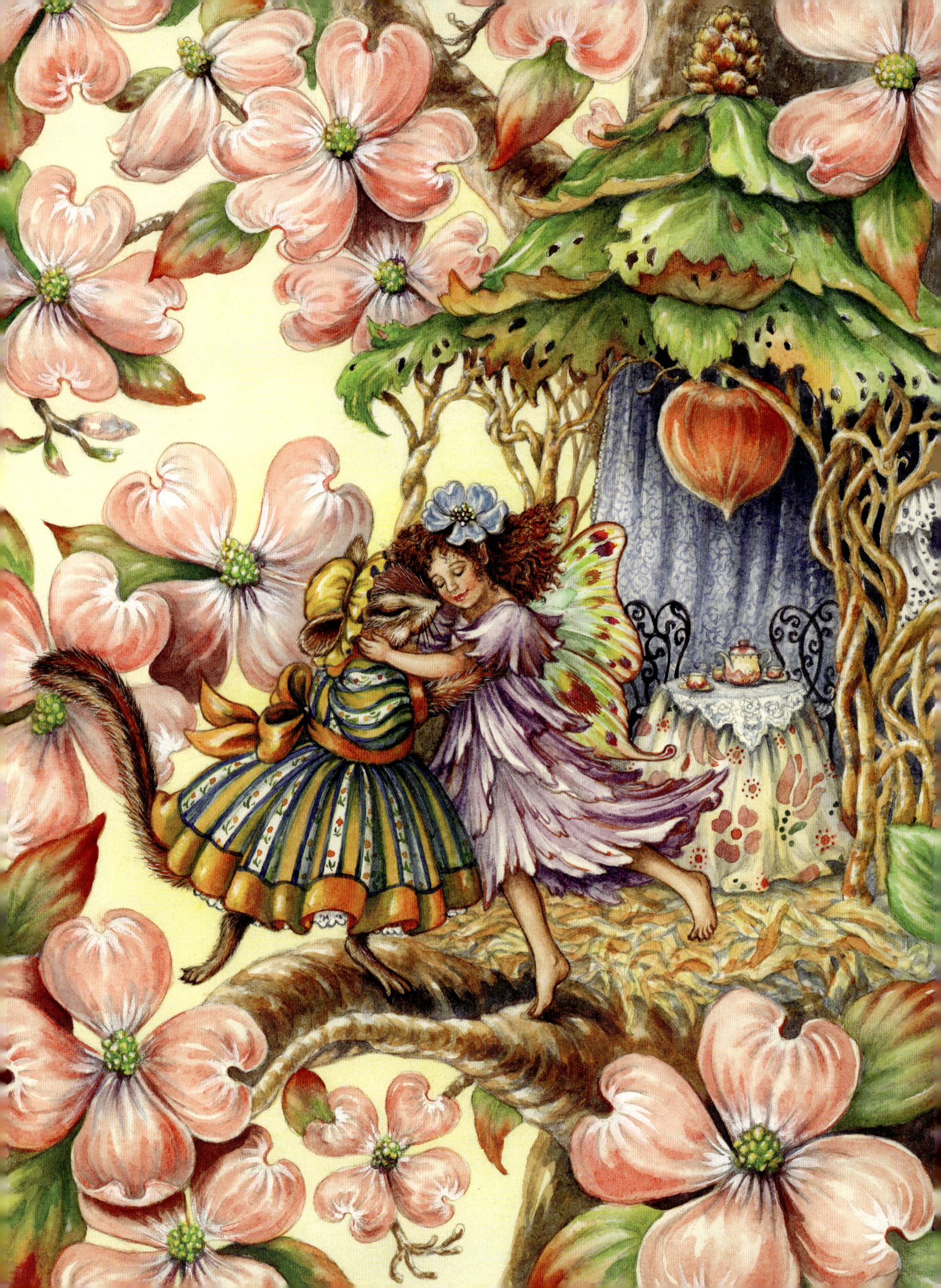

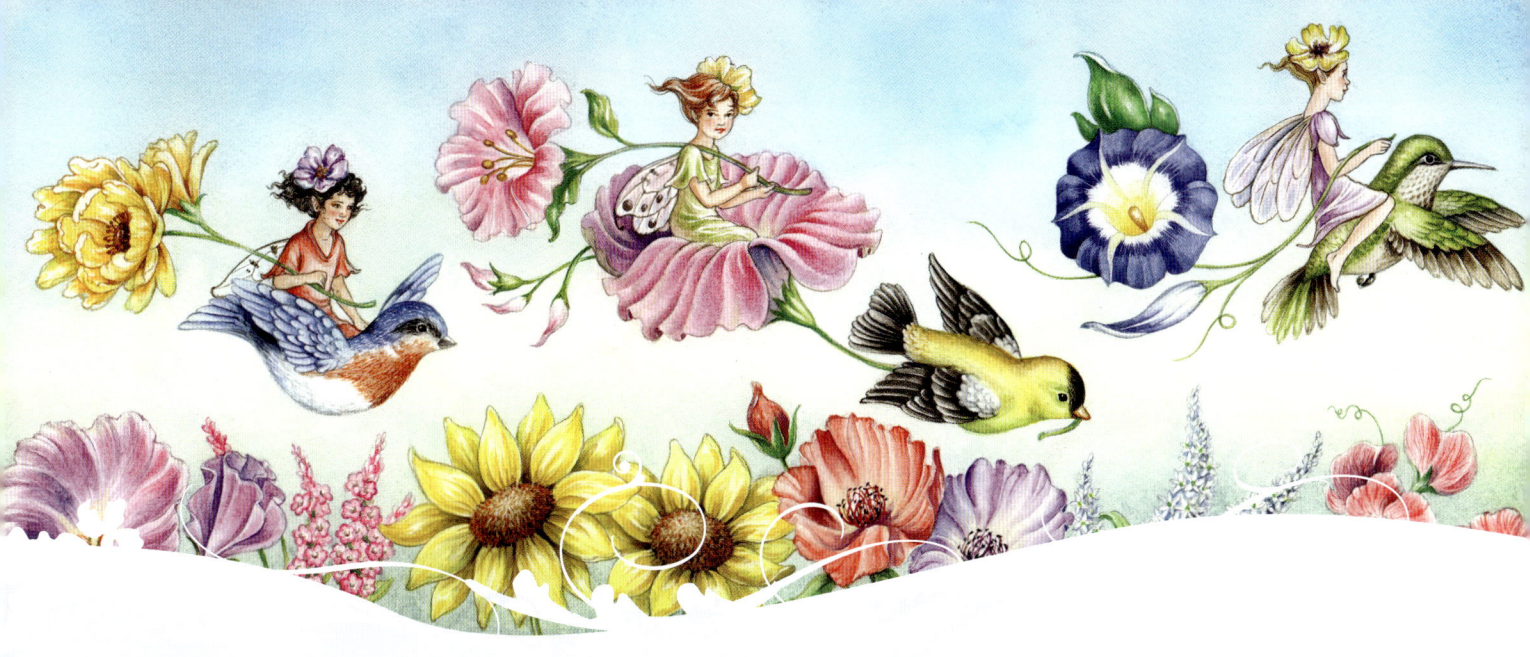

# INTRODUCTION

Has a stroll down a garden path or through the woods ever led you to wonder about the world of fairies? Stepping beyond the path, you may have marveled at an artful arrangement of twigs or leaves and pebbles leading to a gnarled portal. Silky petals opening to the sun might have revealed first tiny toes, then fluttering wings carrying away the creature in the blink of an eye. It's very likely your love of nature led you down that path and your imagination took you off of it to, among other things, reach for this book. It is my wish that these pages will assist you in painting these illusive creatures using practical methods and materials.

The path that led me to create my Fairy Lane images began in the backyard of my childhood home where I imagined tiny worlds inhabited by fairies. In school, I was learning about the balance of nature, and the misuse of technology which threatened it.

Today, threats to nature have increased, but so, thankfully, has the popularity of fairies. We peek into their world, and see joy and mischief in balance. And, when we re-create their spirit in our art, we are in harmony with nature, too.

Keep in mind that your results will not come through magic, but through good, hard work. And fairies differ from one another, just as people do. My approach to drawing fairies has been to observe the movements and moods of my own children. (After all, with the addition of wings, any child can become a fairy.)

Wherever you get your inspiration, remember that these demonstrations are only paths. When you are ready to step off them, new worlds of knowledge and skill will open up to you.

*Barbara Lanza*

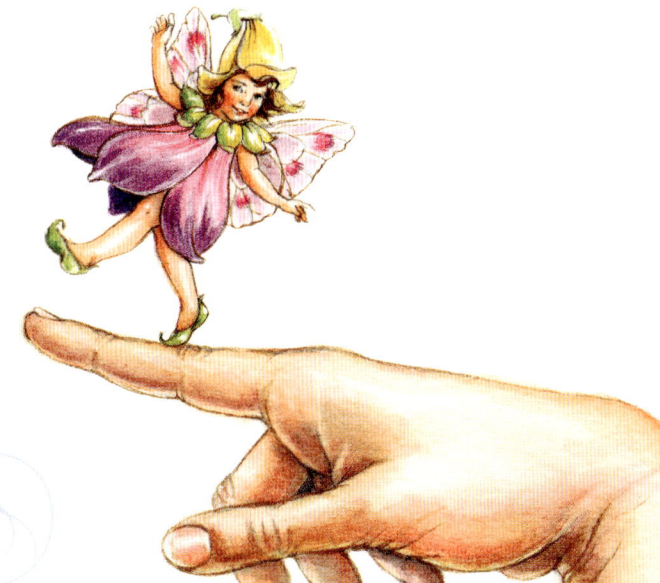

# MATERIALS

## BRUSHES

There are good, inexpensive synthetic brushes on the market for acrylics, but buy sable brushes if you can for watercolors. They are more economical in the long run. The most important aspect about brushes is how well they hold their points, and you can expect points that last from the better brushes. Test them while shopping, as most stores will provide a cup of water. Most of the paintings in this book are 11" × 8½" (28cm × 22cm) and, except for the large background washes, do not require large brushes. For background washes, use a 1½-inch (38mm) flat. The Winsor & Newton Series 7 Miniatures are handy for creating fine details. For maximum control, use a no. 2 miniature round. When painting fur, a no. 1 fan brush does a beautiful job. Use a stipple brush to create a mottled effect for backgrounds or to create the texture of leaves. Simply dip the brush in thick pigment, tap it a few times on scrap paper to remove excess pigment and let the remaining pigment dry slightly. Tap the stipple brush up and down to add texture.

## PALETTES

For watercolors, circular plastic trays containing ten small wells and one large well in the center allow you to easily mix colors in the center. Use a separate tray for each color group to keep your colors harmonious. Arrange the pigments from warm to

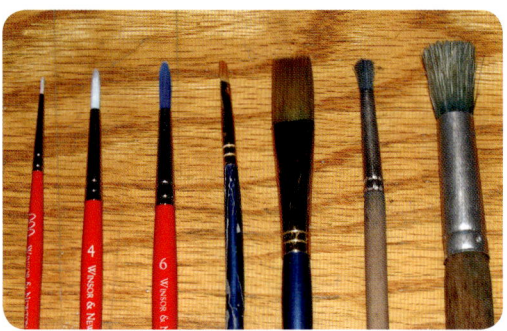

**Sable Brushes for Watercolor**

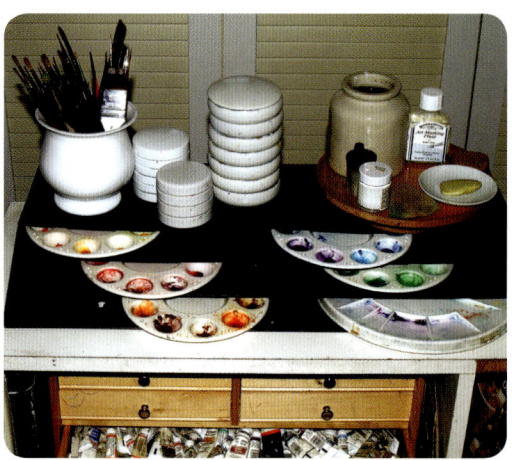

**Acrylic and Stipple Brushes**

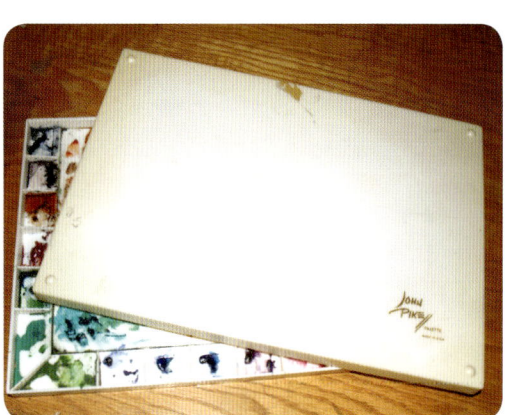

**Acrylics and Acrylic Palette**

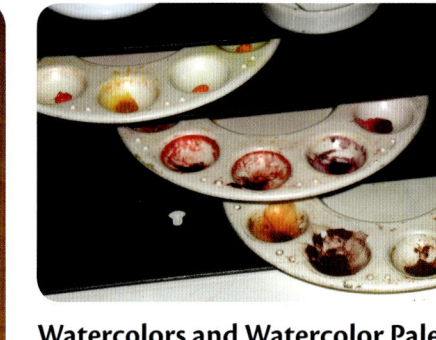

**Watercolors and Watercolor Palette**

A simple document holder that you get at office supply stores is an easy and convenient way to store your palettes.

cool hues. After any prolonged storage, use an eyedropper or brush to add a bit of water to each well of dried color, bringing back the pigments' creamy consistencies before painting.

For acrylics, a simple lidded palette works well. Simply select the colors you want to use and add them to the palette when you're ready to paint. Cover unused colors with a damp paper towel before closing the lid.

## MASKING FLUID

Applying masking fluid over foreground elements takes the worry out of creating even background washes. After the fluid dries, it becomes a protective barrier. It can be used for both watercolors and acrylics and can be either white or tinted.

Remove masking fluid using frisket squares or your fingertips. Simply apply the fluid with inexpensive bristle brushes (or ancient sable ones) dipped in soap.

Before removing masking fluid, make sure that any remaining pigment on it is dry, or better yet, removed carefully with a damp tissue. Otherwise stray pigment may get on your painting during the removal process.

## PAPER

There are so many exciting papers. Art supply stores are the best places to see and feel samples, and sometimes companies will send you free ones. Catalogs show textures as well as possible, but experimentation is the only way to find the paper for you. I've been very happy with 140-lb. (300gsm) Winsor & Newton hot-pressed paper for both watercolor and acrylics. Its satin finish absorbs well, is a nice bright white and can take lots of abuse.

## PENCILS

Have a range of pencils with a soft (B) and medium (HB) lead. Begin your drawing with the softest lead (such as a 2B) because it easily erases away. Use an HB lead once you're happy with your sketch.

## PAINT RAGS

Cotton diapers are the best! So absorbent. Mine are twenty-four years old, the age of my first child. In absence thereof, big box stores carry packages of soft rags, or there is always that sentimental T-shirt with which you hate to part. You can also use two-ply bathroom tissue or facial tissue to absorb color where it has pooled.

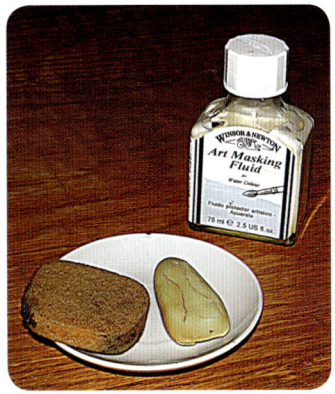

**Masking Fluid, Soap and Square Masking Fluid Pickup**

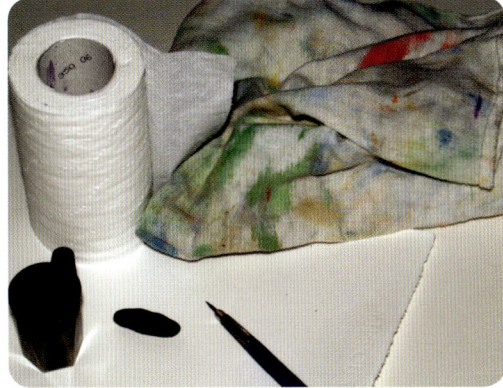

**Pencil, Kneaded Eraser, Pencil Sharpener, Paper Towels, Rags and Paper**

# COLOR

Learning about color is a lifelong pursuit. Here are some basic facts to get you on your way or to refresh your memory:

**Hue** is another name for color.

**Tint** is a color to which white has been added. If you're working in watercolor, you can also add more water to the pigment to lighten.

**Shade** is a color to which black or gray has been added.

**Key color** is the dominant color in a picture.

**Neutral gray** is a mixture of black and white.

**Chroma** is the brightness or dullness of a color.

**Value** is the lightness or darkness of a color.

**Temperature** is the warmness or coolness of a color.

Understanding these basics will help you decide which colors are best suited to the type of fairy you wish to portray. For instance, a quiet, peaceful fairy would wear and be surrounded by serene colors such as cool violets, blues and greens. An assertive fairy would wear and be surrounded by aggressive, passionate colors such as yellows, oranges and reds.

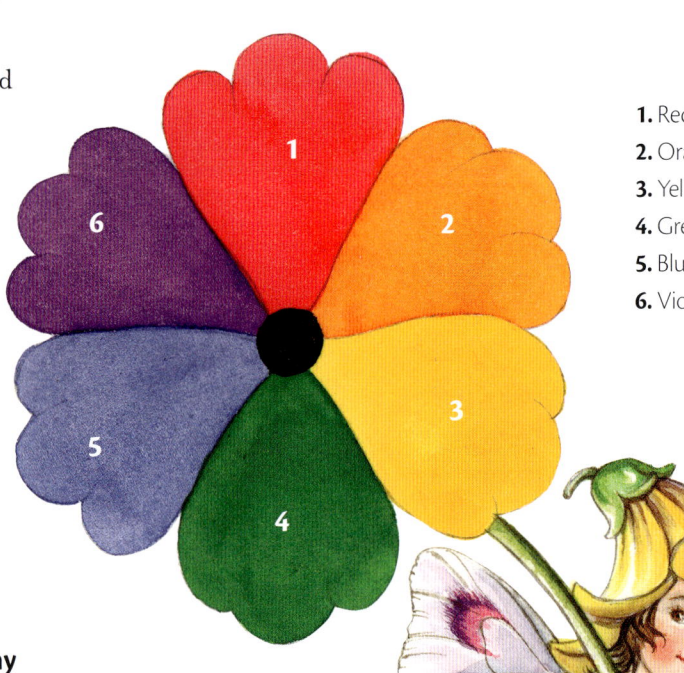

**1.** Red
**2.** Orange
**3.** Yellow
**4.** Green
**5.** Blue
**6.** Violet

## The Color Wheel and Color Harmony

The color wheel is a wonderful visual tool for creating color harmony. By just glancing at the color wheel, you can select compatible color schemes that make your fairies nearly fly off the page.

- *Primary colors* are those that cannot be made by mixing other colors. They are yellow, red and blue.
- *Secondary colors* are created by mixing primary colors. They are orange, green and violet.
- *Tertiary colors* are those made by mixing primary colors with a secondary color. Red and orange become red-orange, yellow and orange become yellow-orange.
- *Complementary colors* are colors opposite one another on the color wheel. Red and green are complements, as are blue and orange and yellow and violet.

# PAINT

Both watercolors and acrylics lend themselves to magical effects, and product quality is a must. Begin with a basic color palette by selecting at least two of each of the primaries, a few oranges and greens, and Payne's Gray and Carbon Black if you're working in acrylic or Payne's Gray and Ivory Black if you work in watercolor.

There are two whites that I like to use: Titanium White for acrylics and Chinese White for watercolor. Experiment to see which medium you prefer, and gradually add to your supply. I use Winsor & Newton and Holbein's watercolors, and I use Golden and Winsor & Newton's acrylics. Experiment with a variety of paints to find the brands and pigments that work best for you.

## Full Palette of Liquid Acrylics

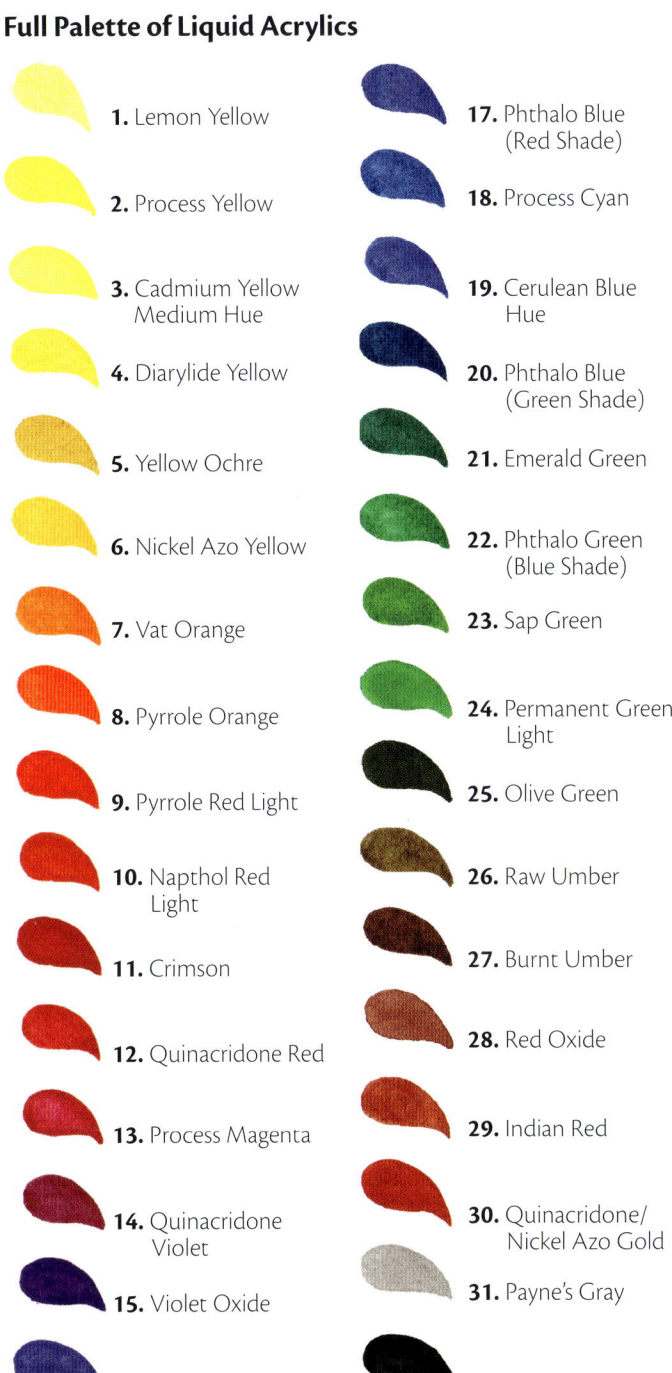

1. Lemon Yellow
2. Process Yellow
3. Cadmium Yellow Medium Hue
4. Diarylide Yellow
5. Yellow Ochre
6. Nickel Azo Yellow
7. Vat Orange
8. Pyrrole Orange
9. Pyrrole Red Light
10. Napthol Red Light
11. Crimson
12. Quinacridone Red
13. Process Magenta
14. Quinacridone Violet
15. Violet Oxide
16. Ultramarine
17. Phthalo Blue (Red Shade)
18. Process Cyan
19. Cerulean Blue Hue
20. Phthalo Blue (Green Shade)
21. Emerald Green
22. Phthalo Green (Blue Shade)
23. Sap Green
24. Permanent Green Light
25. Olive Green
26. Raw Umber
27. Burnt Umber
28. Red Oxide
29. Indian Red
30. Quinacridone/Nickel Azo Gold
31. Payne's Gray
32. Carbon Black

## Full Palette of Watercolors

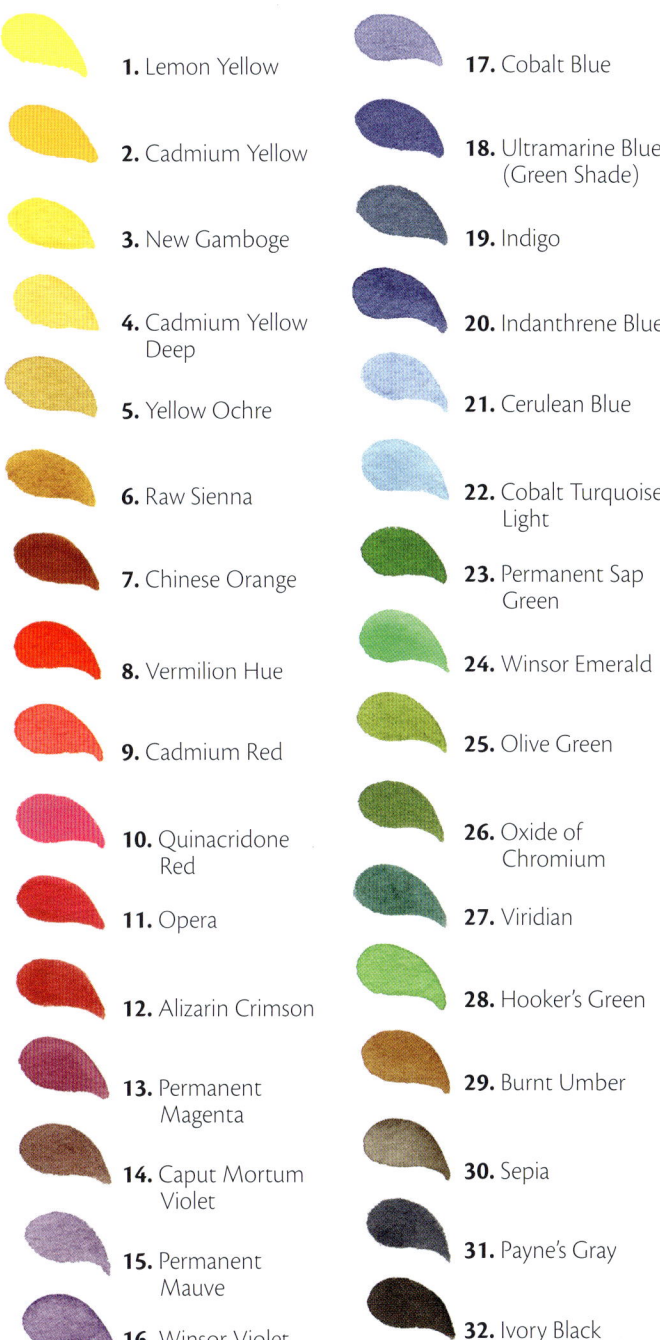

1. Lemon Yellow
2. Cadmium Yellow
3. New Gamboge
4. Cadmium Yellow Deep
5. Yellow Ochre
6. Raw Sienna
7. Chinese Orange
8. Vermilion Hue
9. Cadmium Red
10. Quinacridone Red
11. Opera
12. Alizarin Crimson
13. Permanent Magenta
14. Caput Mortum Violet
15. Permanent Mauve
16. Winsor Violet (Dioxazine)
17. Cobalt Blue
18. Ultramarine Blue (Green Shade)
19. Indigo
20. Indanthrene Blue
21. Cerulean Blue
22. Cobalt Turquoise Light
23. Permanent Sap Green
24. Winsor Emerald
25. Olive Green
26. Oxide of Chromium
27. Viridian
28. Hooker's Green
29. Burnt Umber
30. Sepia
31. Payne's Gray
32. Ivory Black

# GETTING STARTED

Unless you're using a heavyweight watercolor paper 300-lb. (640gsm) or heavier, you'll need to stretch the paper or it will buckle when you apply watercolor washes. Stretching watercolor paper is easy—just anchor the paper down, wet it, and wait for it to dry flat.

Tape down the paper with blue tape, found in most hardware and art supply stores. Get the kind that doesn't tear the paper when you remove it. A flat wash brush works to apply the water. Remove excess water with a sponge or a dry brush and let the paper dry.

### ~YOU WILL NEED~
#### MATERIALS
1½-inch (38mm) flat ~ blue tape ~ hair dryer ~ watercolor paper ~ watercolor paper block backing or other firm surface

## STRETCHING WATERCOLOR PAPER

**1** Secure your watercolor paper to a firm backing with the blue tape.

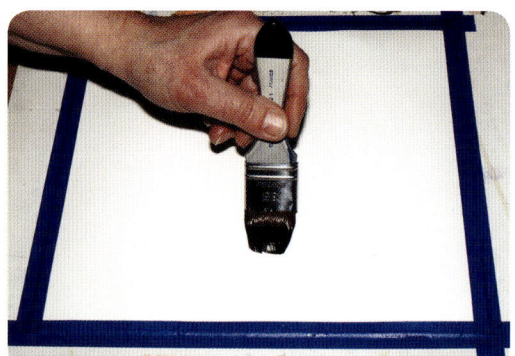

**2** Using a 1½-inch (38mm) flat, apply water horizontally, then vertically to the paper.

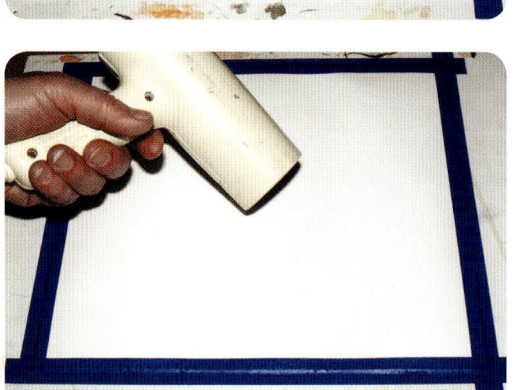

**3** Let the paper dry naturally or use a hair dryer set at medium heat.

### SPEED UP THE DRYING TIME
If you don't want to wait for your watercolor paper to dry, use a hair dryer to make that paper dry faster!

To transfer a drawing to your watercolor paper, make a photocopy of the image and enlarge it to your preferred size. Trace the enlarged image onto tracing paper and transfer it to your watercolor paper using graphite or blue Saral transfer paper. I prefer blue because it lifts more easily when erased and does not reproduce for printing purposes. If the blue or graphite lines are too heavy, press a kneaded eraser on them to remove the excess graphite.

### YOU WILL NEED
#### MATERIALS

Blue tape ~ graphite or blue Saral transfer paper ~ hard-leaded pencil or a ballpoint pen that has run out of ink ~ HB pencil ~ kneaded eraser ~ stretched watercolor paper ~ tracing paper

## TRACING AND TRANSFERRING AN IMAGE

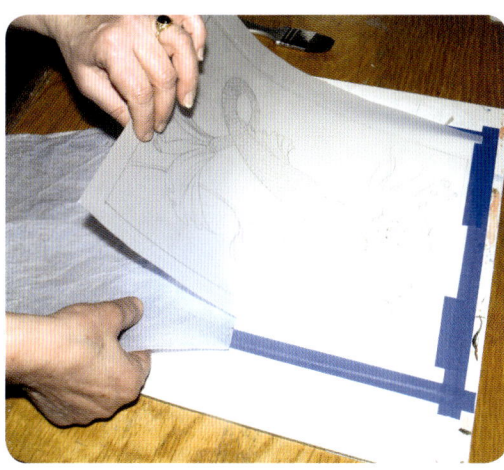

**1** Once you have traced the drawing onto your tracing paper, tape the tracing paper to the top of your watercolor paper. Place your transfer paper face down between your tracing paper and your watercolor paper.

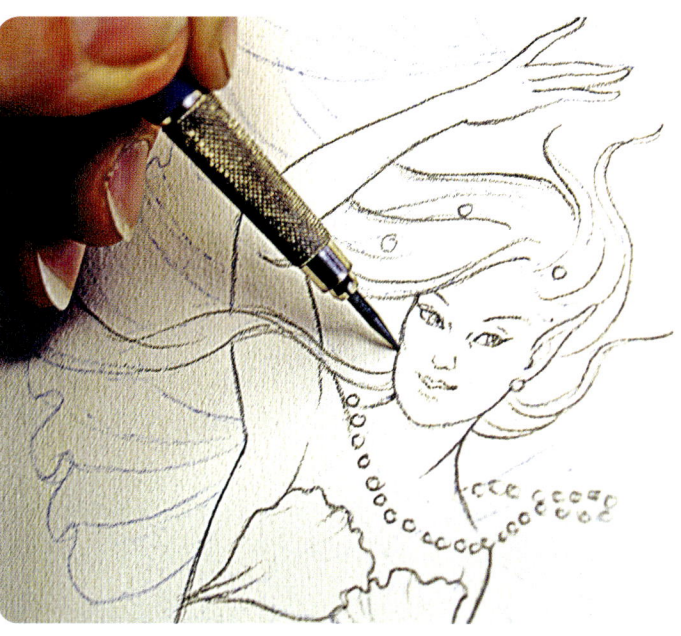

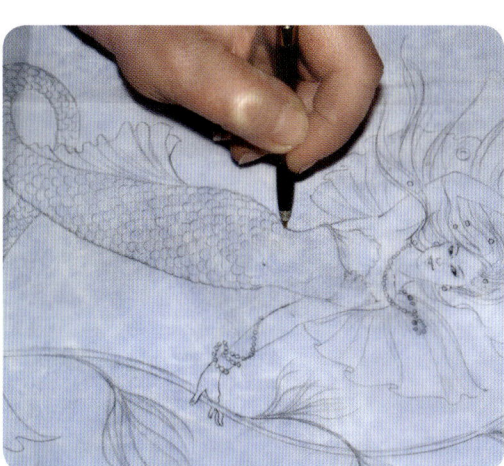

**2** Using a hard-leaded pencil or a ballpoint pen that has run out of ink, go over the lines of your tracing, transferring your image to the watercolor paper below.

**3** Use an HB pencil to carefully redraw and fill in the image. Try not to lose the spontaneity of the original drawing. This is the time to add details to your subjects.

# USING COLOR TO CREATE LIGHT AND SHADOW

After deciding on the type of fairy you want to paint, consider which type of light will suit her best. Painting the effects of light upon her will bring your fairy to life. Light and shadow are dependent on the time of day and the direction of the light. If your fairy is sitting outside in the middle of the day, the contrast between light and shadow will be much stronger than if she were sitting in late afternoon light where there would be less contrast between the lights and shadows.

Regardless of the time of day, any lit object should have the following elements:

**Highlight**: The area where the light hits most directly. This is usually bright white.

**Reflected light**: The light bounced back onto the object from the surface it rests on.

**Cast shadow**: The shadow cast from one object onto another.

**Form shadow**: The areas where light does not hit the object. The coolest, darkest part of the form shadow is the *core shadow*. Think of the core shadow as the opposite of the highlight.

When light falls directly on a subject, it creates *hard-edged* shadows, or very distinct changes from the light to the shadow. When the light is obstructed, it will create *soft-edged* shadows where the transition between light and shadow is more blended and gradual.

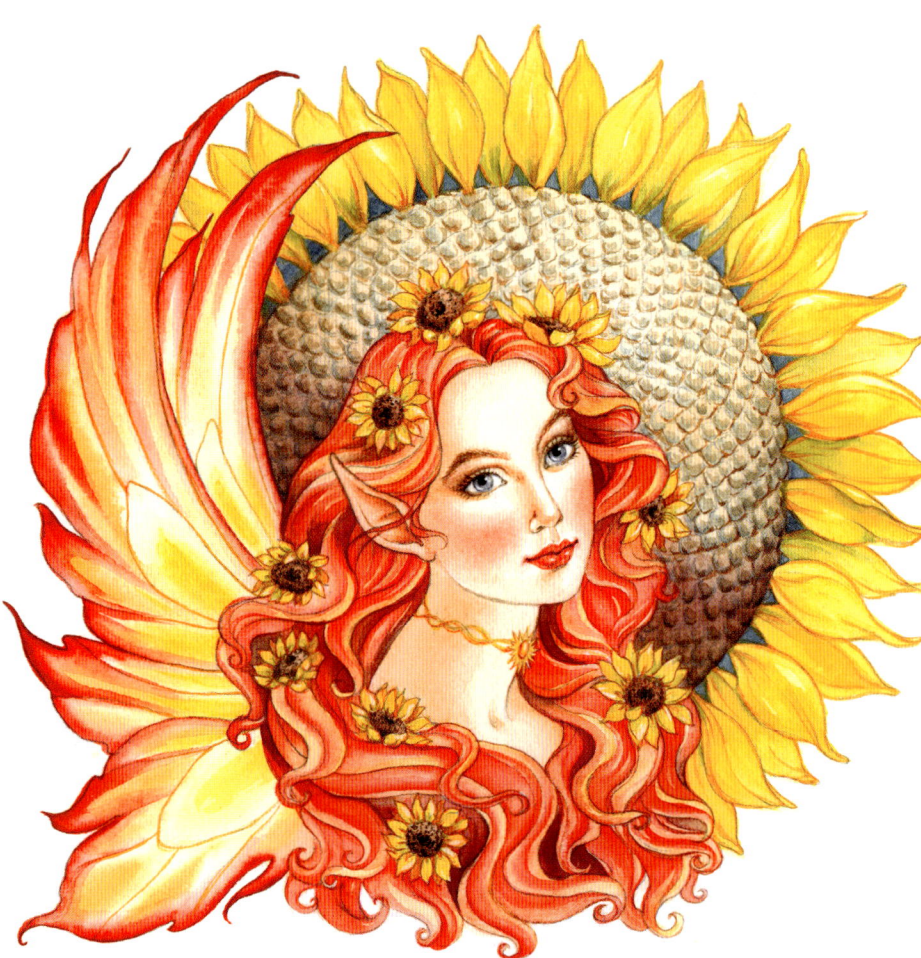

### Using Light, Shadow and Color Together

The light source for the Noon Fairy is overhead and slightly to the right (she is the "Noon" Fairy after all). In addition to the type of shadow we use, the sunflower, the fairy's hair color, and the color of her wings all work together to convey the time of day she represents.

**Highlights** where the light directly hits her face and wings. Even individual sunflower seeds have highlights that gradually turn into darker shadows.

Reddish **reflected light** on the sunflower from her hair.

**Cast shadows** along the inside of her ear and within the folds of her hair.

**Form shadow** along the sides of her face and neck that aren't directly in the light.

**Core shadow** in the dark areas of her hair made with dark shades of red.

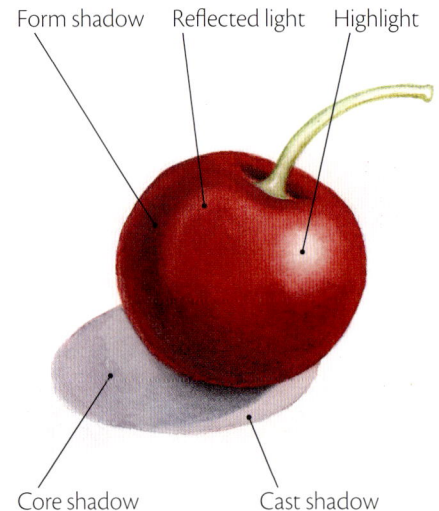

16

A color's hue, value and temperature can be used to create light with such techniques as creating tints and shades of a color. Light tints can be used to suggest the lighter areas while dark shades fill out the areas in shadow.

## ~YOU WILL NEED~
### MATERIALS
No. 1 round ◈ palette ◈ stretched watercolor paper
### PIGMENTS
Ivory Black ◈ Winsor Violet (Dioxazine)

## CREATING TINTS

**1** Mix equal parts of Winsor Violet (Dioxazine) with water.

**2** Add a bit of the same color to another palette well or another area of the paper. This time, mix in more water to create a lighter tint.

**3** Add even more water to the original color to create a very light tint. The possibilities are endless and allow you to create dynamic shadows.

## CREATING A SHADE

**1** In a palette well or on your paper, mix Winsor Violet (Dioxazine) with a very small amount of Ivory Black and enough water to create a creamy consistency. This creates a very dark shade of the color, perfect for a night sky.

**2** Place a bit of the original color in another palette well and add an equal amount of water to create a medium shade.

**3** Place a bit of the medium shade into a third palette well and add an equal amount of water to create a light shade.

### ACRYLIC TINTS AND SHADES
Follow the same technique to create tints with acrylics but instead of adding water to your pigment, add a white acrylic such as Titanium White. To create shades with acrylics, mix your original pigment with a darker color such as Carbon Black or Payne's Gray.

# APPLYING A WASH

One of the most daunting challenges in every watercolor artist's life is learning to apply even washes. However, once the steps are broken down, the mystery is gone. The basic rules, which should not be broken, are as follows:

1. Wait until the shine is gone from your wet surface before applying color.
2. Have enough pigment mixed to cover the intended area; letting the pigment on the paper dry while you mix more pigment will lead to poor results.
3. Direct the flow of your wash by tilting your paper back and forth in all directions.

Take a deep breath (without holding it), throw caution to the wind and begin.

You can create many different kinds of washes for a variety of dynamic backgrounds from a simple flat wash, in which the background is all the same even color, to a gradated wash, in which the background gradually changes from dark to light. We'll start with a gradated wash, one you'll often use in the demonstrations to come.

### YOU WILL NEED

**MATERIALS**
1½-inch (38mm) flat ∾ palette ∾ stretched watercolor paper

**PIGMENTS**
Cerulean Blue ∾ Lemon Yellow

**ACRYLIC WASHES**
Follow the same basic steps to create a wash with acrylic paints, but keep in mind that acrylics will dry faster than watercolors.

## WATERCOLOR WASH

**1** With a 1½-inch (38mm) flat, wet the entire sky area and apply Lemon Yellow at the bottom of the paper. Tilt your board upside down and back and forth to allow the color to fade into the clear water. On your palette, prepare three different tints of Cerulean Blue, by adding increasing amounts of water.

**2** Apply the lightest tint of Cerulean Blue about one-fourth of the way up the paper where the yellow has faded away. Apply the pigment by brushing back and forth. Add a medium tint of Cerulean Blue above the light tint, working as quickly as possible and titling the board side to side and back and forth.

**3** Above the medium tint, add the darkest tint of Cerulean Blue. Turn your board upside down and left to right, allowing the two colors to blend together for even coverage.

# WORKING WET-INTO-WET

As the term suggests, wet-into-wet is the practice of adding one pigment into a painted area that is still wet so the colors will merge. This technique is employed in most watercolor paintings. You can work wet-into-wet with acrylic, but you will have to work faster because of acrylic's quick drying time.

Whether you are painting fairy wings, a dress, or a flower petal, this technique can suggest reflected light. Use the wet-into-wet technique for small detailed areas of your painting or to create interesting background washes.

> ### ~YOU WILL NEED~
> **MATERIALS**
> 1½-inch (38mm) flat ❧ no. 8 round ❧ palette ❧ stretched watercolor paper
>
> **WATERCOLORS**
> Cobalt Blue ❧ Winsor Violet (Dioxazine)

## THE WET-INTO-WET METHOD

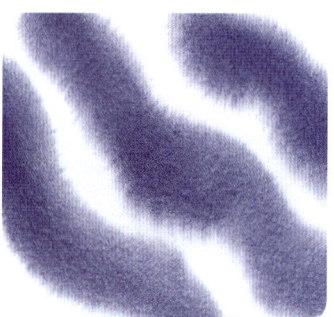

**1** Wet the area you intend to paint with a 1½-inch (38mm) flat. When the sheen has gone, you're ready to add your first color.

**2** Working quickly, apply some Cobalt Blue with a no. 8 round. Notice how the paper's wetness creates soft edges.

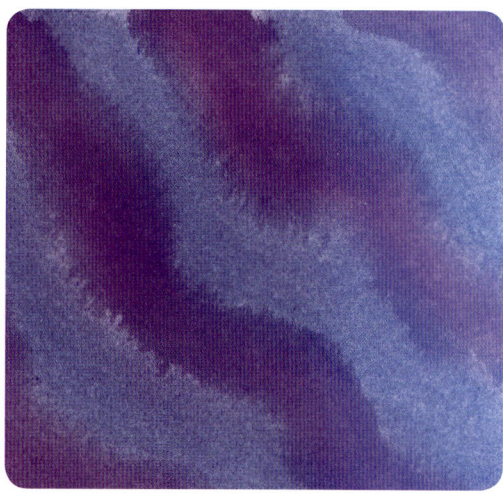

**3** Before the first layer dries, add Winsor Violet (Dioxazine) with the no. 8 round. Tilt your board from left to right to allow the colors to blend softly and seamlessly.

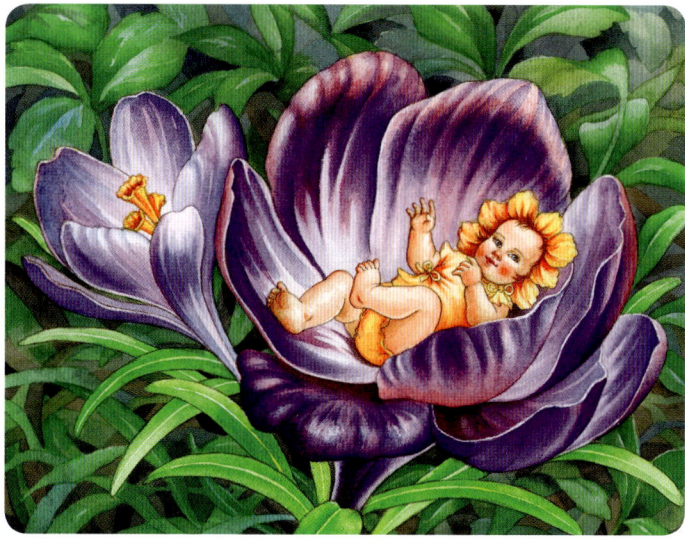

### Work Wet-Into-Wet for Velvety Flower Petals

Working wet-into-wet on this piece helped form the curve of the petals. After applying color to the top of the wet petal, I added a deeper tint to indicate where it turns from the light. The colors will merge on your painted petal as they do on living flower petals. (See page 88 for the full demonstration.)

# CHARGING AND LAYERING

Charging, or adding colors to an area of paper that is still wet, allows your colors to mingle, creating the subtle blend of light and shadow that happens in nature. Consider charging color when you want to paint the shaded part of a petal at the same time you are painting the part that faces the light source.

Because acrylic paint dries quickly and cannot be lifted, you can quickly build layers that will remain fixed. Apply thin layers of liquid acrylics where you want a transparent watercolor effect and opaque layers where you want an opaque effect, as in the delicate shape of Queen Anne's lace.

### ~ YOU WILL NEED ~
**MATERIALS**

½-inch (12mm) stipple brush ~ nos. 000, 0 and 2 round ~ palette ~ stretched watercolor paper

**WATERCOLOR**

Opera

**ACRYLIC**

Carbon Black ~ Cerulean Blue Hue ~ Olive Green ~ Phthalo Blue (Green Shade) ~ Titanium White

## CHARGING WITH ACRYLIC AND LAYERING WITH WATERCOLOR

You can also use charging with acrylics, just remember that you have to work quickly because of acrylic's fast drying time. Likewise, layering with watercolors, also called *glazing*, is a slower process.

## CHARGING WITH WATERCOLORS

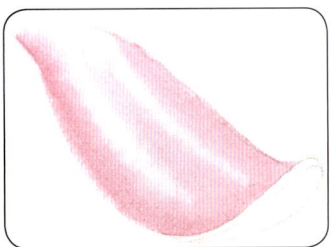

**1** Wet the entire surface with clean water and a no. 2 round. Load the round with Opera. Starting at the petal's bottom, apply paint to the wet petal.

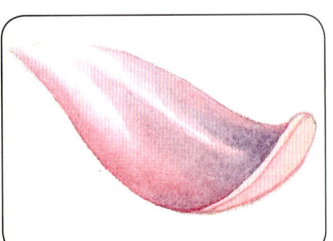

**2** While the paint and the paper are wet, drag the color upwards. Charge a darker tint of Opera into the petal's contours. The darker tint will blend smoothly with the lighter tint.

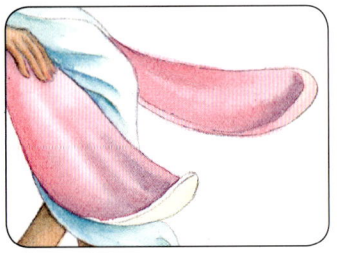

**3** Finish the petal by outlining the edges with a darker tint of Opera on a no. 000 round.

## BUILDING LAYERS WITH ACRYLICS

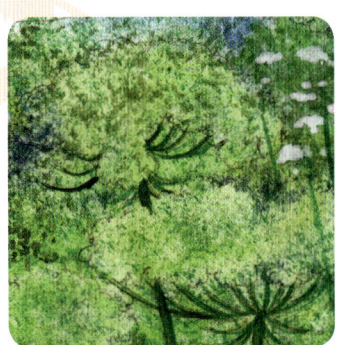

**1** Use a ½-inch (12mm) stipple brush to paint an initial layer of Phthalo Blue (Green Shade) in the shape of a flower and let this dry. Add a second layer of Olive Green.

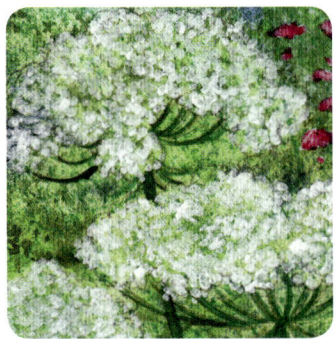

**2** Develop the flower's shadow side with a mixture of Phthalo Blue (Green Shade) and Carbon Black and the ½-inch (12mm) stipple brush. Build the petals with a no. 0 round loaded with Titanium White. Apply a thick layer where the florets face the light and a thin layer as they turn from the light source.

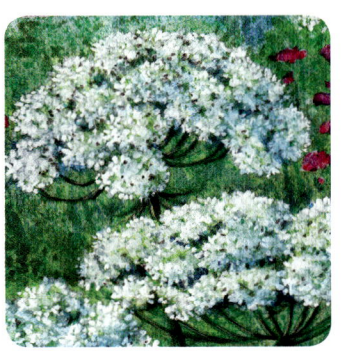

**3** Use a no. 000 round to refine the florets with Titanium White, leaving the background color for depth. When dry, add a medium tint of Cerulean Blue Hue to deepen the shades of the petals. Add a tiny dot of Carbon Black to the center of each floret.

# USING MASKING FLUID

Masking fluid takes the headache out of painting large, loose background washes by creating a barrier over detailed foreground objects.

To apply masking fluid, choose durable and inexpensive brushes, such as student-grade Winsor & Newton University acrylic brushes. Before you load your brush with masking fluid, dip it in water, then rub it in a wet bar of soap. This makes clean-up easier and extends the life of the brush.

If you are applying masking to very fine objects, thin the masking fluid with water. If the foreground objects have less detail, you might not need to mask at all.

Apply masking fluid along the inside edges of an image if the background is smaller than the foreground. If the painting has a large background with little foreground detail, apply the masking fluid over the entire image.

## ~YOU WILL NEED~
### MATERIALS

Bar of soap ~ masking fluid ~ no. 1 acrylic round ~ square masking fluid pickup ~ stretched watercolor paper

**REMOVING MASKING FLUID**
Sometimes the masking peels right off by rubbing it with your fingertips. If not, use a square masking fluid pickup, or you can roll dry masking into a ball for a homemade pickup.

## USING MASKING FLUID

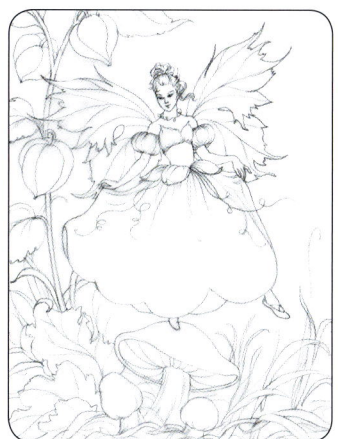

**1** Trace your drawing onto your stretched watercolor paper.

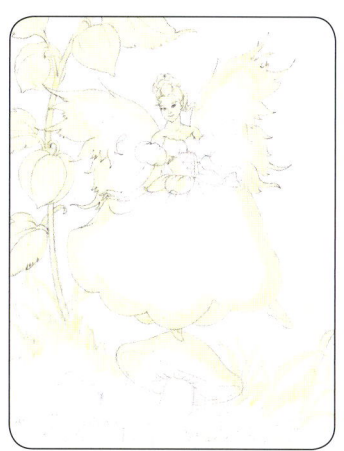

**2** Apply the masking fluid along the edges of the image with a no. 1 acrylic round dipped in water and rubbed in a wet bar of soap.

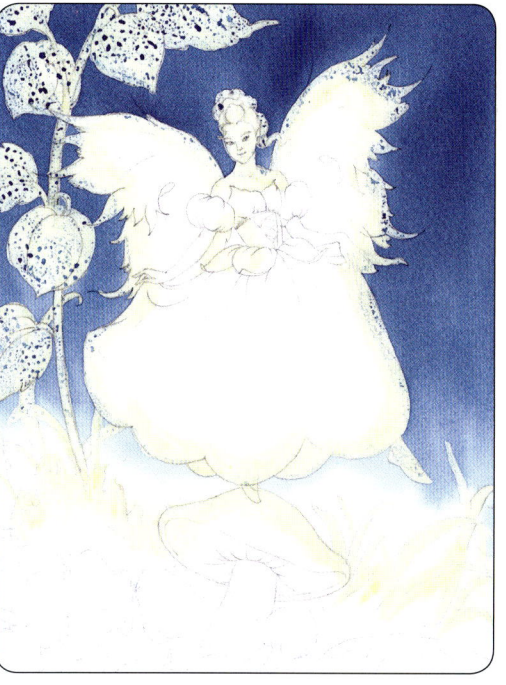

**3** Apply your background treatment, in this case a wash. When the background is completely dry, blot any color that has pooled on top of the mask with bathroom tissue and carefully remove the masking fluid.

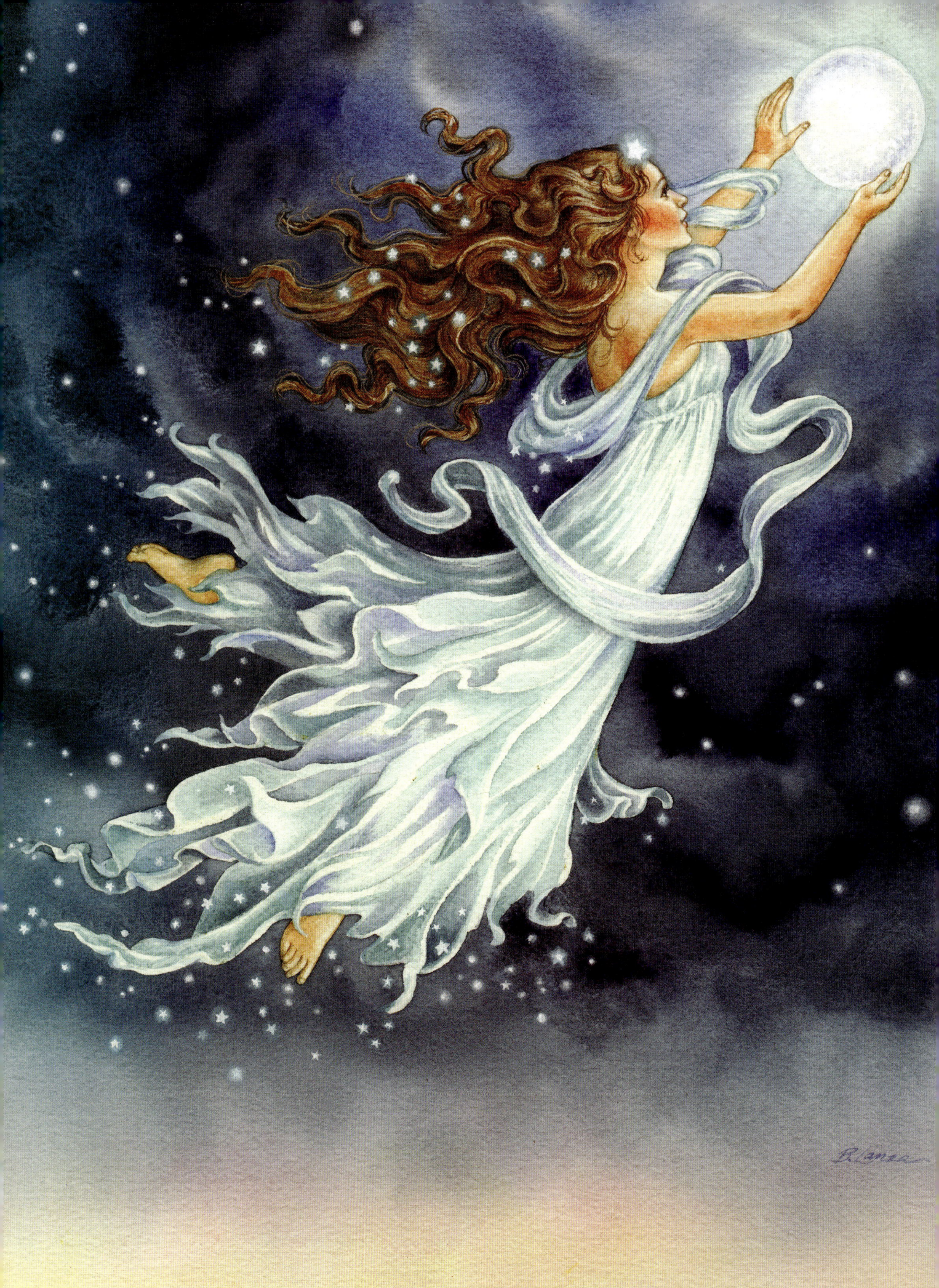

SECTION ONE
# FAIRY FACES & FIGURES

WHAT DO FAIRY FACES AND FIGURES LOOK LIKE? The possibilities are as broad as the many cultures that embrace fairytales. From east to west and north to south fairy features differ just as human features. Though their features change as we circle the globe, the same ideal proportions remain constant. Over the course of this chapter, you'll learn how to create playful and elegant fairy figures.

What makes fairies look different from us has more to do with attitude than anything else. A playful glance or a graceful movement is more indicative of their nature than pointed ears and tapered limbs. Wings can mimic those of a butterfly or fall leaves. Anything goes in their unconventional world, so let your imagination be your guide when drawing them.

A gentle reminder from one who knows and the best advice I can offer you: Don't let fear of falling short keep you from working towards your artistic goals. Negativity is the biggest obstacle to creativity. So, let's loosen up and get started.

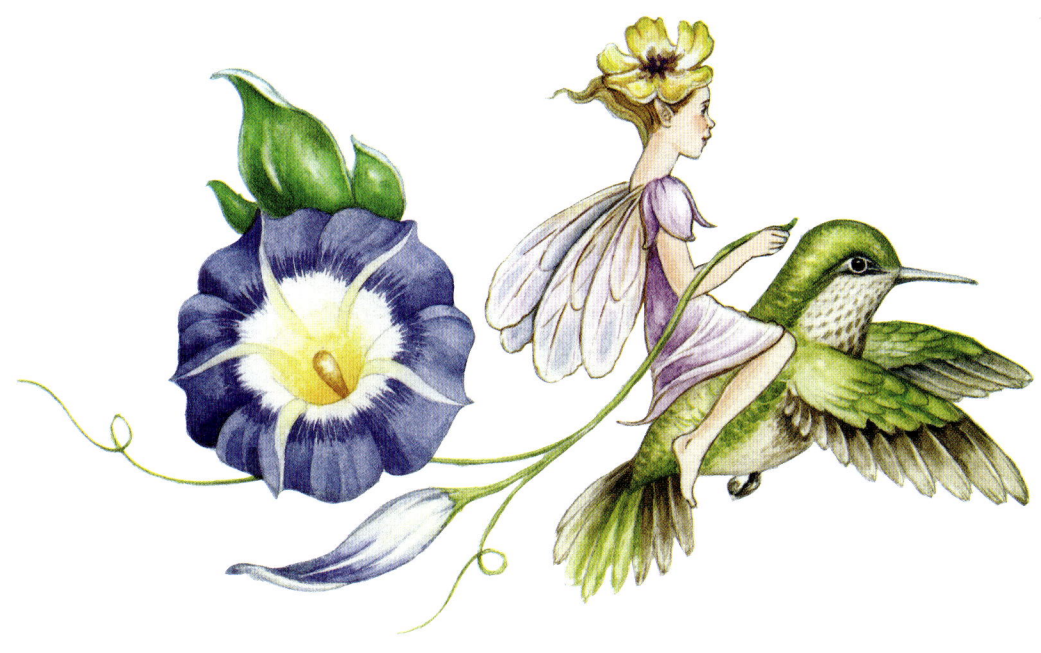

# FAIRY FACES

These exercises follow a formula for ideal proportions, offering basics for creating your own charming fairies. Except for the telltale ears, fairy faces are a lot like human ones.

**BABY FAIRY**

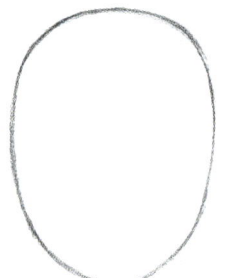 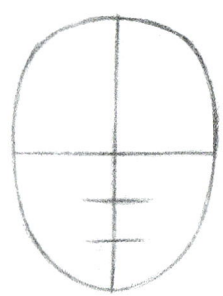 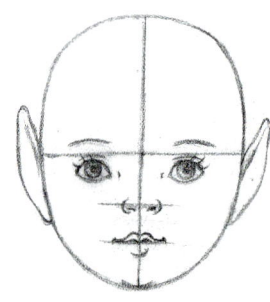

**ADOLESCENT FAIRY**

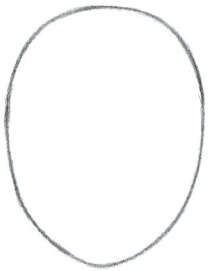 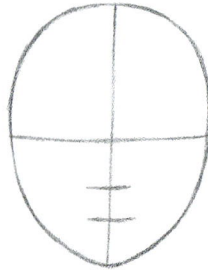 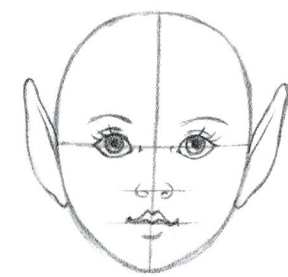

**ADULT FAIRY**

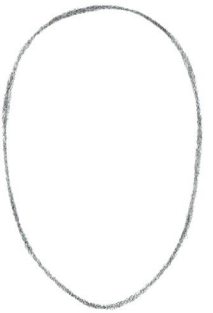 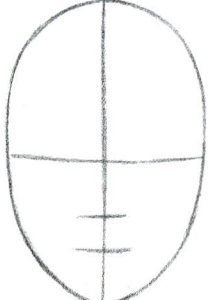 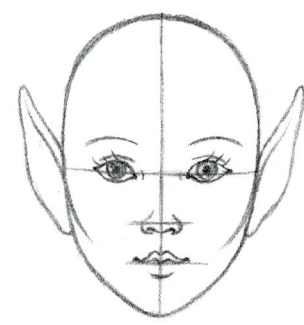

**1** With your pencil, draw an oval that's wider at the top than at the bottom (or chin) and less curved along the sides.

**2** Draw a vertical line down the center of the oval. Then draw a horizontal line halfway down the vertical line to create a guideline for the eyes (the eyeline). At one third of the distance between the horizontal line and the chin, draw a horizontal line for the nose, then draw a horizontal line between the nose and chin for the mouth.

**3** Draw the eyes using the eyeline for a guide, placing them depending on the fairy's age. Add the eyebrows above that. Fill out the nose, then draw the mouth. Indicate the ears, which start at the midpoint between the crown and the chin and end halfway between the nose and the mouth.

# THREE QUARTER HEAD VIEWS

Compare the tilted ovals below. Notice how the oval tapers as the age of the fairy increases. This Baby Fairy is older than the one on the previous page so her eyes are closer to the halfway line.

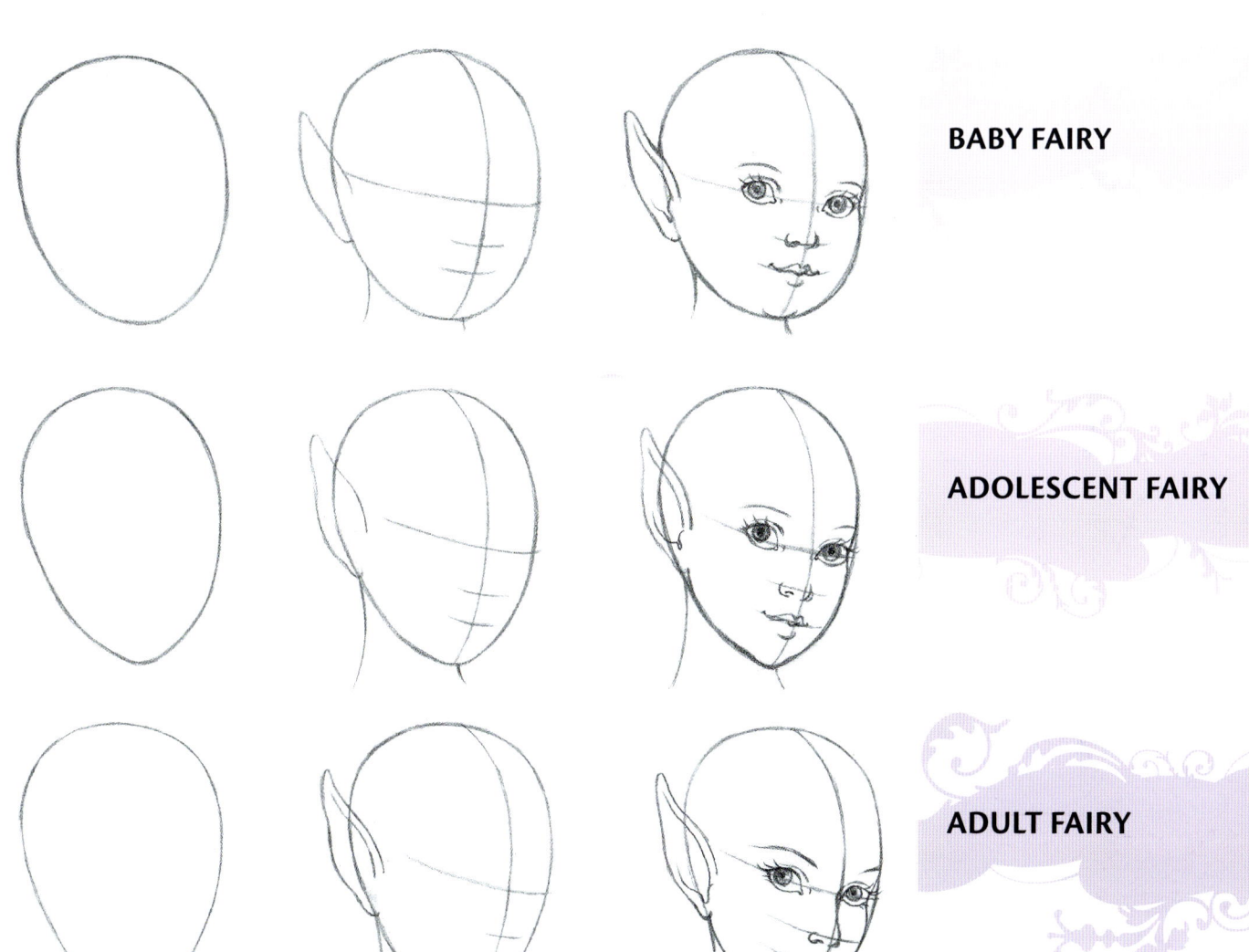

**BABY FAIRY**

**ADOLESCENT FAIRY**

**ADULT FAIRY**

**1** With your pencil, draw an egg-shaped oval that's tilted to the left. The upper part of the oval should be wider than the bottom, or chin. Make the side less curved.

**2** Three quarters from the left side of the oval, add a rounded line from the top of the head to the chin. Draw a horizontal line halfway between the top and bottom of the head for the eyeline. Place the nose line between the eyes and the chin, then add the mouth line between the nose and the chin.

**3** Draw the eyes along the eyeline so the pupils rest just above it. Flesh out the nose and mouth. Add the ears halfway between the crown and the chin.

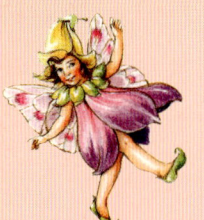

## MINI DEMONSTRATION
# BABY FAIRY: front view

*The proportions of these fairies are similar to ours. Using basic shapes, you can create baby, adolescent and adult fairy figures. After a bit of practice, you can change proportions to emphasize characteristics that suit your fancy.*

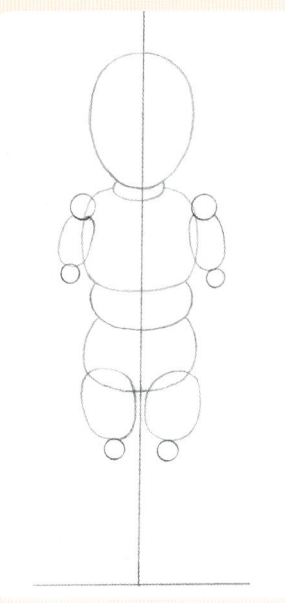

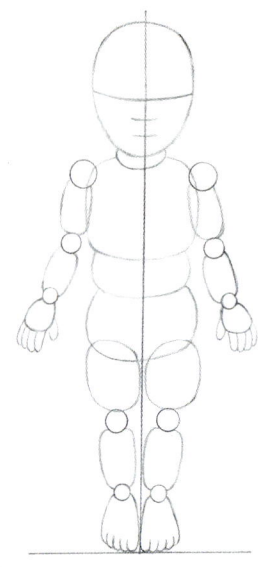

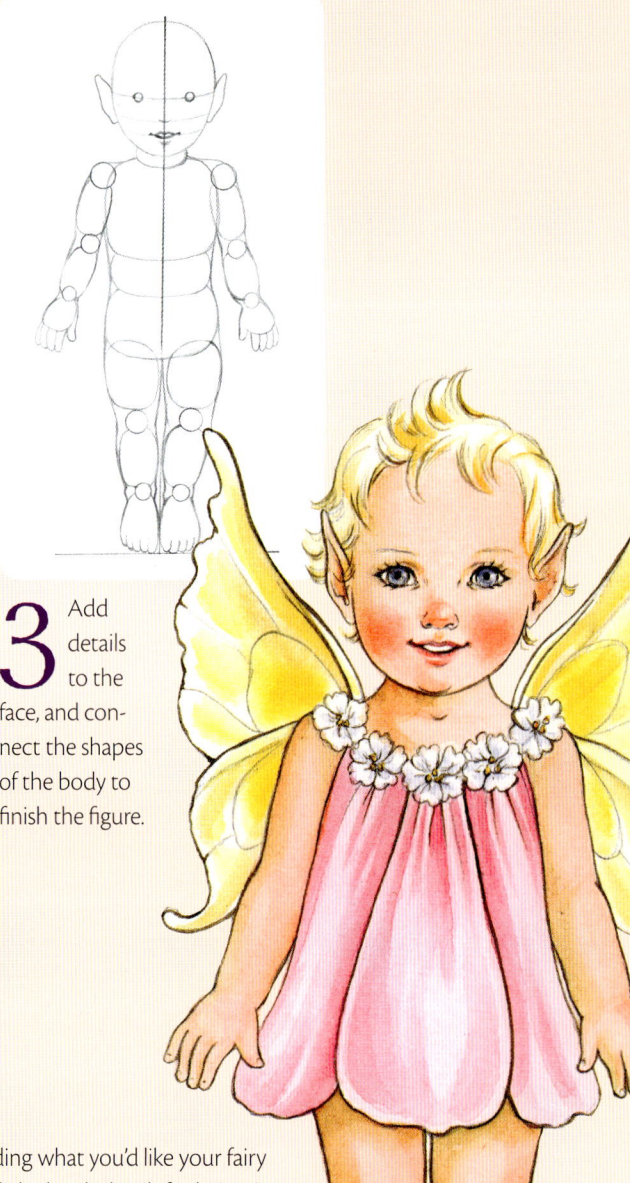

**1** Indicate the midline with a vertical line. Then, add the oval for the head. Measure the head and mark four head lengths along the midline. Draw a horizontal line across the bottom of the vertical one to serve as the ground.

Build the body with ovals and circles of various sizes. Use larger shapes for the larger areas of the body such as the chest. Use smaller shapes for smaller areas such as the neck and elbow joints.

**2** Add the guidelines for the features of the face as you did on page 24.

Continue building the arms and legs. Draw ovals for hands and curved ovals for thumbs and fingers. Draw triangular ovals to indicate feet and curved ovals for toes.

**3** Add details to the face, and connect the shapes of the body to finish the figure.

**4** After deciding what you'd like your fairy to wear, lightly sketch details for hair, wings and clothing. Erase all the guidelines and circles you used to create the figure.

Plan your clothing colors to complement the fairy's hair and skin tones.

## MINI DEMONSTRATION
# ADOLESCENT FAIRY: front view

*Adolescent Fairy is the same size as a ten-year-old girl. The ovals which make up her limbs are more elongated and she is no longer straight in the waist like Baby Fairy.*

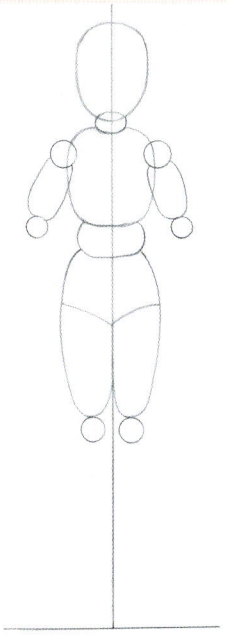
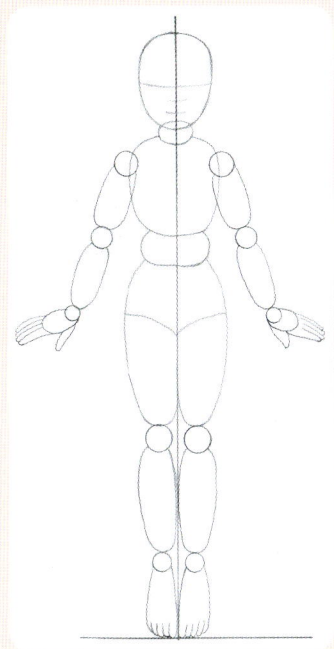
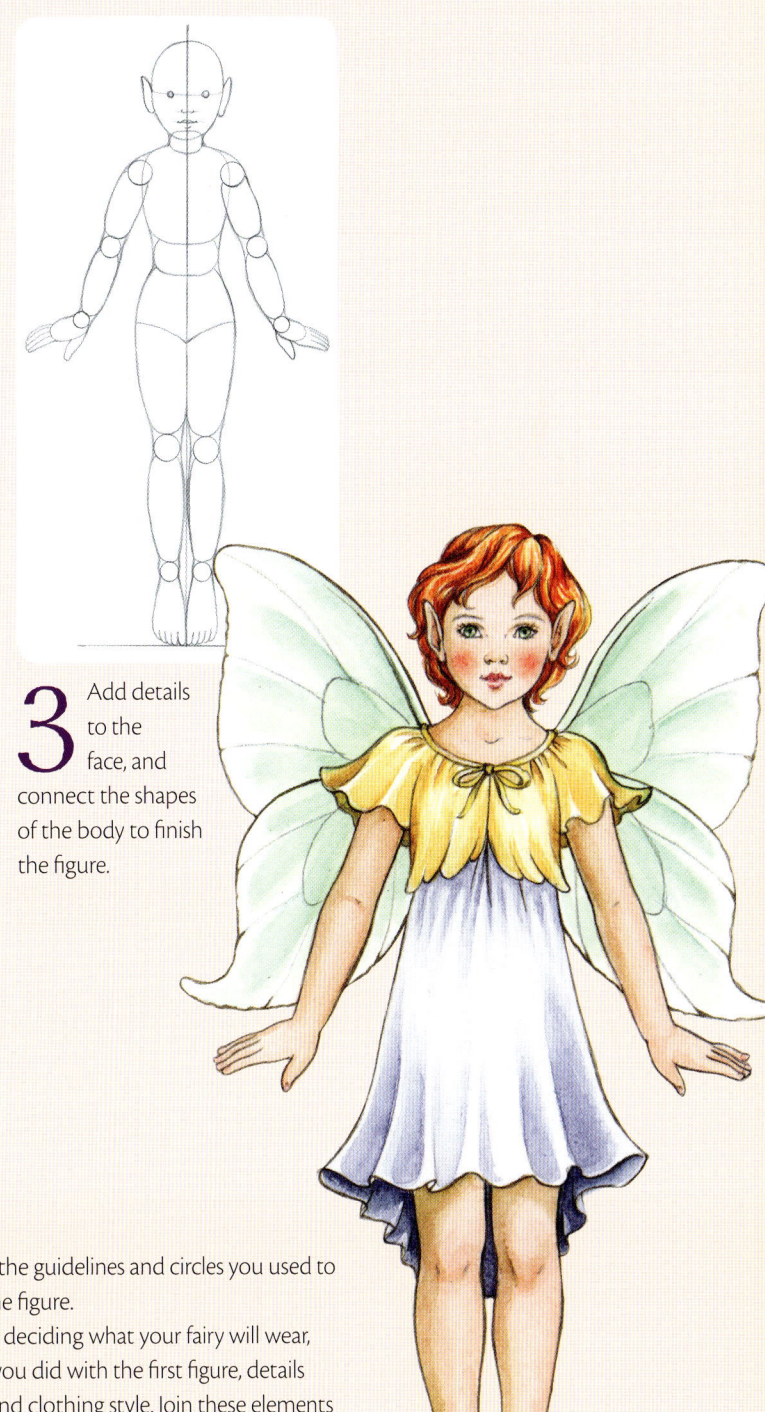

**1** Indicate the midline with a vertical line, then add the oval for the head. Measure the head and mark six head lengths down the vertical line. Draw a horizontal line at the bottom.
  Build the body with ovals and circles of various sizes. Use larger shapes for the larger areas of the body such as the chest. Use smaller shapes for smaller areas such as the neck and elbow joints.

**2** Add the guidelines for the features of the face as you did on page 24.
  Continue building the arms and legs. Draw ovals for hands and curved ovals for thumbs and fingers. Draw triangular ovals to indicate feet and curved ovals for toes.

**3** Add details to the face, and connect the shapes of the body to finish the figure.

**4** Erase all the guidelines and circles you used to create the figure.
  After deciding what your fairy will wear, lightly sketch, as you did with the first figure, details such as her hair and clothing style. Join these elements with colors that complement one another.

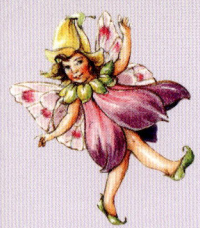

MINI DEMONSTRATION
# ADULT FAIRY: *front view*

*The small waist, longer neck and tapered limbs tell us this is an adult fairy. To create her, you'll follow the same process you used for the baby and adolescent, modifying some of these basics to fit the proportions of an adult.*

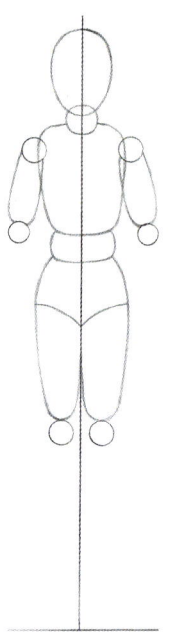
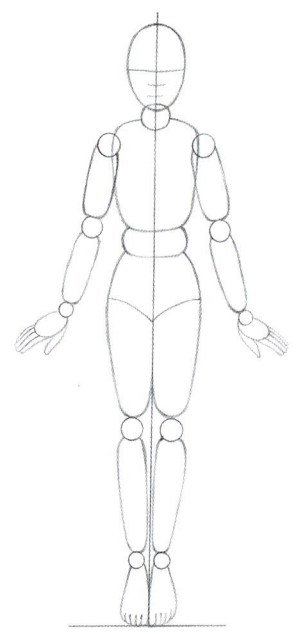
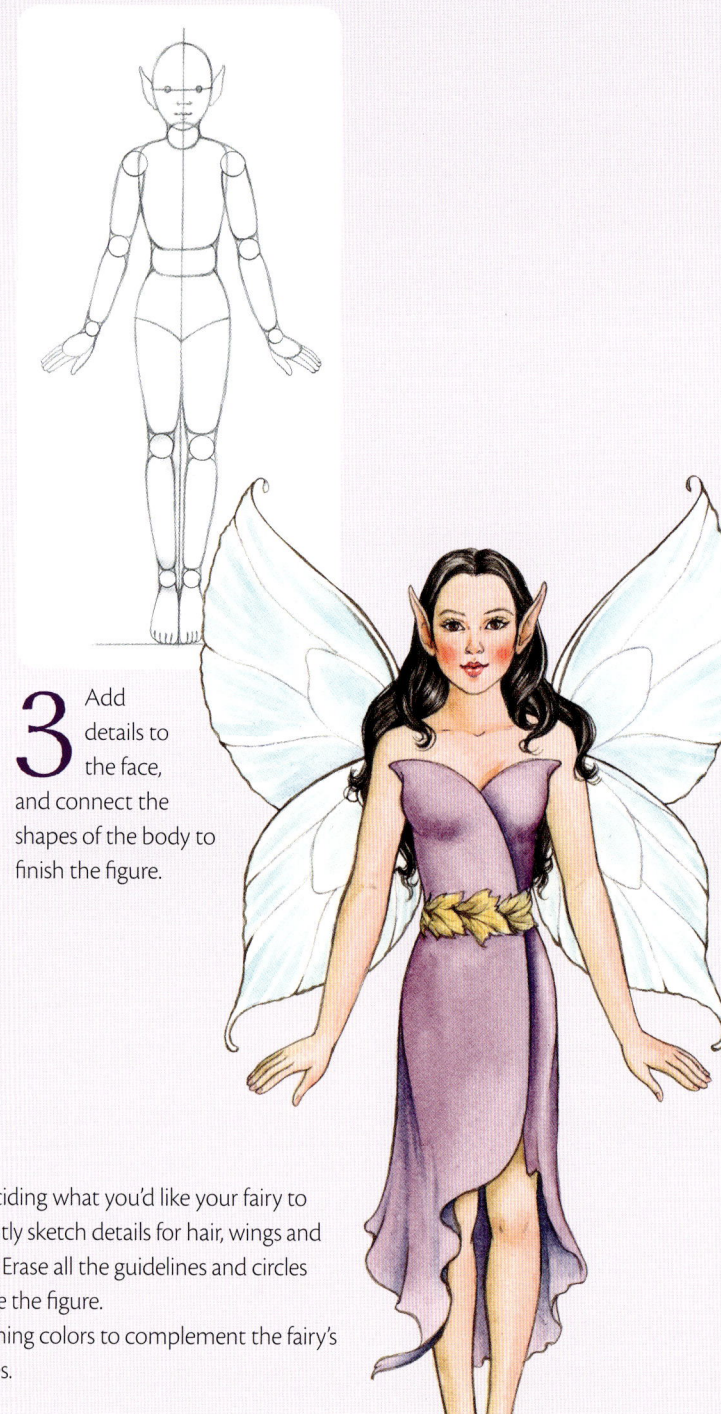

**1** Indicate the midline with a vertical line, then add an oval for the head. Measure the head and mark seven head lengths down the midline. Draw a horizontal line to indicate the ground at the end of the seventh head length.

Build the body with ovals and circles of various sizes. Use larger shapes for the larger areas of the body and smaller shapes for smaller areas. Use a rounded oval for the chest, tapering it down to the waist. Draw an oval for the waist and a rounded oval for the hips, which taper up to the waist.

**2** Add the guidelines for the features of the face as you did on page 24.

Continue building the arms and legs. These ovals should be more long and slender than those of the younger fairies. Draw ovals for hands and curved ovals for thumbs and fingers. Draw triangular ovals to indicate feet and curved ovals for toes.

**3** Add details to the face, and connect the shapes of the body to finish the figure.

**4** After deciding what you'd like your fairy to wear, lightly sketch details for hair, wings and clothing. Erase all the guidelines and circles you used to create the figure.

Plan your clothing colors to complement the fairy's hair and skin tones.

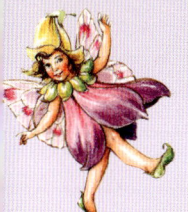

## MINI DEMONSTRATION
# BABY FAIRY: 3/4 view

*While it's important to know how to draw the basic figure, sometimes it's just as easy to trace an object. Now is the time to practice tracing fairies onto 140-lb. (300gsm) hot-pressed watercolor paper. Then you are ready to paint!*

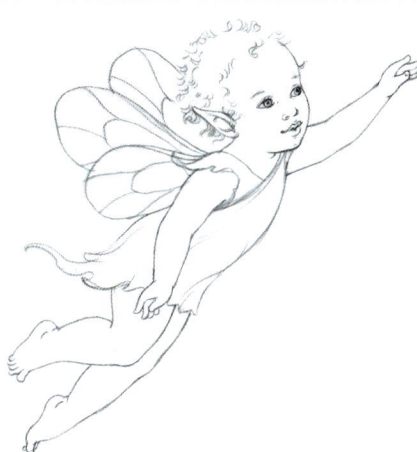
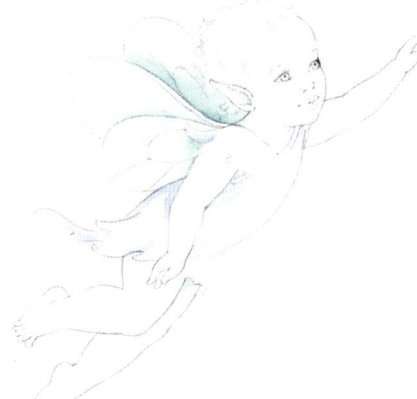
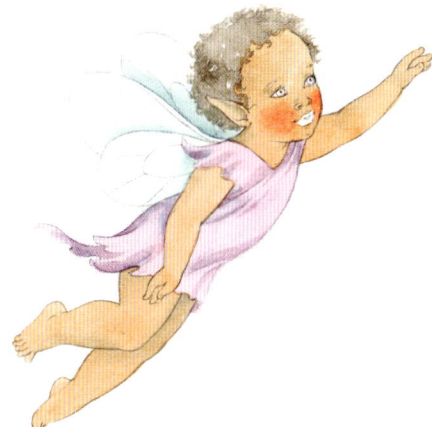

**1** Trace the fairy onto hot-pressed watercolor paper. Using a 2B lead in a mechanical or wooden pencil, draw over the traced image.

**2** Shade the body with a light tint of Indigo with a no. 2 round. Add a light tint of Viridian to the wings where they attach. Apply a light tint of Indanthrene Blue to the folds of the dress.

**3** Use a medium tint of Burnt Umber and Chinese Orange and a no. 2 round to paint the skin. Paint her hair a medium dark tint of Sepia with the no. 2 round. Wet the dress with clear water, then use a medium tint of Permanent Mauve to paint it. When the dress has dried a bit, add a darker Permanent Mauve tint to the lower part and to the folds. Let the tints mingle, using a no. 2 round to drag and blend the colors where needed. Add rosy cheeks with a medium shade of Vermilion Hue, blending outward with clear water.

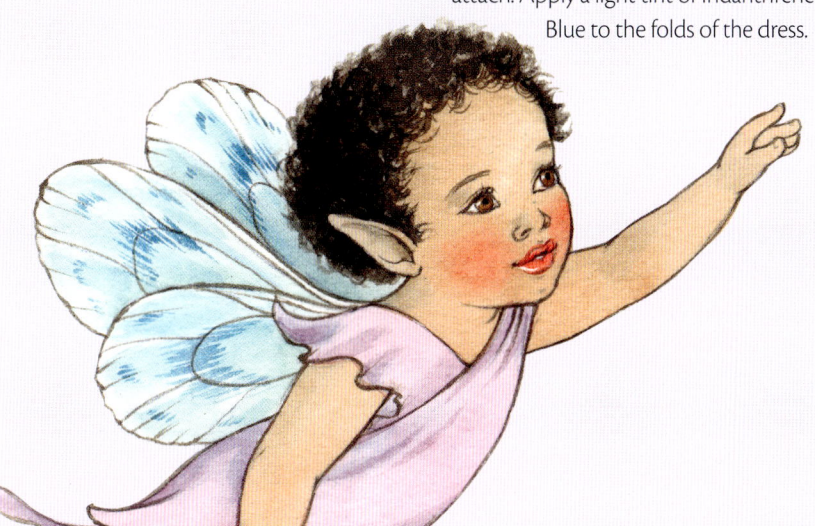

**4** With a no. 000 round, paint around the wings with Cobalt Blue. Use Burnt Umber for her eyes and Bright Red for her lips. With a no. 000 round, paint Cobalt Blue details on the wings. Use the same brush to outline the figure with Sepia.

## MINI DEMONSTRATION
# ADOLESCENT FAIRY: 3/4 view

*It's good practice to paint the shaded areas of your picture first so the shadows will not dominate the final color. If, as the picture progresses, you do apply deeper shadows to the dress, for instance, apply a wash of clean water over the entire dress to "set" the colors.*

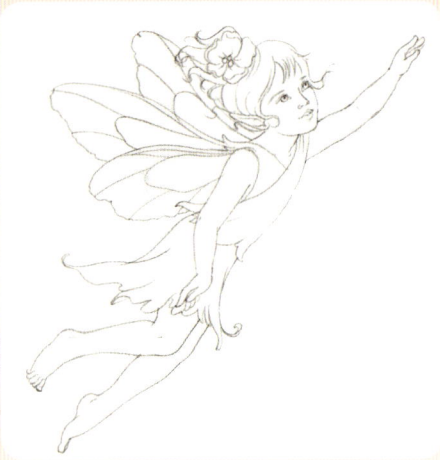 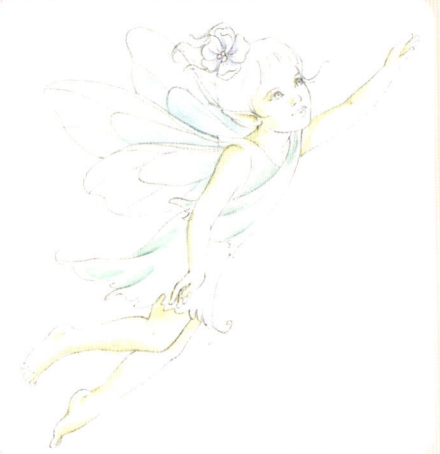 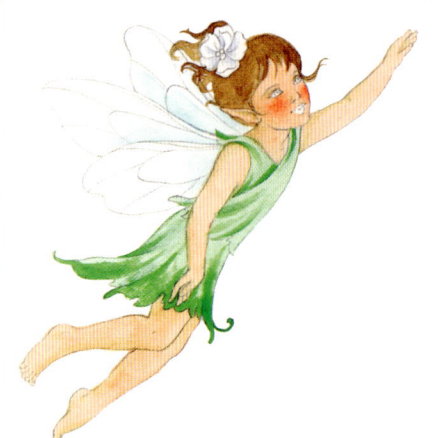

**1** Trace the fairy onto 140-lb. (300gsm) hot-pressed watercolor paper. Using a 2B lead in a mechanical or wooden pencil, draw over the traced image.

**2** With a mixture of Olive Green, Burnt Umber and Chinese Orange, paint the shaded areas of the skin with a no. 1 round. Add a light tint of Viridian to the shaded areas of the dress. Use a light tint of Cobalt Turquoise Light to paint inside the wing's veins and Cobalt Blue to paint the petals of the flower in her hair.

**3** Use a light tint of Permanent Sap Green and a no. 2 round to paint the dress. When the shine is gone, apply a darker tint of this green to the folds at the dress's bottom. Drag the paint where needed with a brush. Paint the cheeks with a no. 1 round and Vermilion Hue. Use a no. 000 round to define strands of her hair with Burnt Umber.

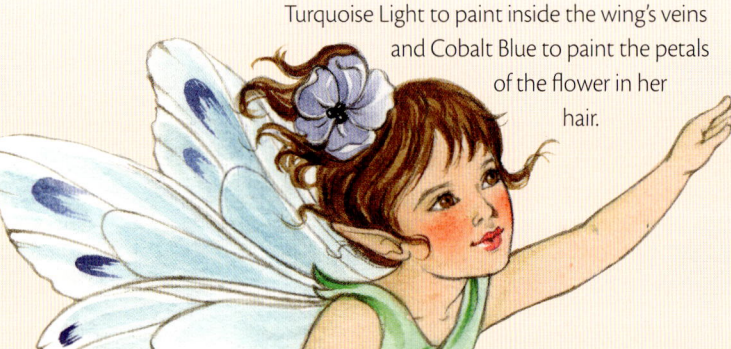

**4** Add flecks of Cobalt Blue to the wings. Paint her eyes with Burnt Umber and use Vermilion Hue for her lips. Using a no. 000 round dipped in a deep tint of Sepia, outline the details and the figure.

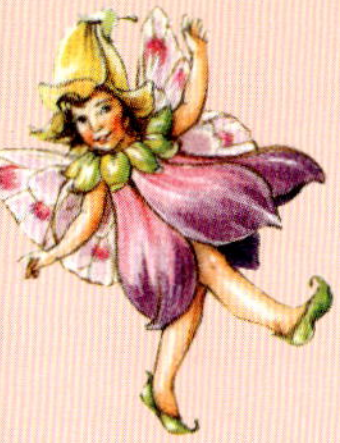

## MINI DEMONSTRATION
# ADULT FAIRY: 3/4 view

*This demonstration is good practice for painting hair. For painting the shaded areas of this fairy's hair, apply Sepia. Using this dark, cool color beneath the final hair color will make the shadow recede as it should.*

**1** Trace the fairy onto hot-pressed watercolor paper. Using a 2B lead in a mechanical or wooden pencil, draw over the traced lines.

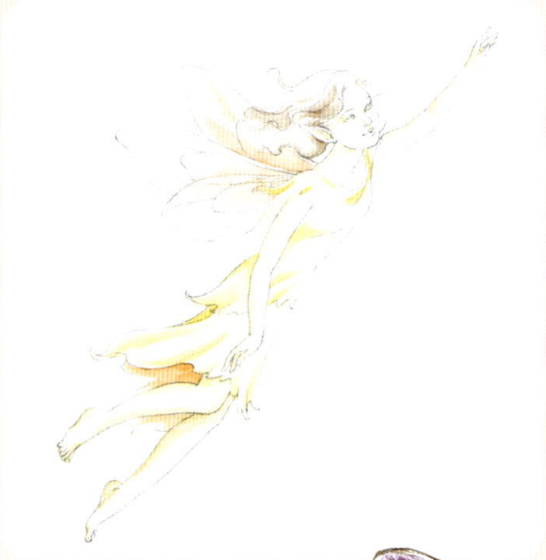

**2** With a pale tint of Olive Green, Chinese Orange and Burnt Umber, paint the shaded areas of the fairy's skin, using a no. 1 round. Shade her hair with Sepia and paint the dress's folds with Raw Sienna. Add Chinese Orange to the wings where they connect with her body.

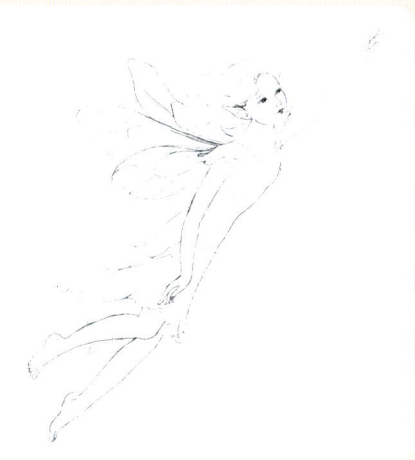

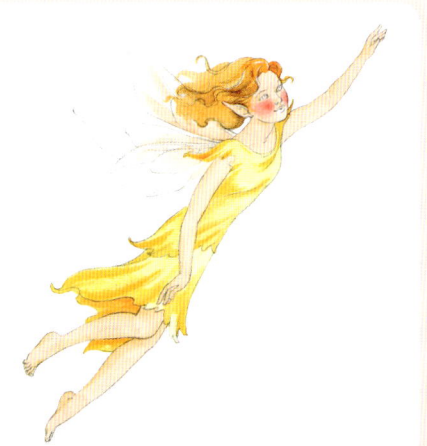

**3** Add Chinese Orange to the fairy's hair with a no. 1 round. Once the first layer is dry, define individual strands with a dark shade of Chinese Orange. Paint the wings with a shade of Viridian. Use a medium tint of Quinacridone Red to paint her cheeks.

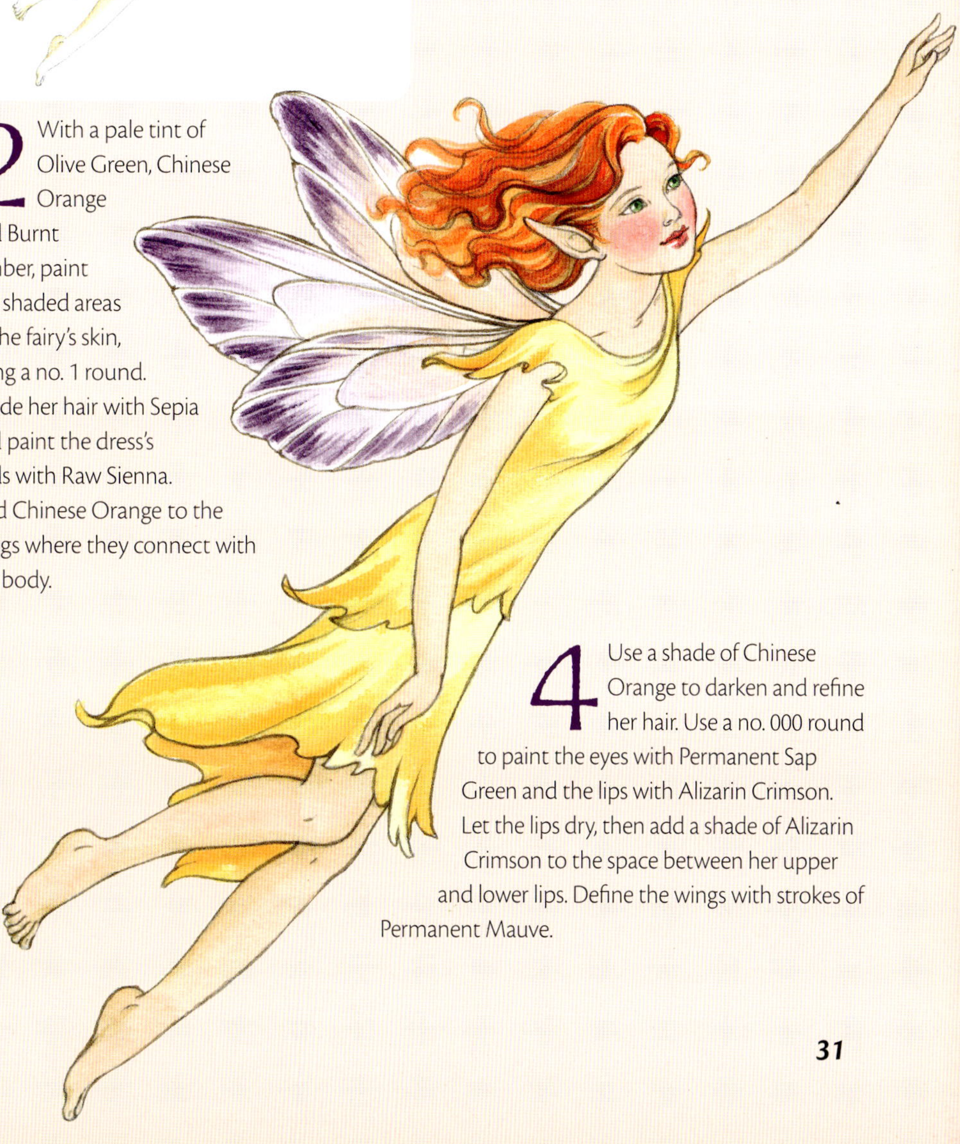

**4** Use a shade of Chinese Orange to darken and refine her hair. Use a no. 000 round to paint the eyes with Permanent Sap Green and the lips with Alizarin Crimson. Let the lips dry, then add a shade of Alizarin Crimson to the space between her upper and lower lips. Define the wings with strokes of Permanent Mauve.

# DEMONSTRATION
# BABY FAIRY in wild rose

*Perhaps you would like to replace this baby's face with that of another. Just be sure the pose is very close to this one as well as the position of the head. Keep in mind that the light source is coming from the right.*

## ~ YOU WILL NEED ~

### MATERIALS
Blue tape ~ hard-leaded pencil or ballpoint pen that has run out of ink ~ HB or 2B graphite pencil ~ kneaded eraser ~ no. 2 miniature ~ nos. 000, 00, 1, 2, and 5 rounds ~ Saral transfer paper ~ stretched watercolor paper ~ tracing paper ~ workable fixative

### PIGMENTS
Alizarin Crimson ~ Burnt Umber ~ Cadmium Red ~ Caput Mortum Violet ~ Chinese Orange ~ Chinese White ~ Cobalt Turquoise Light ~ Indanthrene Blue ~ Olive Green ~ Payne's Gray ~ Permanent Mauve ~ Quinacridone Red ~ Raw Umber ~ Sepia ~ Ultramarine Blue (Green Shade) ~ Vermilion Hue ~ Winsor Violet (Dioxazine) ~ Yellow Ochre

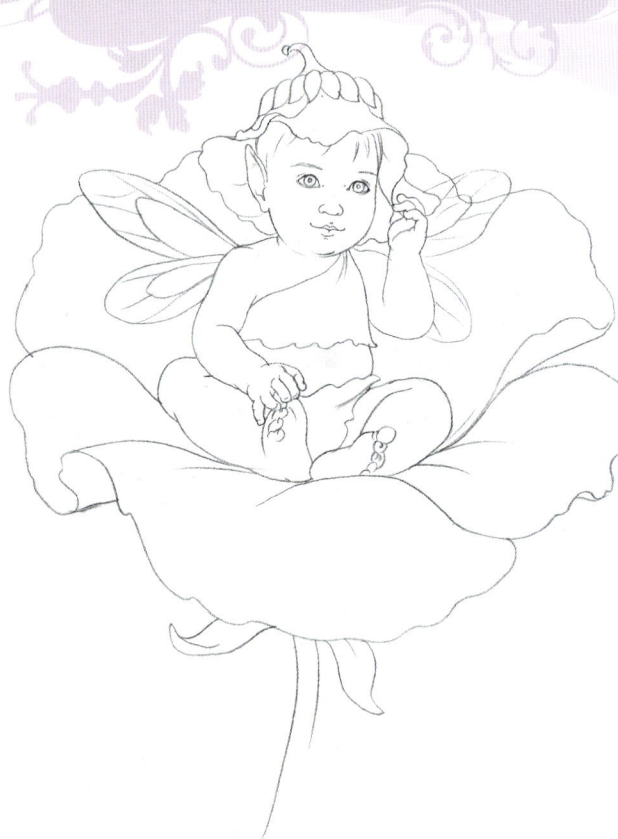

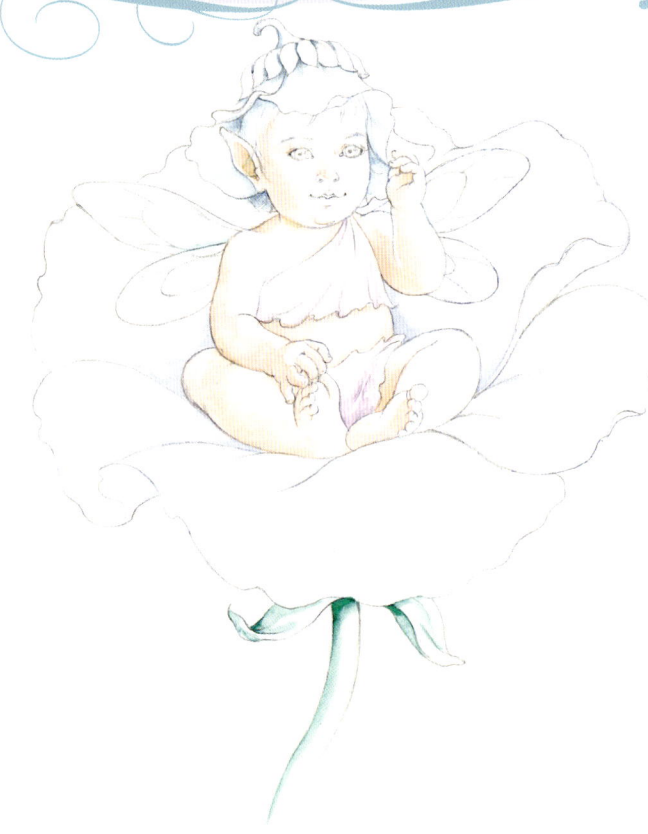

**1** Stretch your watercolor paper and trace the image following the steps on pages 14 and 15. Spray your paper lightly with workable fixative. Let this dry.

**2** Mix together a little Chinese Orange, Burnt Umber, Vermilion Hue and Olive Green and paint the shaded areas of the skin with a no. 1 round. Paint the shadow areas of the flower hat with Payne's Gray and the no. 1 round. Paint the shaded area around the fairy and the folds of the petals with Ultramarine Blue (Green Shade). Paint the shaded areas of the baby's outfit with Winsor Violet (Dioxazine).

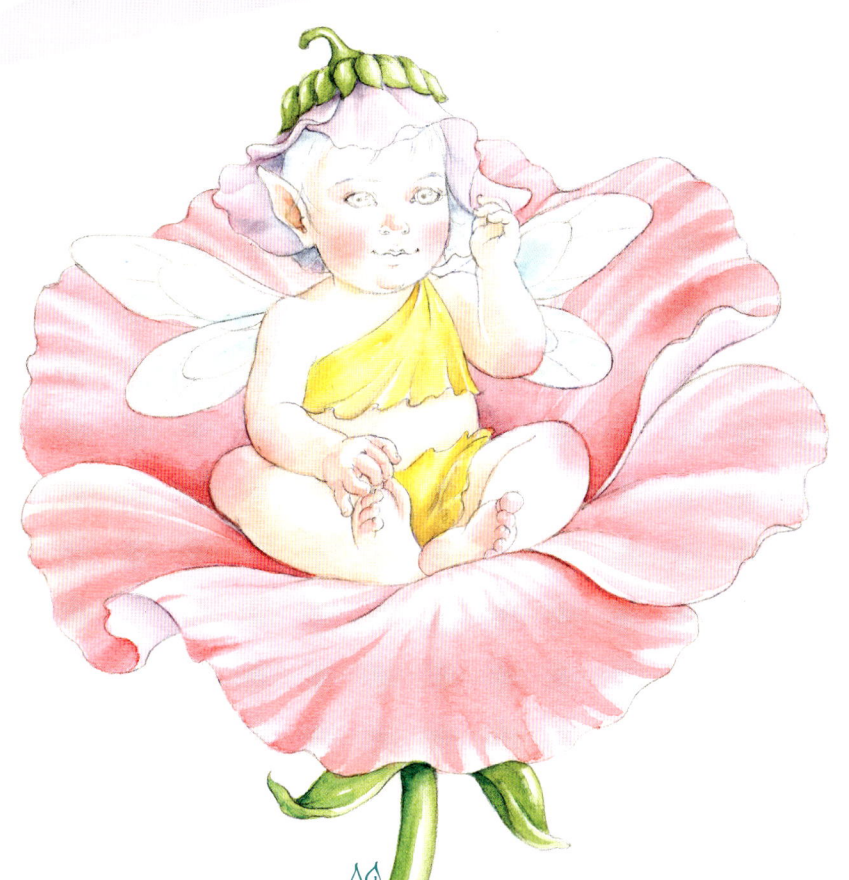

**3** Use a no. 5 round loaded with a medium tint of Quinacridone Red to paint the entire rose. Paint the baby's cheeks with Quinacridone Red. When dry, use a no. 1 round to add Olive Green to the stem and leaves. Wet the knees, toes, elbows and fingers and charge in Quinacridone Red. Add Cadmium Red to the nose, eyelids and ear. Shade the legs with a faint tint of Payne's Gray. Add Winsor Violet (Dioxazine) behind the baby. Strenghten the shadow under the hat with Payne's Gray. Paint the outfit using New Gamboge. Paint between the wing's veins with a light tint of Cobalt Turquoise Light.

To create the color on the rose petals, follow the steps in the technique demonstration on this page.

Follow the steps in the detail demonstration on this page to create the fairy hat.

## TECHNIQUE DEMONSTRATION — Painting Flower Petals

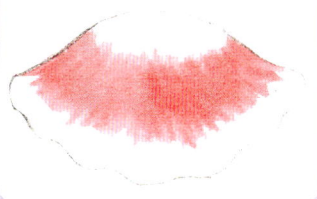
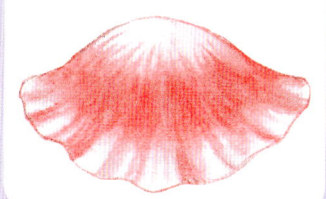
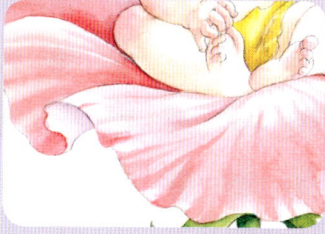

**1** Wet the front petal. When the sheen is gone, paint a horizontal band of Quinacridone Red along the center of the petal using a no. 2 round.

**2** Using a no. 2 miniature, drag Quinacridone Red from the center of the band to the top of the petal and then toward the outer edge of the petal. Outline the petal in Quinacridone Red with a no. 000 round.

**3** Repeat this process on all the petals. While the petals are still wet, charge Alizarin Crimson into the shaded areas on each side of the baby. Add some tints of Winsor Violet (Dioxazine) to the undersides of the petals on the left and right.

## DETAIL DEMONSTRATION — Fairy Hat

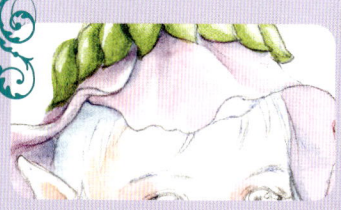
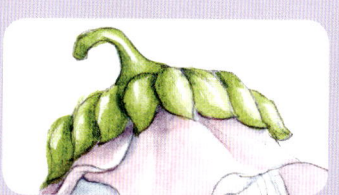

**1** With a no. 1 round, paint a medium tint of Permanent Mauve on the petals of the flower hat. Blend to white paper highlights with a brush dipped in clear water.

**2** Add Olive Green to the top of the flower hat, again leaving the white highlights.

**4** With a no. 00 round, paint the hair with a Yellow Ochre and Raw Umber mixture. Use Permanent Mauve to add more definition to the flower hat petals, shading underneath the petals with Ultramarine Blue (Green Shade) and Payne's Gray. Add more contrast to the petals by painting stronger tones of Permanent Mauve where they overlap. Using a no. 000 round, paint the baby's lips with Vermilion Hue, leaving a white paper highlight across the lower lip. Paint the center of the lips with Caput Mortum Violet.

*To create the baby's eyes, see the technique demonstration on this page.*

**5** Further define the figure using a no. 000 round dipped in a dark tint of Sepia along the outer edge of the fairy's skin. Use Quinacridone Red to paint between the veins of the baby's wings, creating a transparent effect When dry, paint streaks of Indanthrene Blue on the wings. Blend the wings with clear water. Outline the wings and the veins with Cobalt Turquoise Light. Add more Quinacridone Red to the areas of the petals that turn from the light, especially in the areas under the fairy's legs. Using a no. 000 round loaded with a medium dark tint of Quinacridone Red, outline the petals with a double line to indicate thickness.

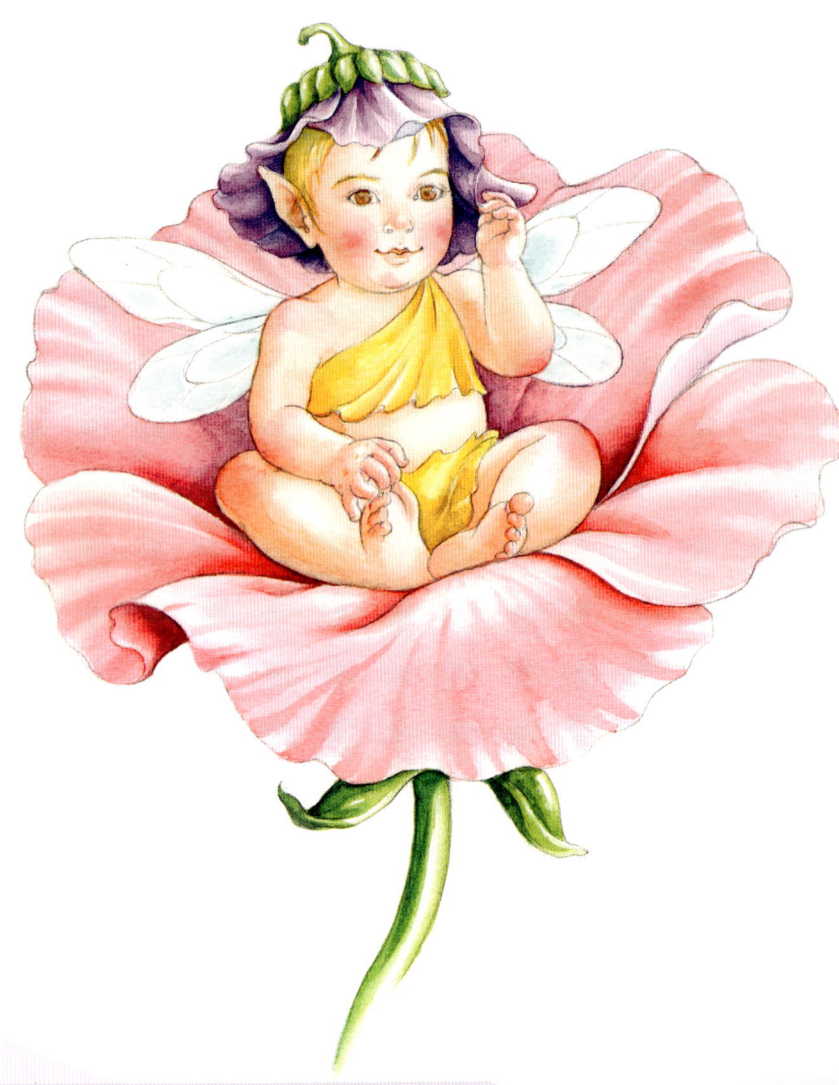

## TECHNIQUE DEMONSTRATION — *Painting Fairy Eyes*

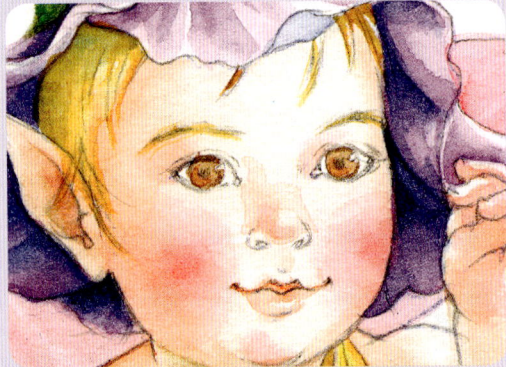

**1** Paint the baby's eyes with a no. 000 round using Burnt Umber, keeping white paper for highlights.

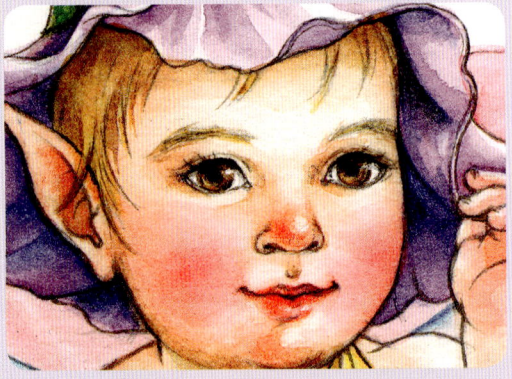

**2** Using a no. 000 round, add highlights to the eyes by mixing a bit of Yellow Ochre with Chinese White and painting a crescent opposite the white highlights. When dry, outline the eye with Sepia with a no. 000 round and paint the eyebrows with delicate short strokes.

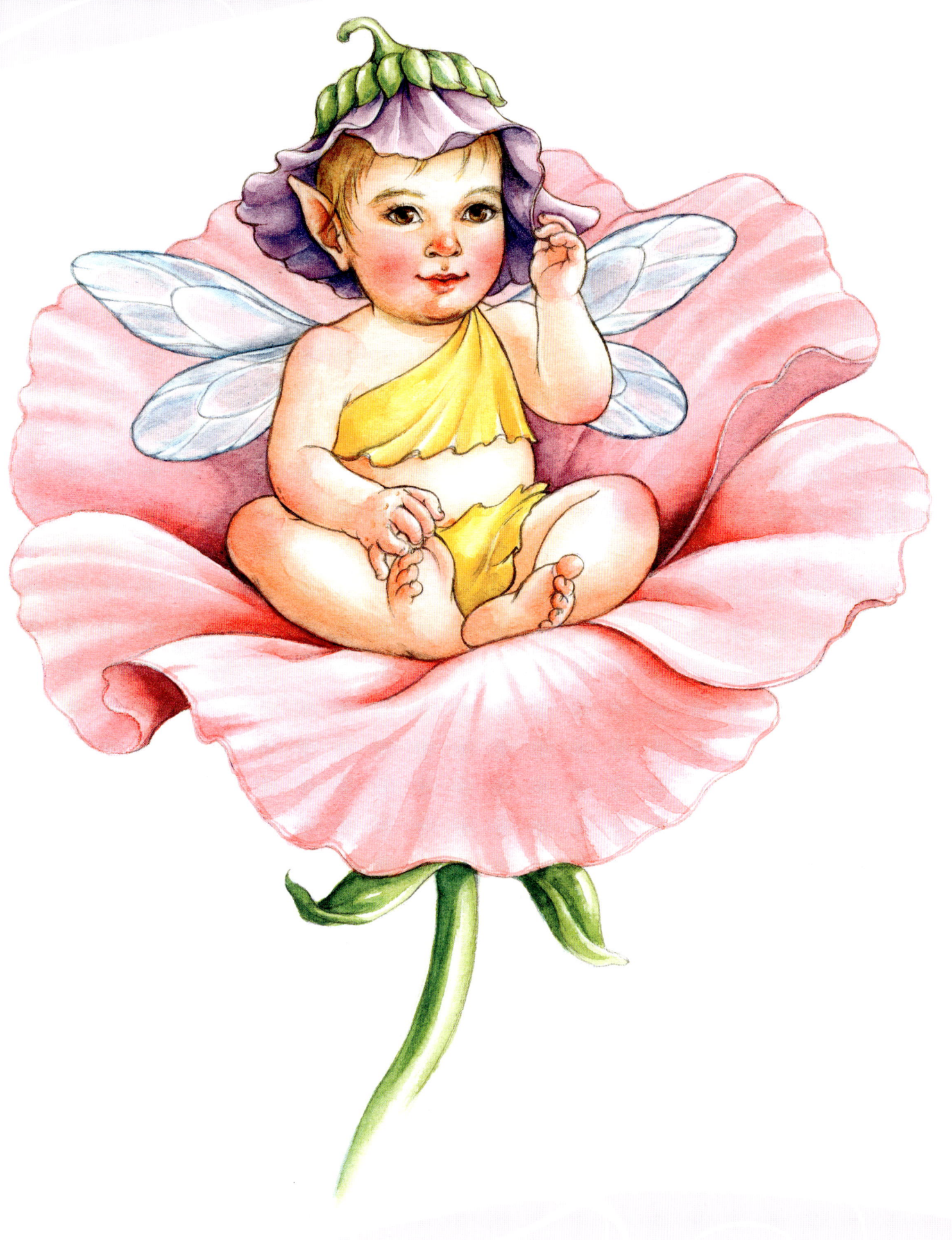

## DEMONSTRATION
# ADOLESCENT FAIRY on hydrangea

*Have fun changing colors if you like. Since this is a redheaded fairy, I thought to include some freckles, but perhaps you have something else in mind. Experiment with your own color combinations on scrap paper or just take colors from a favorite piece of fabric or photograph.*

### ~ YOU WILL NEED ~
#### MATERIALS
Blue tape ~ hard-leaded pencil or ballpoint pen that has run out of ink ~ HB or 2B graphite pencil ~ kneaded eraser ~ no. 2 miniature round ~ nos. 000, 00, 1 and 4 rounds ~ Saral transfer paper ~ stretched watercolor paper ~ tracing paper

#### PIGMENTS
Alizarin Crimson ~ Burnt Umber ~ Cadmium Red ~ Caput Mortum Violet ~ Chinese Orange ~ Chinese White ~ Cobalt Turquoise Light ~ Indigo ~ Olive Green ~ Permanent Magenta ~ Permanent Mauve ~ Permanent Sap Green ~ Sepia ~ Ultramarine Blue (Green Shade) ~ Viridian ~ Winsor Violet (Dioxazine)

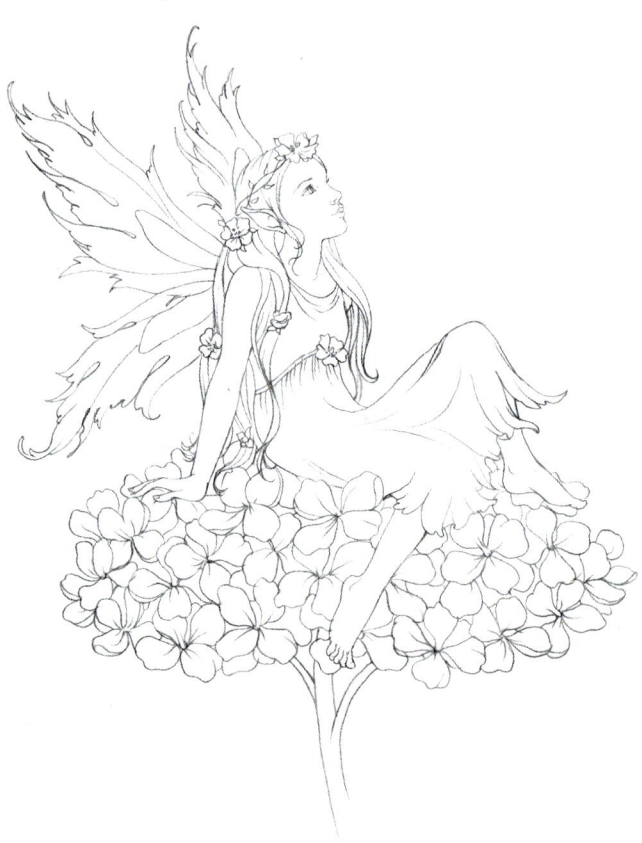

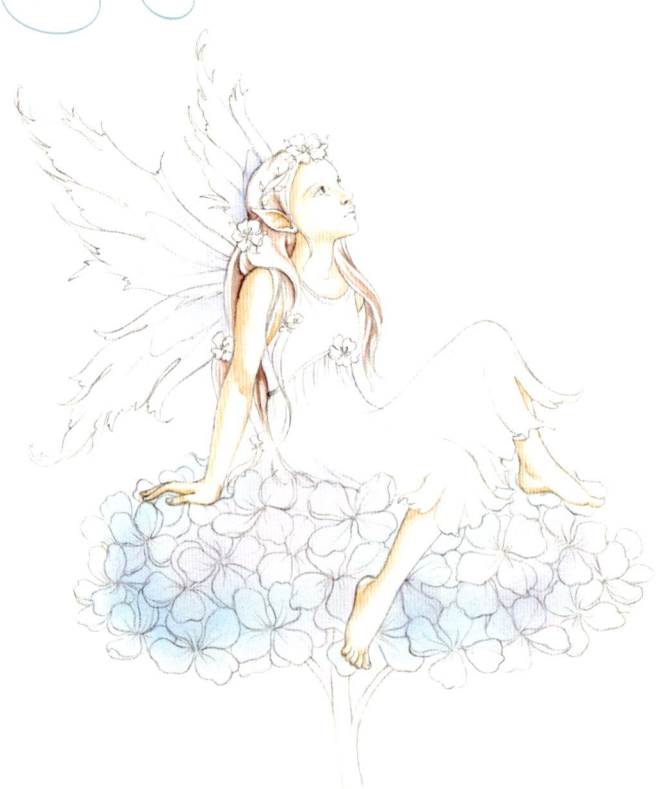

**1** Stretch your watercolor paper and trace the image following the steps on pages 14 and 15.

**2** Wet the entire flower. When the sheen is almost gone, charge in Cobalt Turquoise Light in some areas and Winsor Violet (Dioxazine) in others with a no. 4 round. Add a pale tint of Ultramarine Blue (Green Shade) between the veins of the wings, blending outward with clear water. Use more pale Ultramarine Blue (Green Shade) to paint the inner creases of the dress folds. Shade the fairy's hair with Caput Mortum Violet.

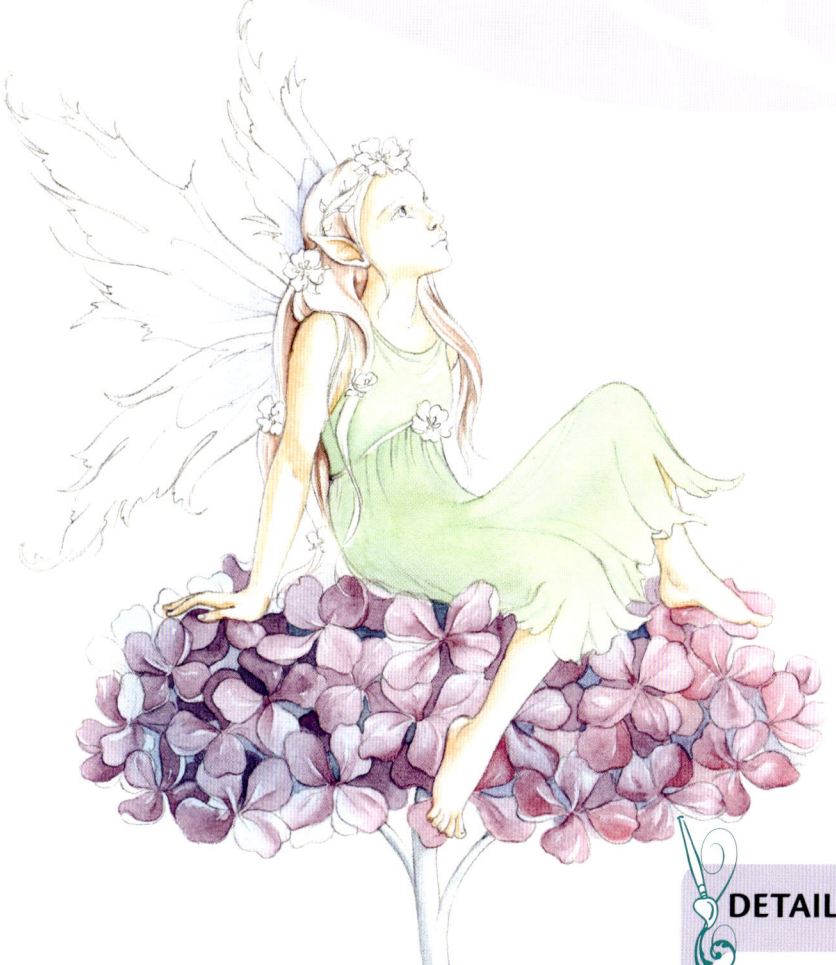

**3** When dry, shade the area under the outermost petals with a no. 2 miniature using cooler shades of the same colors, such as Permanent Mauve, Ultramarine Blue (Green Shade) and Indigo. Dilute Permanent Sap Green and paint the fairy's dress. Use Indigo to paint the shaded side of the stem.

*To create color on the petals, follow the steps for the detail demonstrations on this page.*

## DETAIL DEMONSTRATION — Light Petals

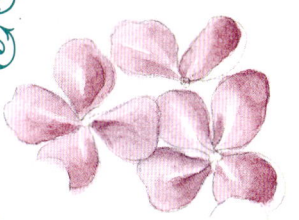 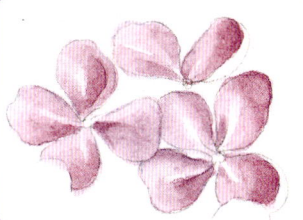

**1** On the petals of hydrangea florets that face the light, apply a mixture of a medium tint of Permanent Mauve and Permanent Magenta.

**2** Apply color to the contours, letting the pigment pool in the more concave parts of the petals.

## DETAIL DEMONSTRATION — Dark Petals

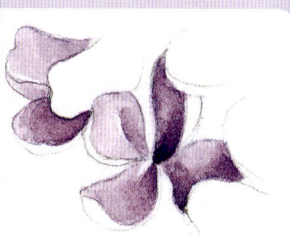 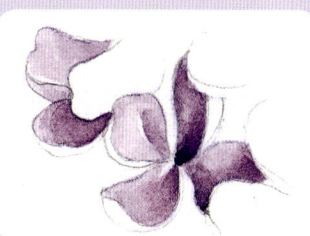

**1** For the petals on the left side of the hydrangea flower head, use Winsor Violet (Dioxazine) following the technique for Light Petals.

**2** Apply color to the contours, letting the pigment pool in the more concave parts of the petals.

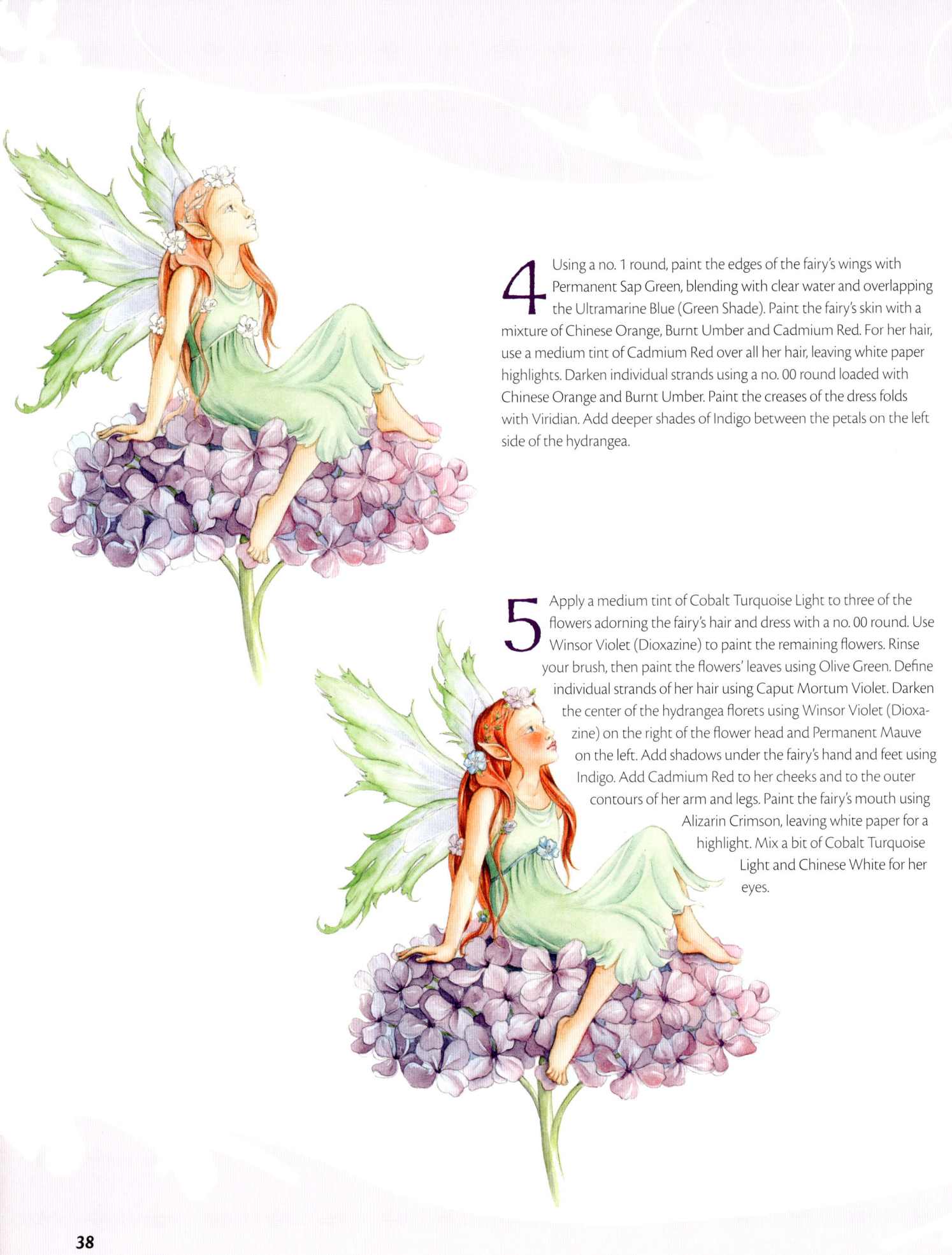

**4** Using a no. 1 round, paint the edges of the fairy's wings with Permanent Sap Green, blending with clear water and overlapping the Ultramarine Blue (Green Shade). Paint the fairy's skin with a mixture of Chinese Orange, Burnt Umber and Cadmium Red. For her hair, use a medium tint of Cadmium Red over all her hair, leaving white paper highlights. Darken individual strands using a no. 00 round loaded with Chinese Orange and Burnt Umber. Paint the creases of the dress folds with Viridian. Add deeper shades of Indigo between the petals on the left side of the hydrangea.

**5** Apply a medium tint of Cobalt Turquoise Light to three of the flowers adorning the fairy's hair and dress with a no. 00 round. Use Winsor Violet (Dioxazine) to paint the remaining flowers. Rinse your brush, then paint the flowers' leaves using Olive Green. Define individual strands of her hair using Caput Mortum Violet. Darken the center of the hydrangea florets using Winsor Violet (Dioxazine) on the right of the flower head and Permanent Mauve on the left. Add shadows under the fairy's hand and feet using Indigo. Add Cadmium Red to her cheeks and to the outer contours of her arm and legs. Paint the fairy's mouth using Alizarin Crimson, leaving white paper for a highlight. Mix a bit of Cobalt Turquoise Light and Chinese White for her eyes.

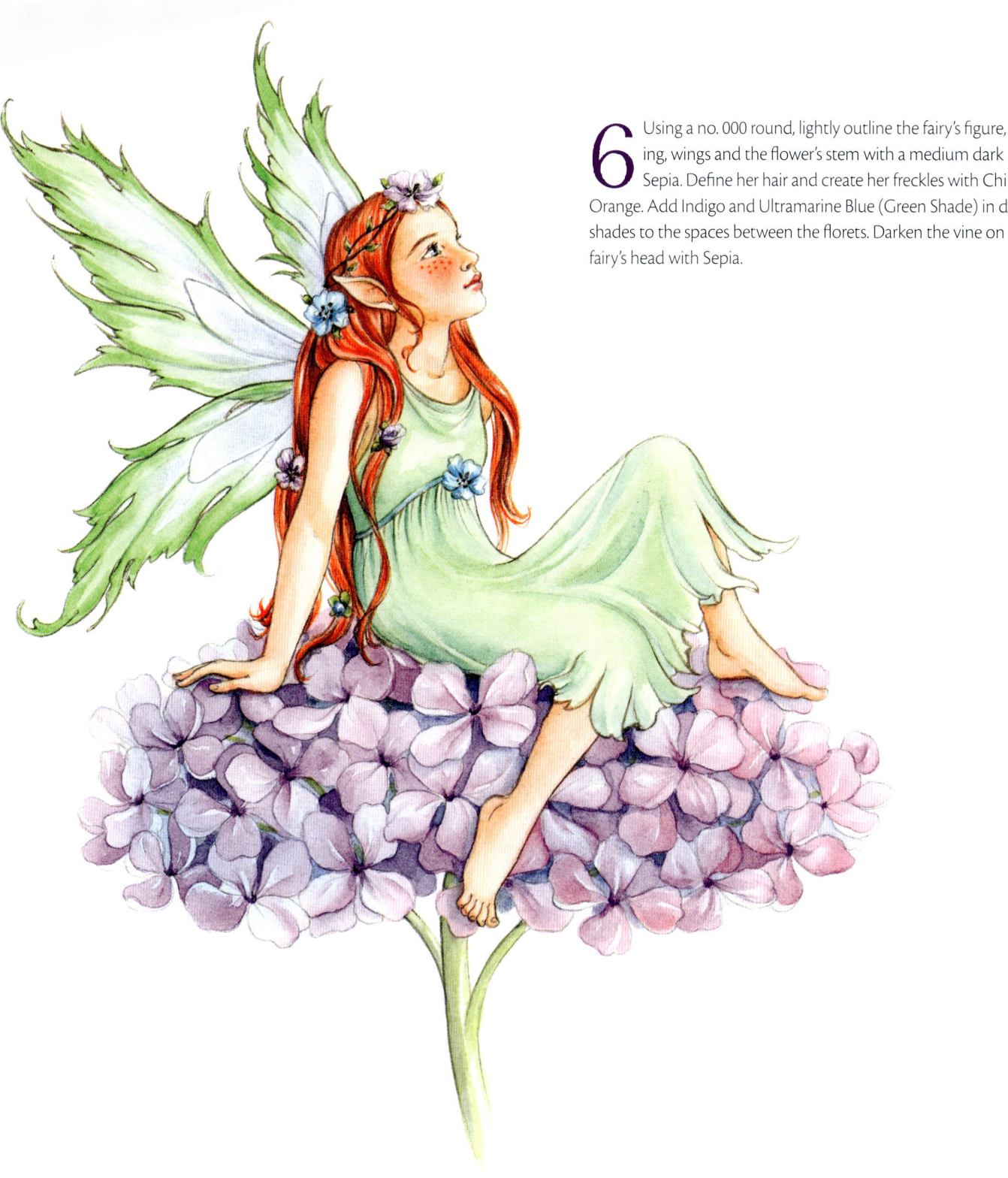

**6** Using a no. 000 round, lightly outline the fairy's figure, clothing, wings and the flower's stem with a medium dark tint of Sepia. Define her hair and create her freckles with Chinese Orange. Add Indigo and Ultramarine Blue (Green Shade) in darker shades to the spaces between the florets. Darken the vine on the fairy's head with Sepia.

# DEMONSTRATION
# ADULT FAIRY on windflower

Here you have an opportunity to practice charging color into petals. The way you apply the color and fine brushstrokes will make the fairy's wings appear translucent. Remember to select colors for the flower and dress that complement your fairy's skin tone.

## ~ YOU WILL NEED ~
### MATERIALS
Blue tape ~ hard-leaded pencil or ballpoint pen that has run out of ink ~ HB or 2B graphite pencil ~ kneaded eraser ~ nos. 000, 00, 0, 1 and 2 rounds ~ Saral transfer paper ~ stretched watercolor paper ~ tracing paper ~ workable fixative

### PIGMENTS
Burnt Umber ~ Cadmium Red ~ Caput Mortum Violet ~ Chinese Orange ~ Chinese White ~ Cobalt Turquoise Light ~ New Gamboge ~ Olive Green ~ Opera ~ Oxide of Chromium ~ Quinacridone Red ~ Sepia ~ Ultramarine Blue (Green Shade) ~ Vermilion Hue ~ Viridian ~ Yellow Ochre

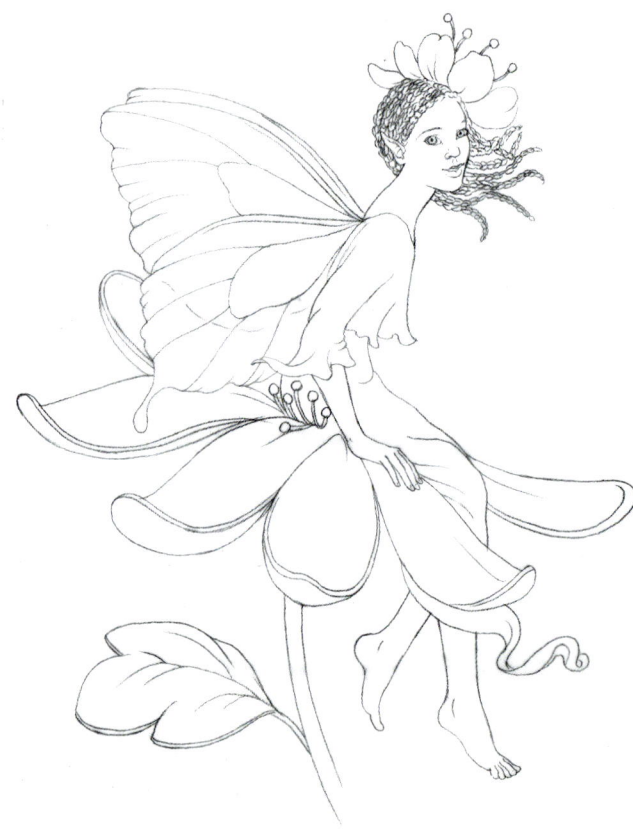

**1** Stretch your watercolor paper and trace the image following the steps on pages 14 and 15. Spray your paper lightly with workable fixative.

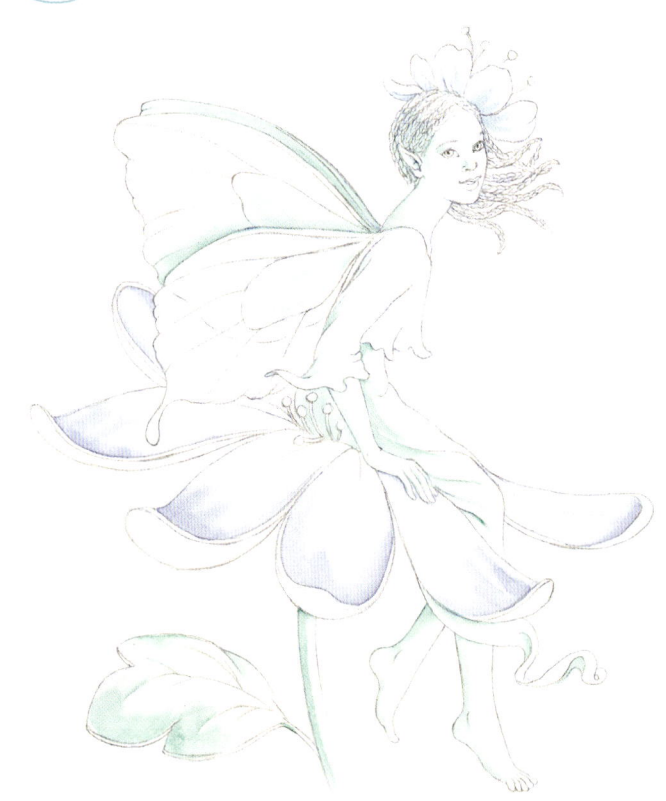

**2** Using a no. 1 round, shade the side of the fairy's skin on the left using a light tint of Viridian. Rinse the brush, then paint the shaded parts of the petals using Ultramarine Blue (Green Shade).

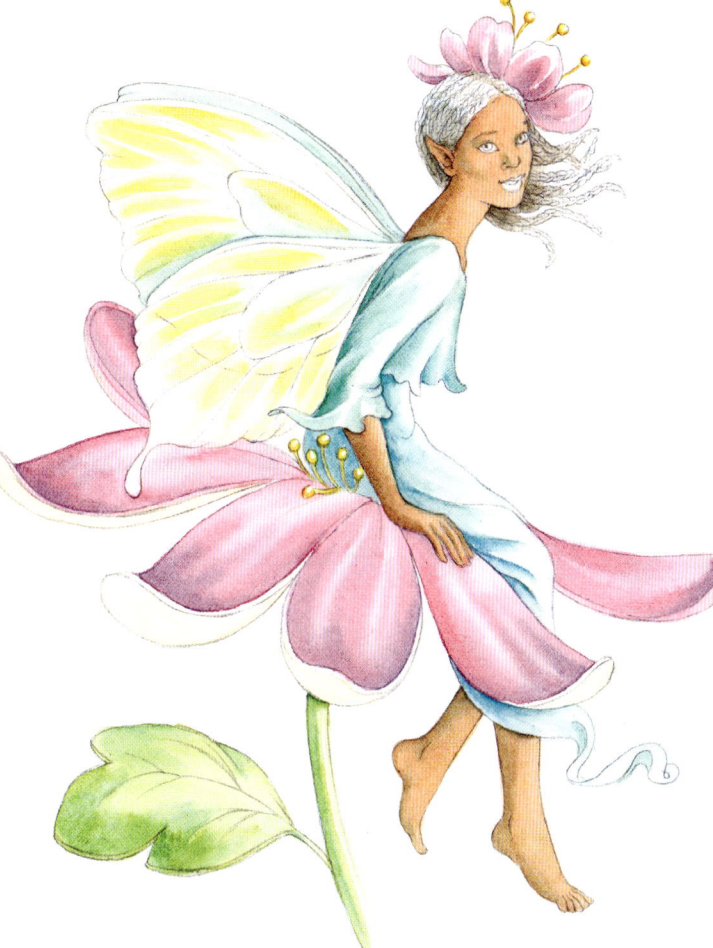

**3** In a palette well, mix the fairy's skin tone using Burnt Umber, Vermilion Hue and Chinese Orange and then apply the mixture using a no. 1 round. Test the mixture on scrap paper to be sure it remains transparent. Add Olive Green to the stem and the leaf following the contours of the leaf's veins. Use a mixture of New Gamboge and Yellow Ochre and a no. 0 round to paint the flower's stamens and to create streaks in the fairy's wings, leaving white around the veins. Using a no. 1 round, add a medium tint of Sepia to the fairy's hair behind her ear and chin.

*To create the color for the flower petals and the fairy's flower hat, follow the steps in the detail and technique demonstrations on this page.*

## DETAIL DEMONSTRATION — Flower Hat

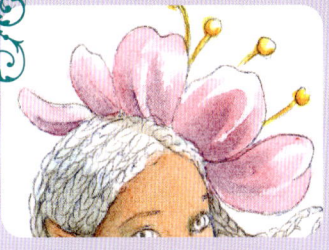

**1** Using a no. 1 round, paint a pale tint of Ultramarine Blue (Green Shade) on the underside of the flower petals, leaving white paper for highlights.

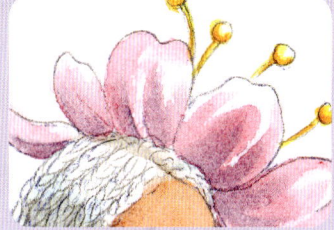

**2** When dry, add a darker tint of Opera to the petals with a no. 1 round. Apply a mixture of New Gamboge and Yellow Ochre to the stamen, leaving white paper highlights.

## TECHNIQUE DEMONSTRATION — Charging Petals

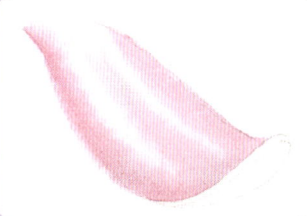

**1** Using a no. 2 round, wet the entire flower surface with clean water. Load the same brush with a medium tint of Opera and charge the pigment into the petal, beginning at the cup-shaped bottom.

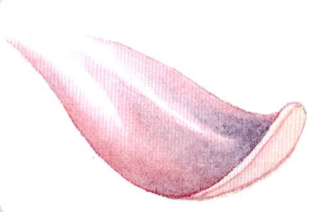

**2** Drag the pigment upwards on the left, center and right sides, leaving white paper highlights. While still wet, charge a darker tint of Opera into the contours of the petal.

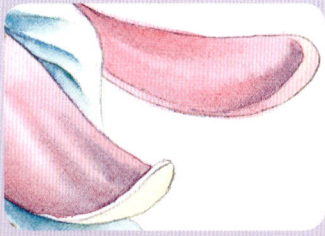

**3** With a no. 000 round, outline the edges of the petal with a still darker tint of Opera. Next, paint the undersides of petals with a very pale tint of New Gamboge for reflected light.

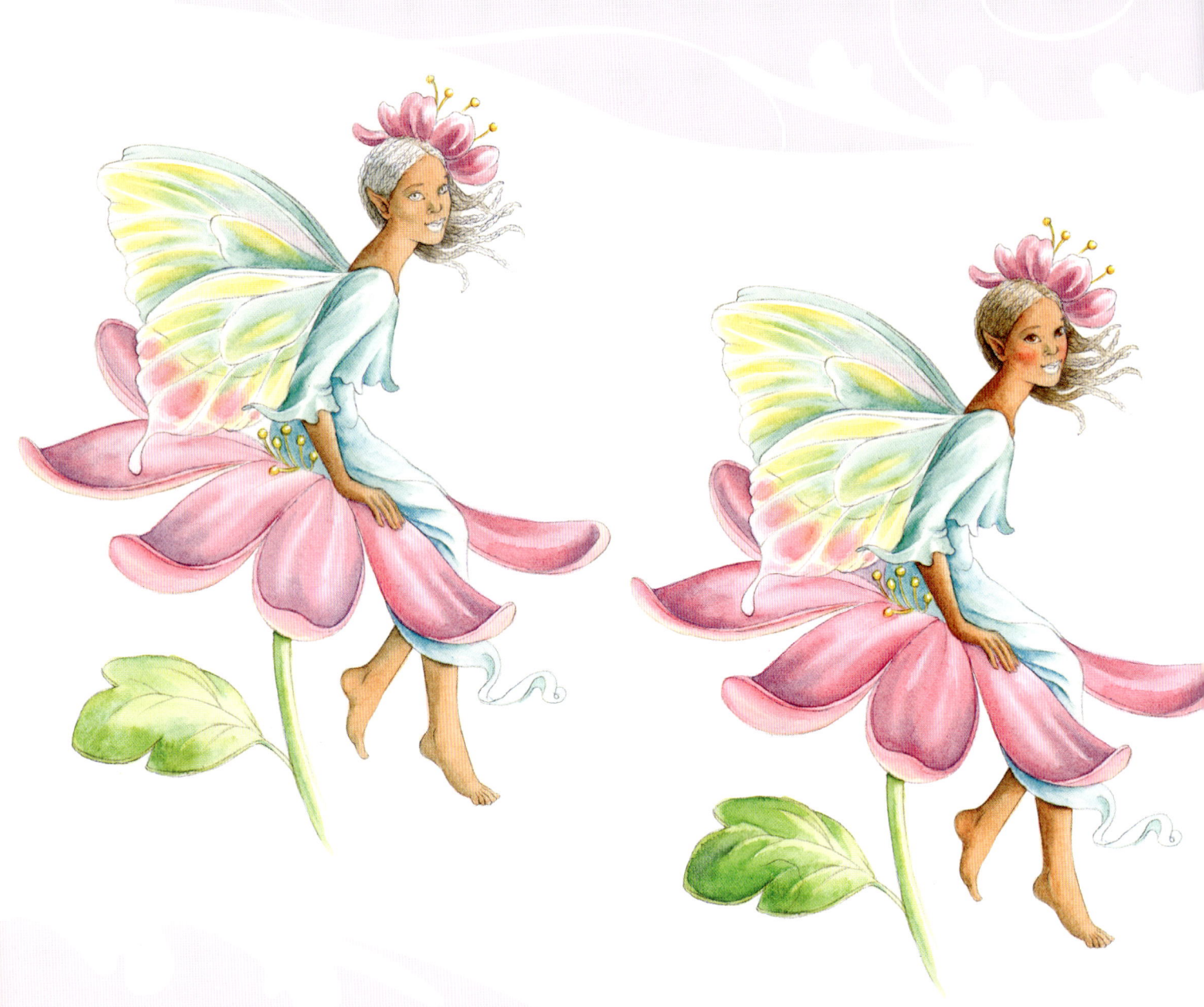

**4** With a mixture of Cobalt Turquoise Light and Viridian, paint the fairy's dress with a no. 1 round. Apply the color to the darkest areas such as the folds and the creases and the left side of the dress, blending outward using clear water. Add Opera and Cobalt Turquoise Light to the lower left portion of the wings for a transparent effect. So that the color will not bleed from one petal to the next, begin adding more Opera to the first two petals on the right.

**5** Using the same process, continue painting the remaining petals with Opera. Add Burnt Umber to the fairy's hair and eyes, leaving white paper for highlights. Mix Chinese Orange and Burnt Umber and wash this onto her skin with a no. 1 round. Add Quinacridone Red to her cheeks using a no. 00 round. Add Oxide of Chromium to the spaces between the veins of the leaf and to the left side of the stem. After the paint dries, apply clear water over the wings. Blend the colors and allow them to set.

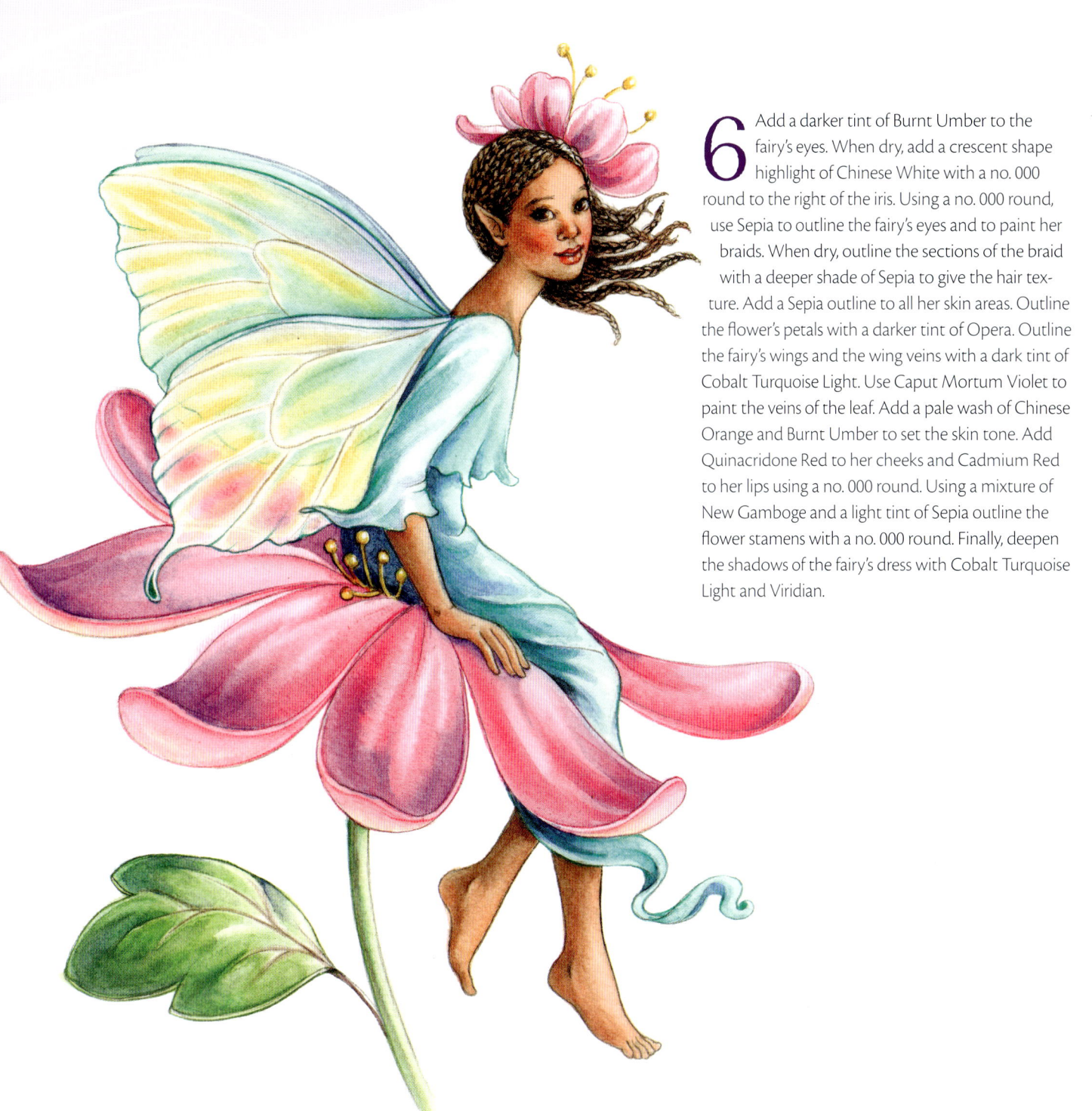

**6** Add a darker tint of Burnt Umber to the fairy's eyes. When dry, add a crescent shape highlight of Chinese White with a no. 000 round to the right of the iris. Using a no. 000 round, use Sepia to outline the fairy's eyes and to paint her braids. When dry, outline the sections of the braid with a deeper shade of Sepia to give the hair texture. Add a Sepia outline to all her skin areas. Outline the flower's petals with a darker tint of Opera. Outline the fairy's wings and the wing veins with a dark tint of Cobalt Turquoise Light. Use Caput Mortum Violet to paint the veins of the leaf. Add a pale wash of Chinese Orange and Burnt Umber to set the skin tone. Add Quinacridone Red to her cheeks and Cadmium Red to her lips using a no. 000 round. Using a mixture of New Gamboge and a light tint of Sepia outline the flower stamens with a no. 000 round. Finally, deepen the shadows of the fairy's dress with Cobalt Turquoise Light and Viridian.

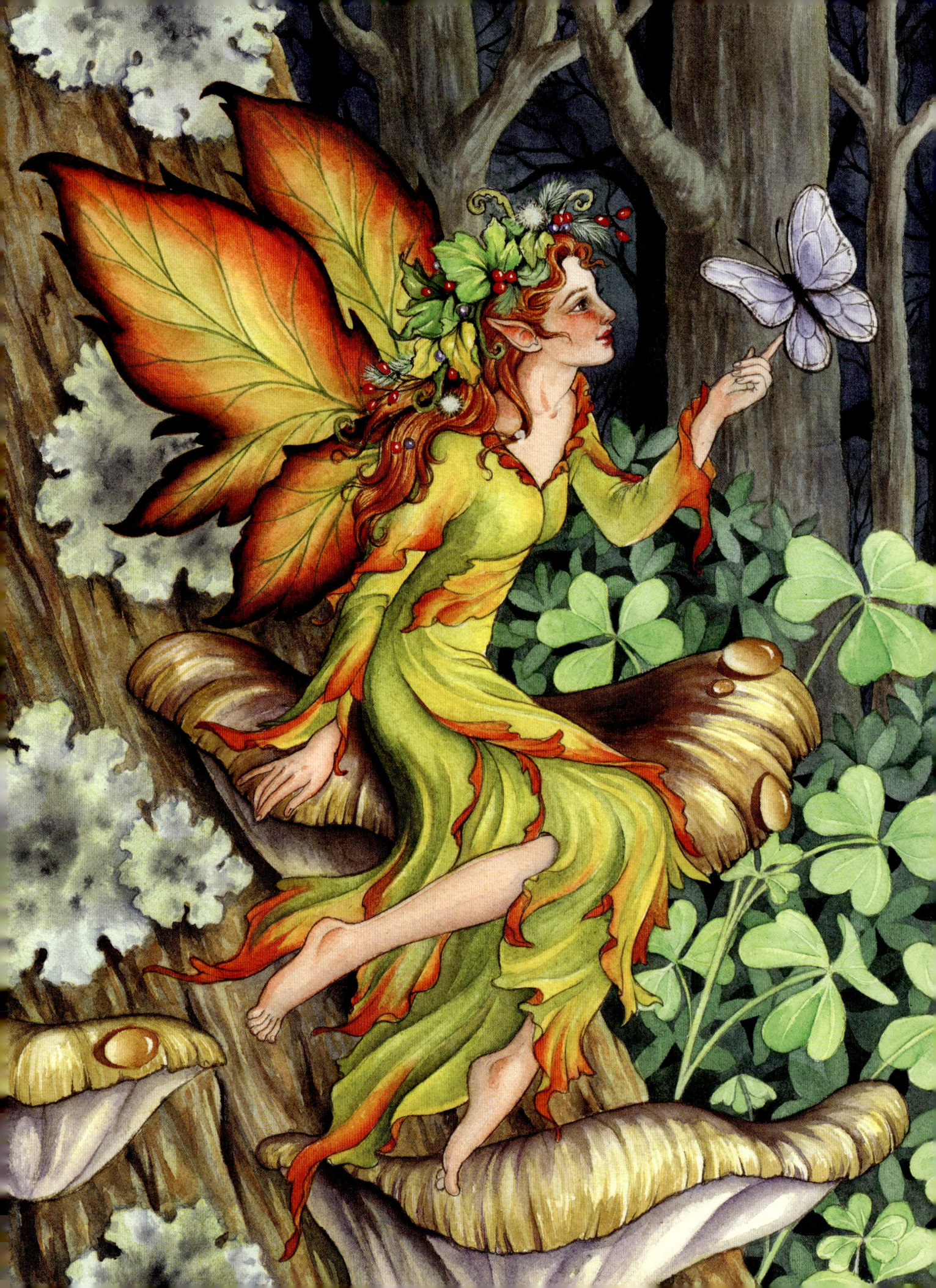

SECTION TWO

# FAIRY TYPES

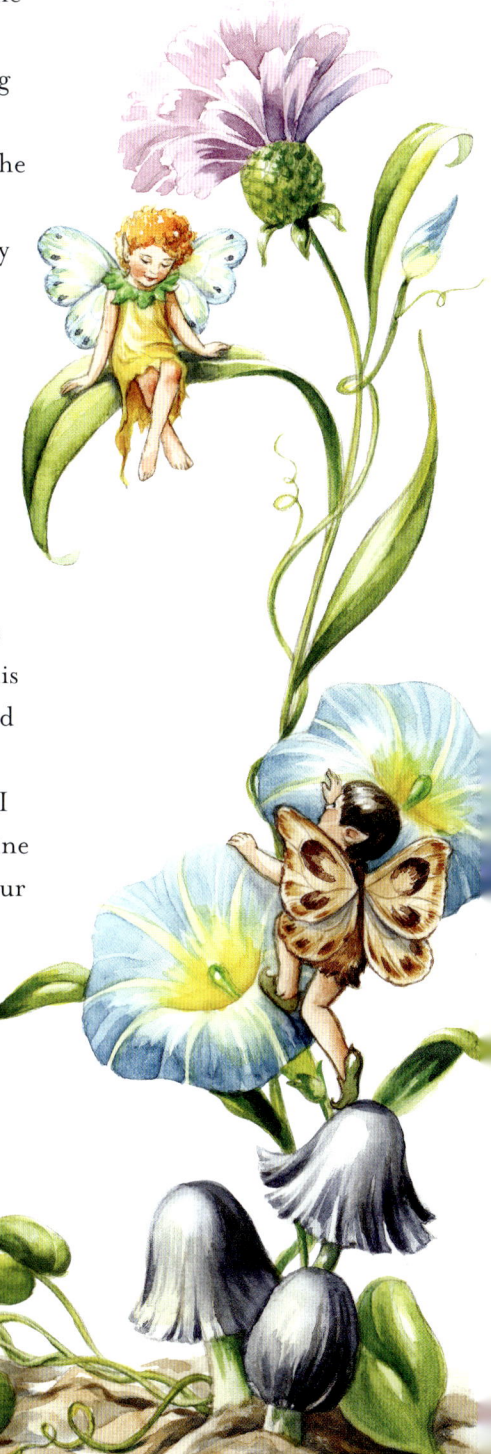

H OW MANY TYPES OF FAIRIES ARE THERE? More than anyone could imagine because they are needed everywhere. Included here are some of the most important fairies in my view.

In this chapter, we have demonstrations for painting fairies of the elements — Earth, Wind, Water and Fire; the seasons — Spring, Summer, Fall and Winter; and the times of day — morning, noon and night.

Each of these demonstrations offers the opportunity to learn techniques for depicting the world around us embodied in these unique creatures.

First, let's visit Morning, Noon and Night Fairies. Wanting to evoke the mood of each time of day, I chose a morning glory, a sunflower and the night blooming moonflower. Their simple, round shapes seemed best to showcase each of these closeups.

One summer night, I invited friends to dinner on the patio. Moonflower buds seemed about to unfurl as they do so gracefully. I was hopeful we'd get to watch this happen. At sunset I looked over, but the buds remained tight. Dinner by candlelight and lively conversation distracted my gaze. It was only after our guests left and I put on lights for cleaning up, that I saw the gorgeous vine in full bloom. I had to resist the impulse to run after our friend's car.

# DEMONSTRATION
# MORNING FAIRY

A morning glory has just unfurled revealing Morning Fairy, ready to face the day. Her upward glance shows her eagerness to play in her bountiful and fragrant garden. Surrounded by cool colors she seems to glow. In this demonstration you will learn to use contrast to focus on your main subject.

### ~YOU WILL NEED~

#### MATERIALS
1½-inch (38mm) flat ❧ blade ❧ blue Saral transfer paper ❧ blue tape ❧ facial tissue ❧ hair dryer ❧ hard-leaded pencil or ballpoint pen that has run out of ink ❧ HB or 2B graphite pencil ❧ no. 2 miniature round ❧ nos. 000, 00, 0, 1 and 2 rounds ❧ stretched watercolor paper ❧ tracing paper

#### PIGMENTS
Burnt Umber ❧ Cadmium Red ❧ Chinese Orange ❧ Cobalt Blue ❧ Cobalt Turquoise Light ❧ Indigo ❧ Ivory Black ❧ New Gamboge ❧ Olive Green ❧ Payne's Gray ❧ Permanent Magenta ❧ Permanent Sap Green ❧ Quinacridone Red ❧ Raw Sienna ❧ Sepia ❧ Ultramarine Blue (Green Shade) ❧ Viridian ❧ Winsor Violet (Dioxazine)

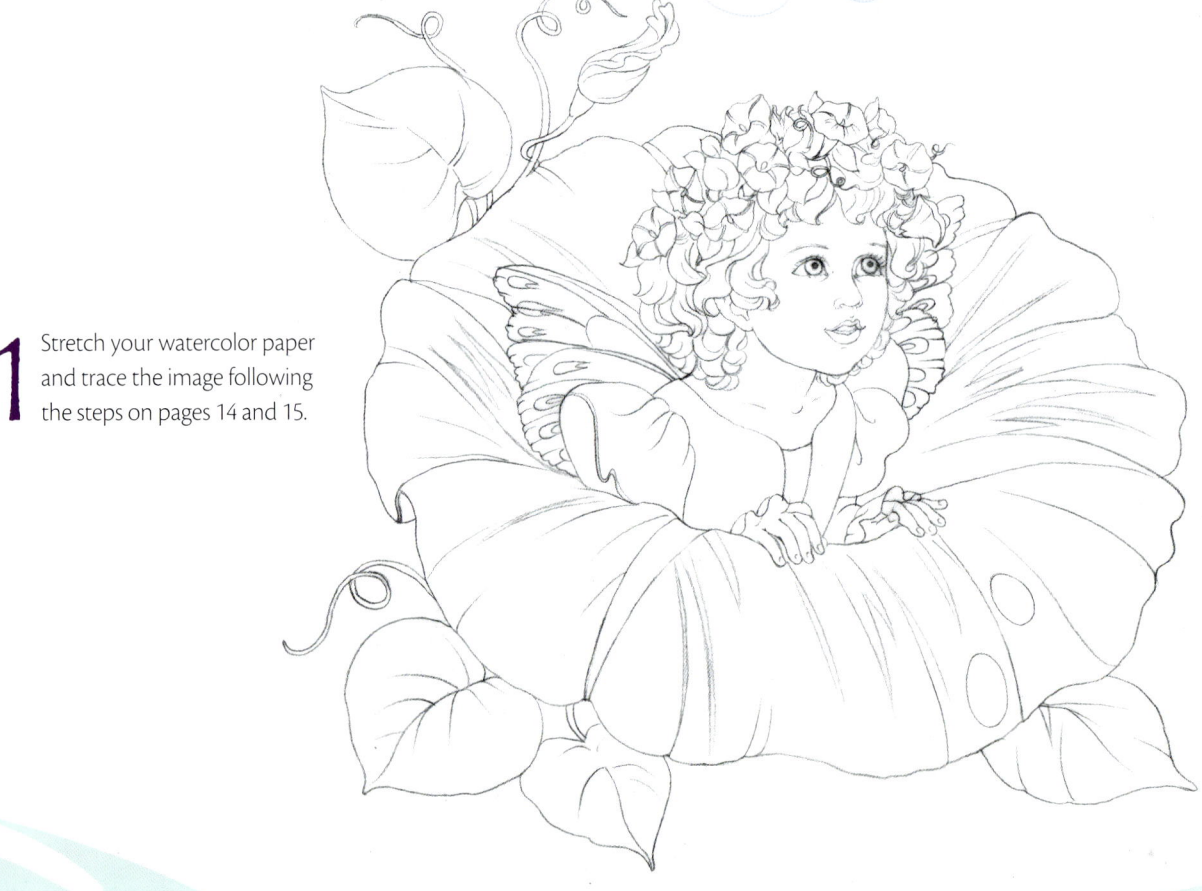

**1** Stretch your watercolor paper and trace the image following the steps on pages 14 and 15.

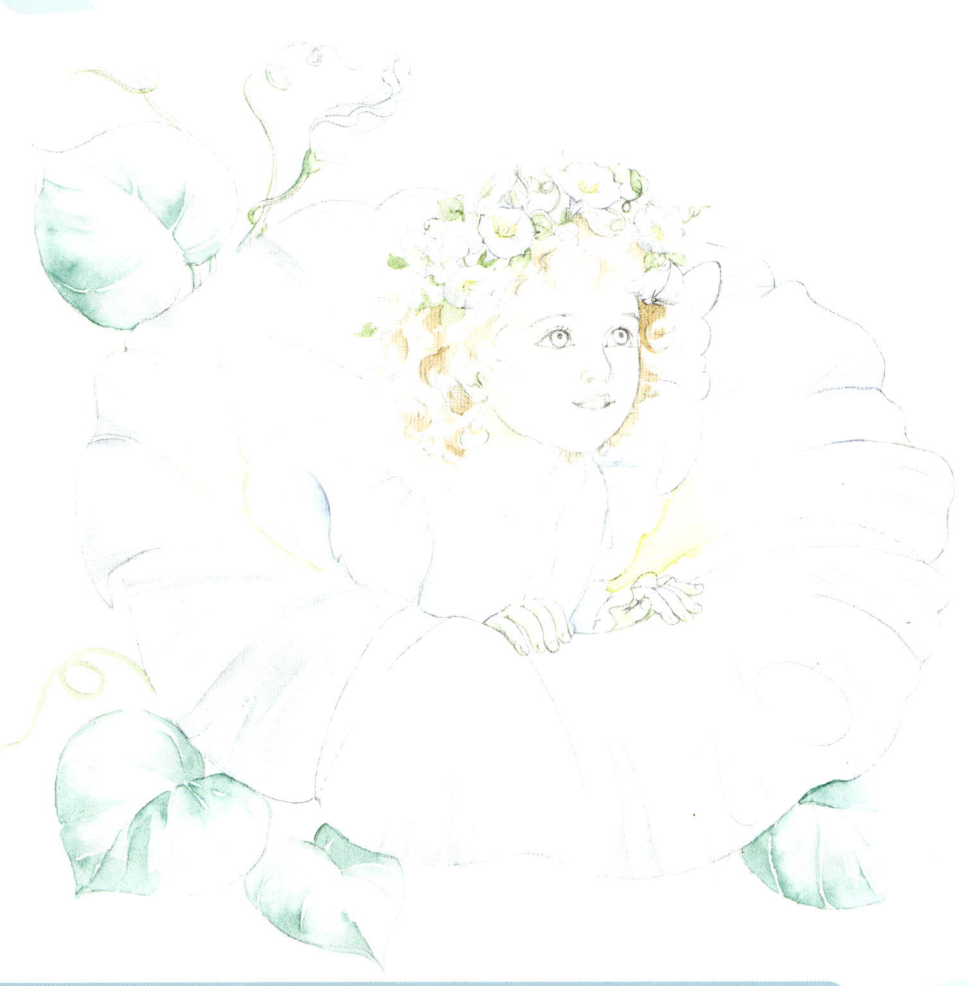

**2** Paint the inside of the flower petals with New Gamboge, blending outward with a no. 1 round loaded with clear water. In a palette well, mix a small amount of Burnt Umber, Chinese Orange and Olive Green and shade the areas on the left side of the fairy's face and neck. Next, paint the shaded folds of the flower with Payne's Gray, making wider stripes at the flower's outer edges and tapering the stripes towards the flower's center. Use Indigo on a no. 0 round to shade the ruffles in the fairy's sleeves and between the upper and lower portions of the wings. Add a mix of Raw Sienna and Sepia to the dark areas of the fairy's curls.

*Create the morning glory leaves following the detail demonstration on this page.*

## DETAIL DEMONSTRATION — *Morning Glory Leaves*

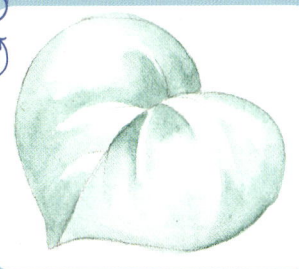

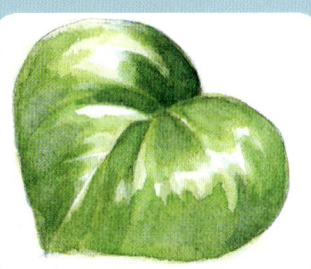

**1** Using a no. 1 round, apply a medium tint of Viridian to shade the left and right side of the center vein. Leave white paper highlights by blending the edges of the color with clear water.

**2** Using a no. 1 round, apply Olive Green to the leaves, leaving the leaf veins and highlights white. When dry, add Permanent Sap Green to the stem end of the leaf and charge it with Indigo. With the same brush, add Permanent Sap Green to the left side of the leaf, next to the highlight.

**3** Add a thin glaze of New Gamboge to the fairy's hair. When her cheeks have dried, glaze her flesh with a light combination of Burnt Umber, Chinese Orange and Quinacridone Red. With a no. 1 round, add a stronger concentration of Olive Green to the leaves on each side of the center vein.

*When her hair has dried, create her rosy cheeks by following the steps in the technique demonstration on this page.*

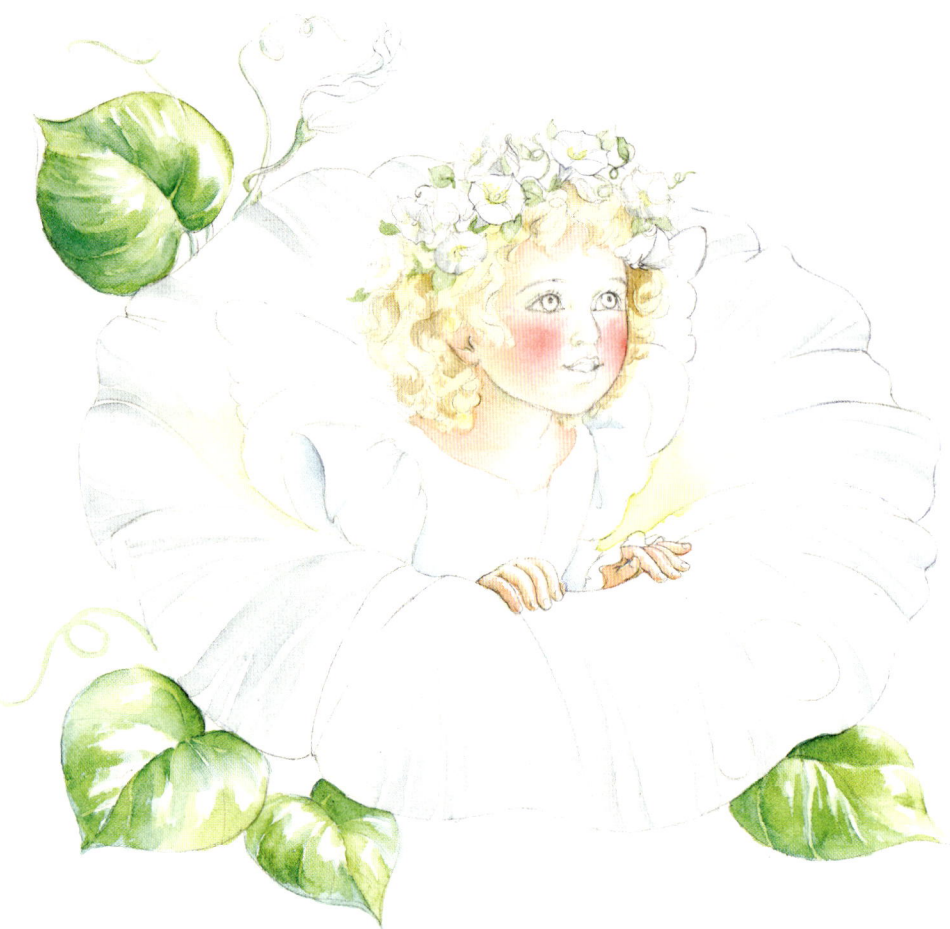

## TECHNIQUE DEMONSTRATION — *Painting Fairy Cheeks*

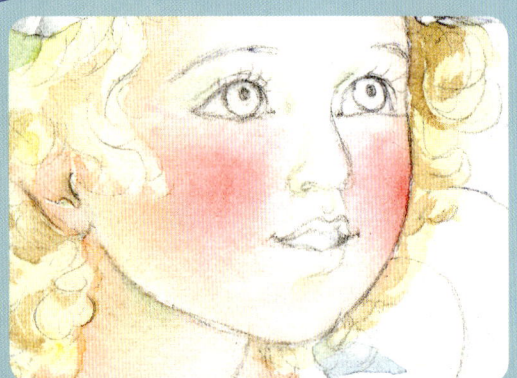

**1** Wet the fairy's cheeks and apply, a small circle of Quinacridone Red with a no. 0 round.

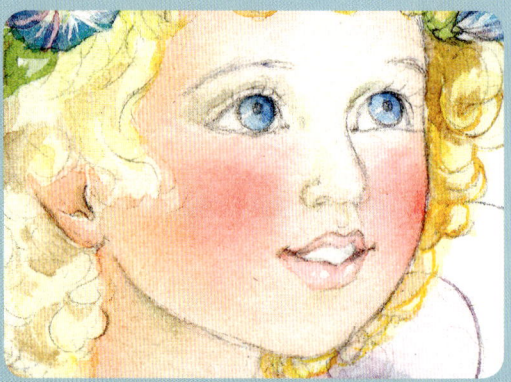

**2** Blend outward with clear water, if necessary. If you apply too much, blot evenly with a facial tissue and start over.

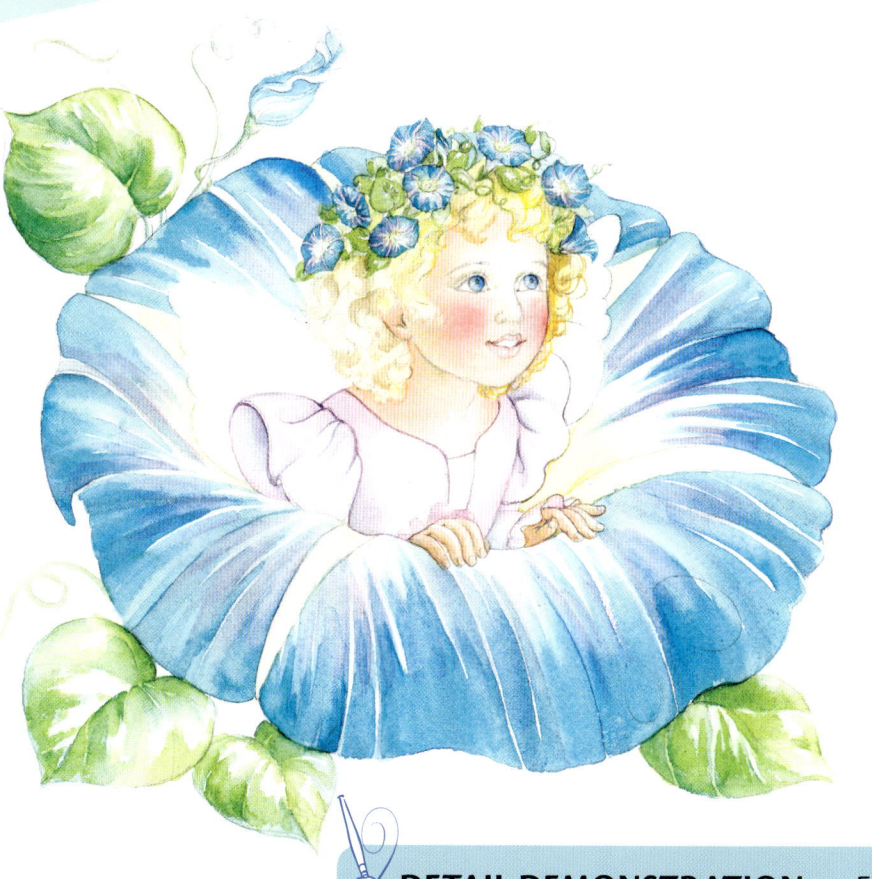

**4** Apply Winsor Violet (Dioxazine) to the fairy's dress using a no. 1 round. Using a no. 000 round, paint her irises with Cobalt Blue, adding a darker shade on the right side of the pupil. Using a no. 000 round, paint the fairy's curls with New Gamboge. With the same brush dipped in a dark tint of a Raw Sienna and Sepia mixture, outline individual strands of her hair once the hair has dried.

*Create the fairy's wreath and the color for the morning glory following the detail and technique demonstrations on this page.*

## DETAIL DEMONSTRATION — *Flower Wreath*

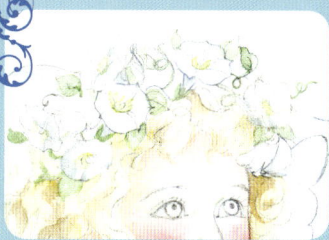 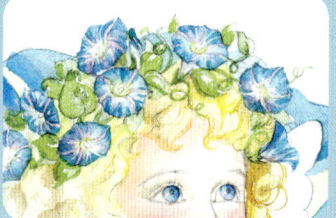 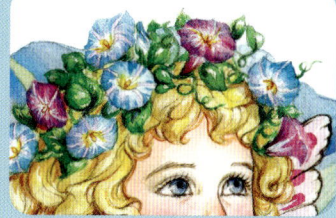

**1** Using a no. 0 round, paint a medium tint of Cobalt Turquoise Light on the outer edge of the flowers. Using clear water, drag the color towards the center, leaving white paper highlights.

**2** Paint the leaves using the same technique described in the detail demonstration on page 47. When dry, use a no. 0 round to add Permanent Sap Green to the leaves for more contrast.

**3** Using a no. 0 round, add darker tints of Cobalt Turquoise Light and Permanent Magenta to the flower ripples. When dry, paint the flower centers with New Gamboge and paint streaks in the flowers with Quinacridone Red.

## TECHNIQUE DEMONSTRATION — *Painting Flower Petals*

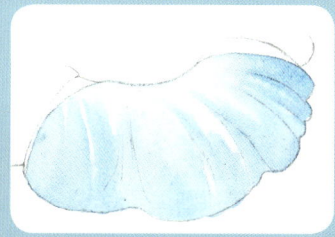 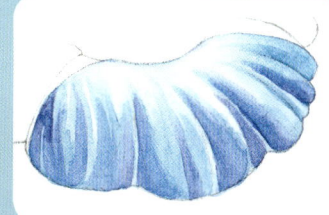 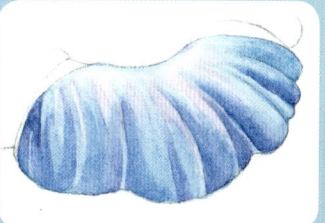

**1** Apply clean water to one section of the flower with a no. 2 round. When the shine has gone, apply a medium wash of Cobalt Turquoise Light with a no. 1 round, starting at the outer edge and lifting as you reach the flower center.

**2** Once the shine has disappeared, use your no. 1 round to lay in dark streaks of Cobalt Turquoise Light one section at a time. Using a no. 1 round, add dark streaks of Ultramarine Blue (Green Shade).

**3** When the petals have completely dried, add Winsor Violet (Dioxazine) streaks with a no. 1 round where the petals curve outward.

## DETAIL DEMONSTRATION — *Fairy Wings*

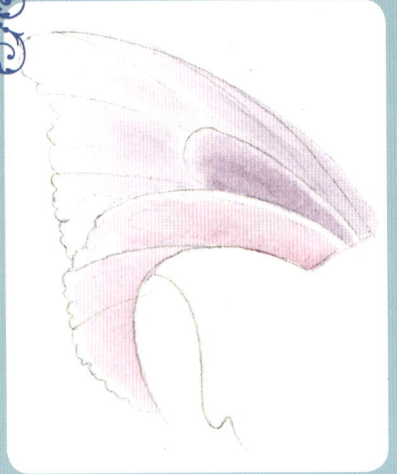 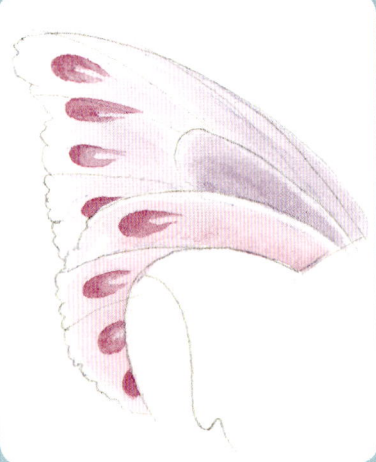 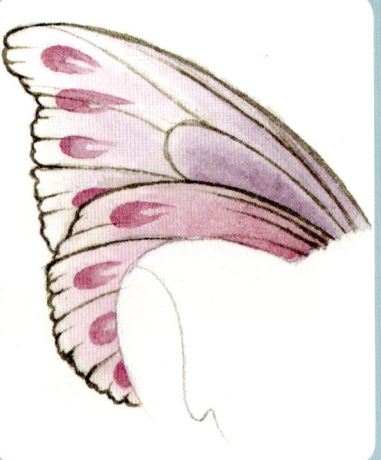

**1** Paint between the veins of the top part of the wing with a no. 2 miniature loaded with Winsor Violet (Dioxazine). When dry, use the same brush loaded with a medium tint of Permanent Magenta to paint the inside of the lower wing, dragging the color outward. Let dry.

**2** Use a no. 00 round loaded with a dark tint of Permanent Magenta to paint crescents of color near the edge of the wing. When dry, add more Permanent Magenta and Winsor Violet (Dioxazine) towards the inside of the wing.

**3** When dry, use a no. 000 round to paint a medium tint of Sepia on the wing veins. Use a darker tint of Sepia to outline the outer edge of the wing. Let dry. Add a clear water wash over the entire wing to set the colors.

## TECHNIQUE DEMONSTRATION — *Painting Dewdrops*

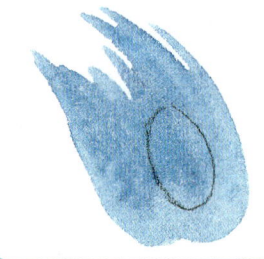 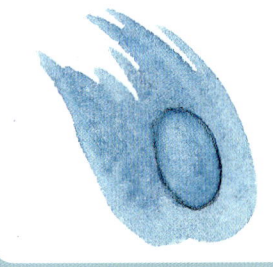 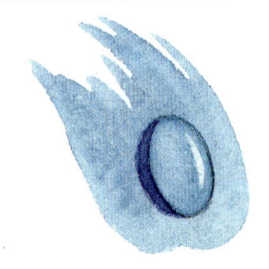

**1** When you're sure the flower is completely dry, pencil in oval dewdrop shapes. Wet each dewdrop thoroughly.

**2** Using a no. 00 round, charge in a deep concentration of Cobalt Turquoise Light on the side facing the light source. Using a clean wet brush, bring the color towards the left side of the droplet. Let dry.

**3** Paint the cast shadow on the left side of the dewdrop using a no. 000 round loaded with a dark tint of Cobalt Turquoise Light and Ultramarine Blue (Green Shade). Using a blade, scratch an arc in the darkest area.

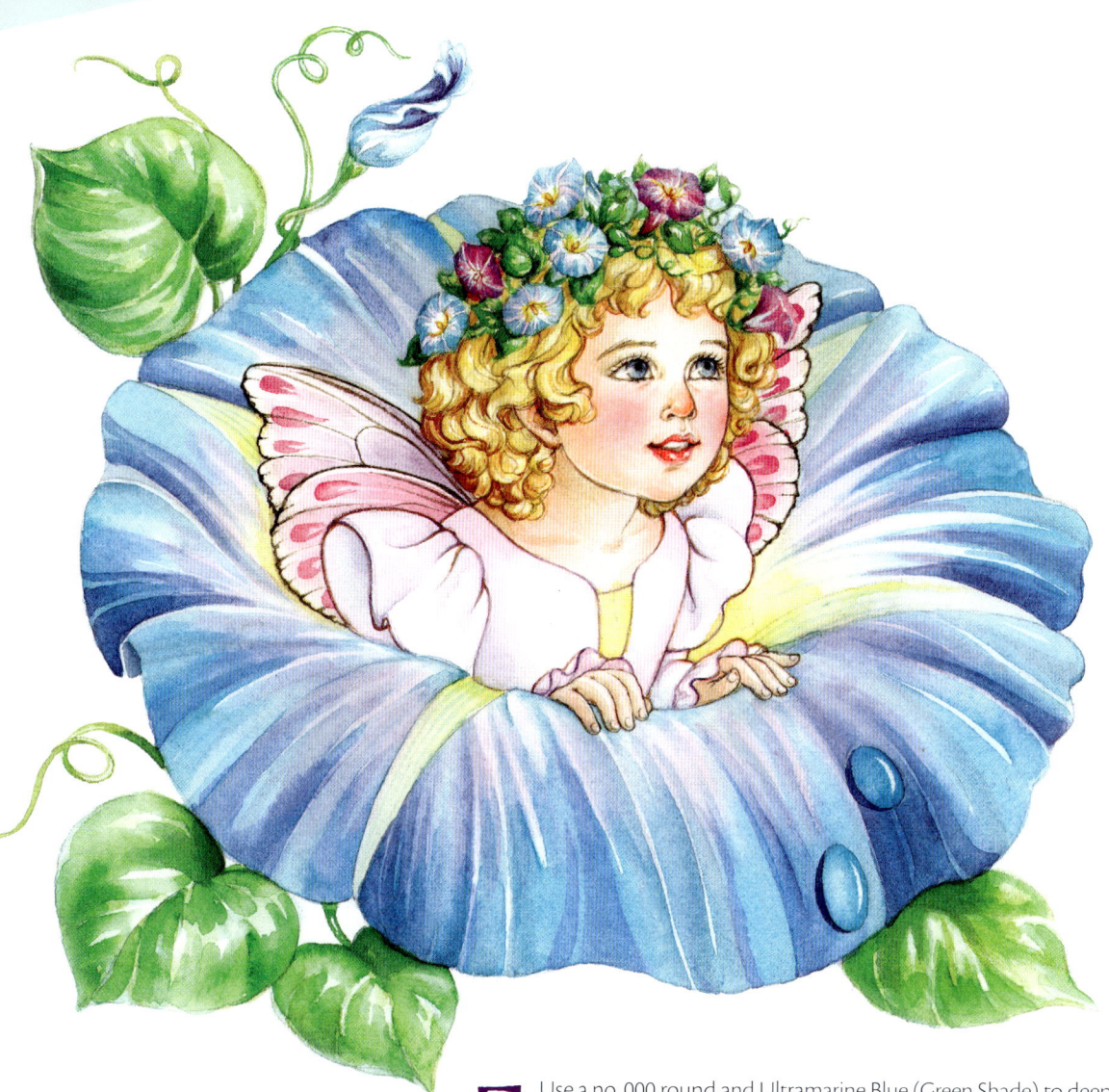

**5** Use a no. 000 round and Ultramarine Blue (Green Shade) to deepen the flower's ripples, working wet-into-wet with more concentrated color. With the same size brush, define the fairy's hair with a medium concentration of a Raw Sienna and Sepia mixture. Next, use Quinacridone Red on a no. 000 round to paint the fairy's lips. Using the same size brush, outline the iris in a medium dark tint of Sepia and paint the pupils using Ivory Black. Wet the end of the fairy's nose with a no. 000 round and charge in Cadmium Red, leaving a white paper highlight on the left side.

Finally, using a no. 000 round, paint around the edges of the figure with a mixture of Chinese Orange, Burnt Umber and Sepia. Load a medium brush with clear water and apply it carefully over the entire flower. Deepen your greens and add Indigo to the leaf parts under the flower and the areas turning from light.

*To create the dewdrops on the flower and the fairy's wings, follow the steps in the technique and detail demonstrations on the previous page.*

## DEMONSTRATION
# NOON FAIRY

*Here is Noon Fairy at the hottest part of a late summer day. The deep reds of her hair and wings pulse with heat. Behind her the petals of the sunflower evoke the flames of its namesake. Yet, from the center of this composition she stares at us with eyes calm and cool.*

### ~ YOU WILL NEED ~

#### MATERIALS
Blue tape ~ hard-leaded pencil or ballpoint pen that has run out of ink ~ HB or 2B graphite pencil ~ kneaded eraser ~ no. 2 miniature round ~ nos. 0, 00, 000, 1 and 2 rounds ~ Saral transfer paper ~ stretched watercolor paper ~ tracing paper ~ workable fixative

#### PIGMENTS
Alizarin Crimson ~ Burnt Umber ~ Cadmium Red ~ Cadmium Yellow ~ Caput Mortum Violet ~ Chinese Orange ~ Chinese White ~ Cerulean Blue ~ Cobalt Blue ~ Indigo ~ Ivory Black ~ Lemon Yellow ~ New Gamboge ~ Olive Green ~ Payne's Gray ~ Quinacridone Red ~ Sepia ~ Vermilion Hue ~ Yellow Ochre

**1** Stretch your watercolor paper and trace the image following the steps on pages 14 and 15. Spray the image lightly with a workable fixative and let it dry.

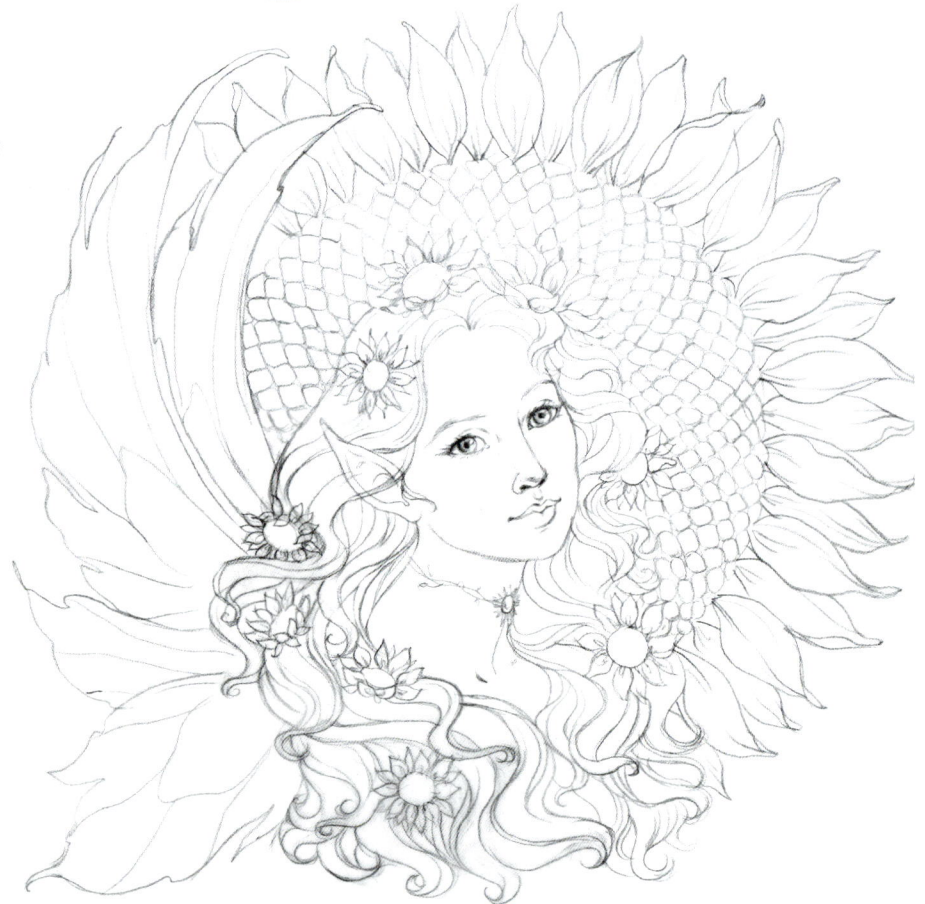

52

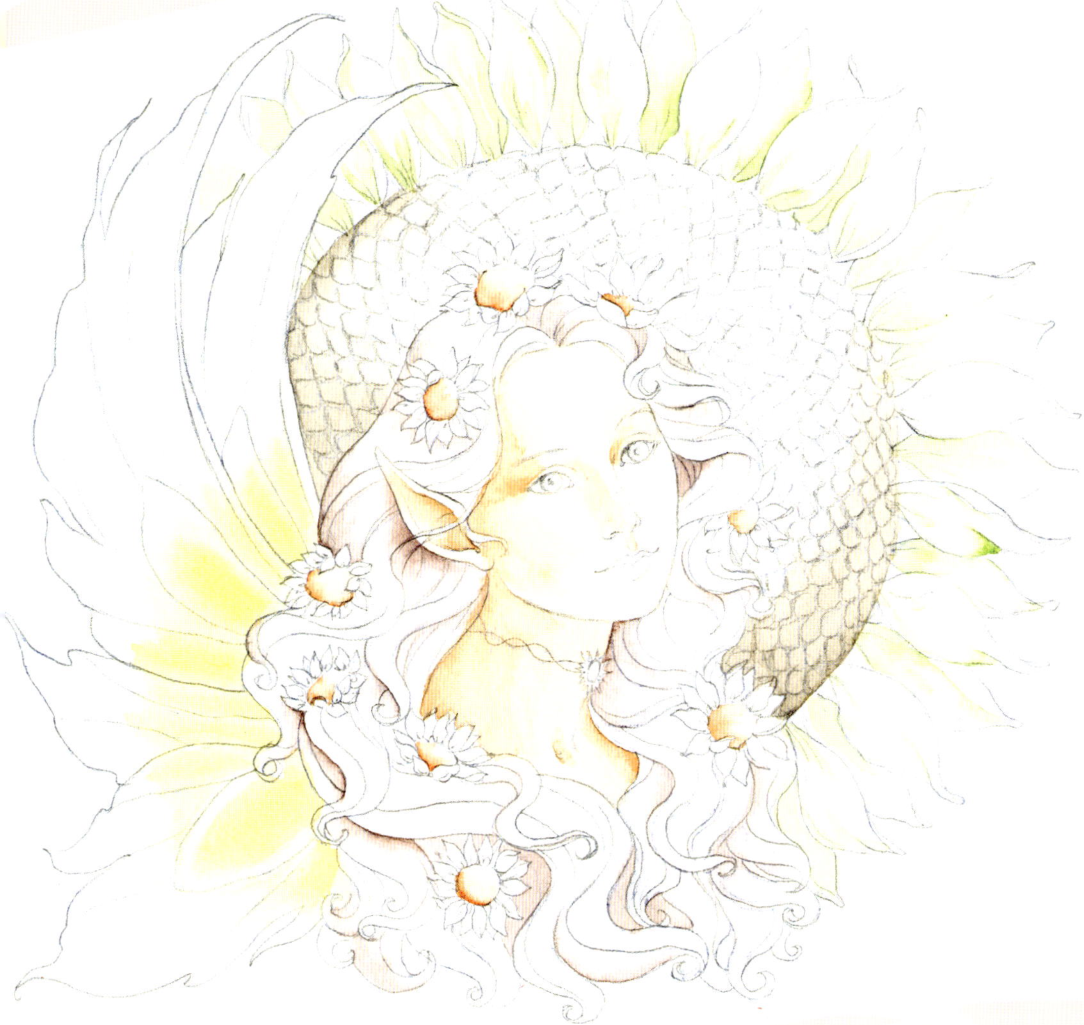

**2** Mix Burnt Umber with Sepia. With your no. 2 round, apply a tint of this mixture to the seedhead of the large flower where it turns from the light source coming from the upper right. Apply a medium tint of New Gamboge to the petals, wing centers and bases, making sure to create delicate shapes in the petals.

*Follow the steps in the technique demonstration on this page to create the fairy's skin tone.*

## TECHNIQUE DEMONSTRATION — *Creating Fairy Skin Tone*

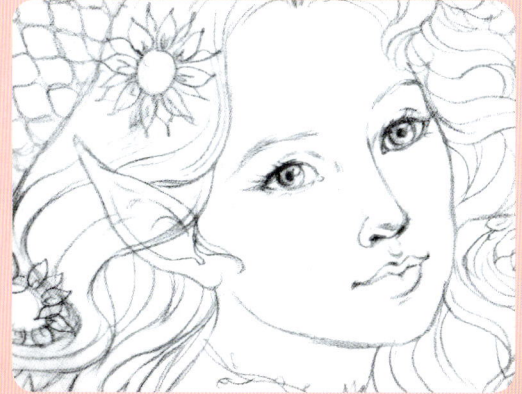

**1** With a no. 1 round loaded with clear water, wet the skin area.

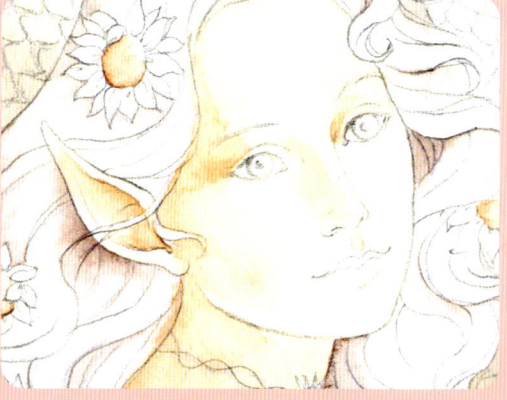

**2** Mix a bit of Chinese Orange with Burnt Umber then add Olive Green. Apply this to her skin with the same brush. Keep the color thinner and lighter where the skin faces the sun by adding water to the mixture before painting those areas.

## TECHNIQUE DEMONSTRATION — *Painting Fairy Hair*

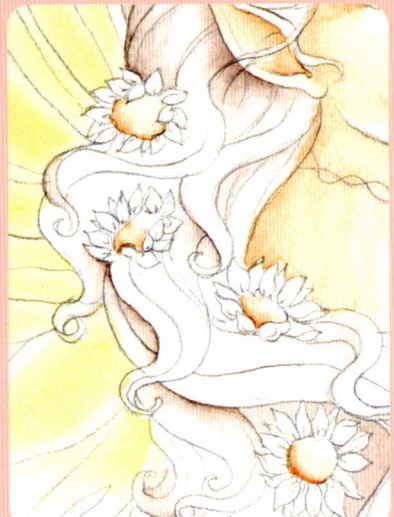
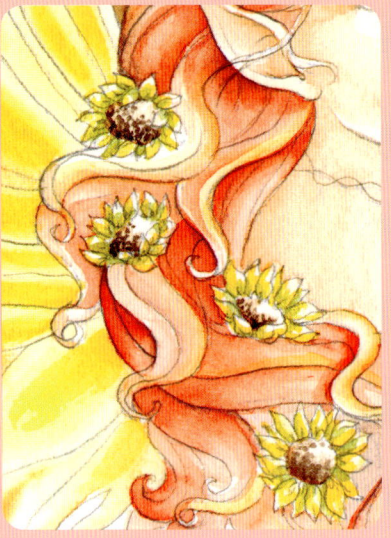
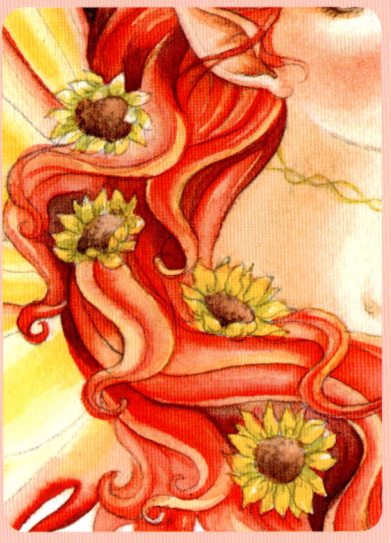

**1** With a no. 2 miniature, use Caput Mortum Violet to shade the fairy's hair. Highlight individual strands with New Gamboge. When dry, use a medium tint of Quinacridone Red on the other strands.

**2** Let dry. Brush clear water with a no. 1 round over the hair to set the color. Once dry, begin adding a stronger concentration of Quinacridone Red to the strands behind the lighter ones.

**3** Finally, deepen the shadows in her hair with a mixture of Caput Mortum Violet and Sepia loaded on a no. 000 round.

## DETAIL DEMONSTRATION — *Small Flowers*

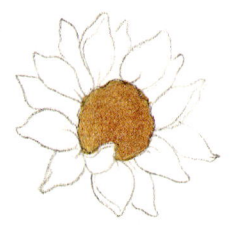
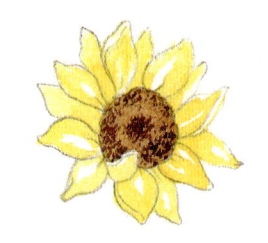
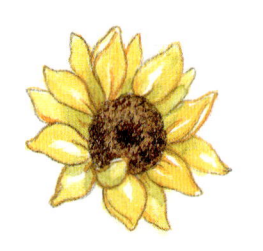

**1** With a no. 0 round, paint a mixture of Chinese Orange, Burnt Umber and Yellow Ochre in the centers of the flowers in the fairy's hair and let dry.

**2** Load a no. 00 round with Burnt Umber and dot the flower centers to suggest seeds. Using a no. 00 round, paint the flower petals with Cadmium Yellow, leaving white paper highlights.

**3** With a no. 00 round, darken the flower centers using Sepia. Shade between the petals with a mixture of Lemon Yellow and Indigo. Highlight some of the petal edges with Chinese White, then outline the petals using a no. 000 round loaded with Chinese Orange.

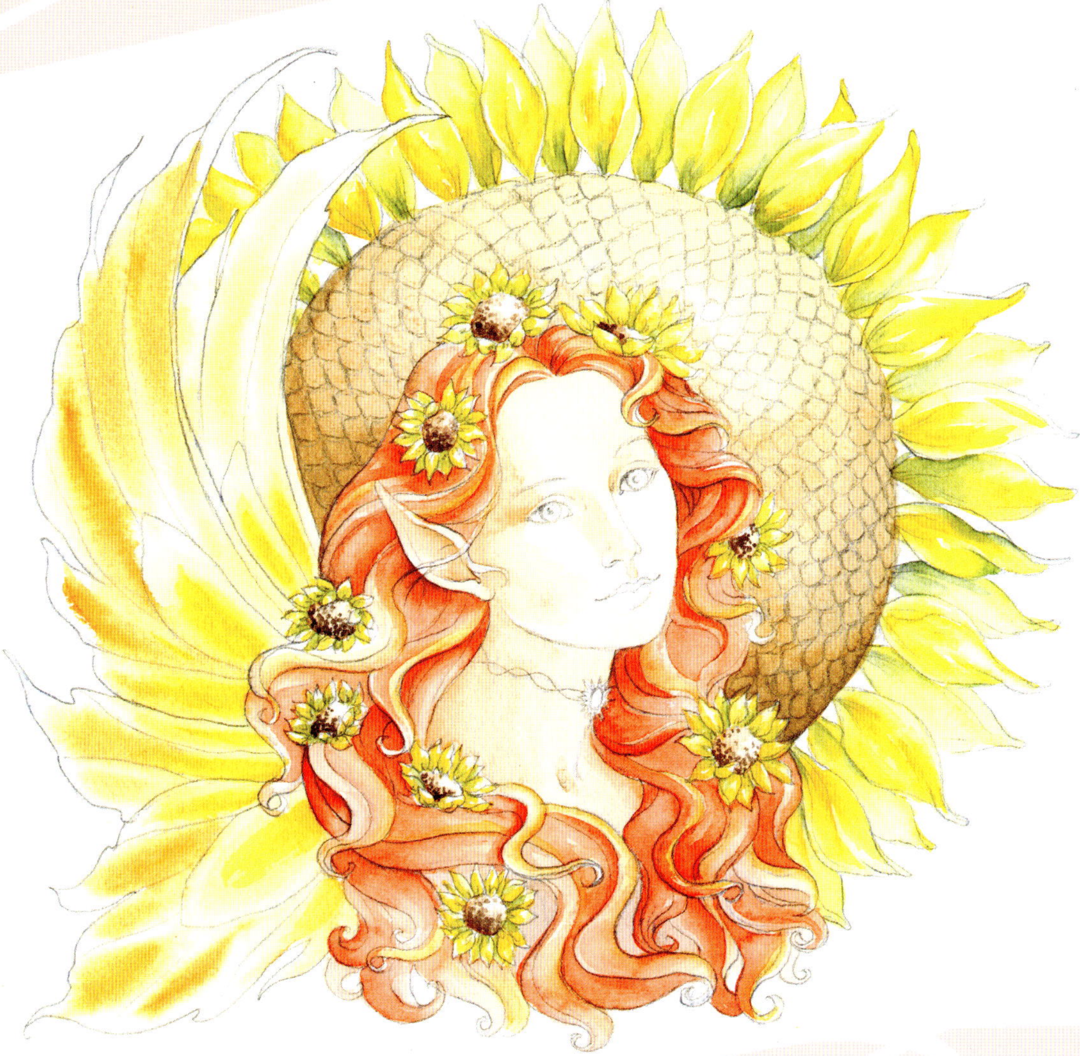

**3** Paint a mixture of Burnt Umber and Chinese Orange on the seed center, making sure to maintain the feeling of roundness by keeping the upper portion a paler tint of the pigment. Use Payne's Gray to paint the shaded area of the petals where they overlap.

🖌 *To create the fairy's hair and the small flowers in her hair, follow the technique and detail demonstrations on page 54.*

🖌 *To define her eyes, follow the detail demonstration on this page.*

## DETAIL DEMONSTRATION — *Fairy Eyes*

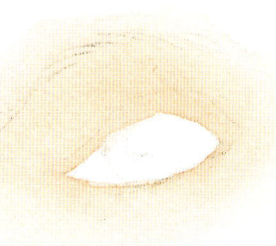 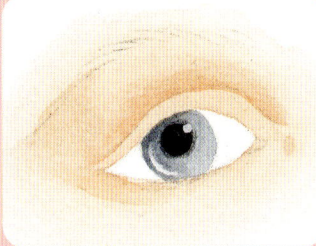 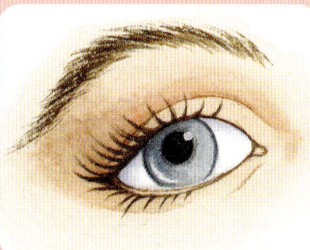

**1** With a no. 2 round, apply a flesh tone mixture of Burnt Umber, Chinese Orange and Cadmium Red around the eye.

**2** Using a no. 0 round, paint the irises with Indigo, adding a darker shade where the iris turns from the light. Using a no. 1 round, apply a darker skin tone to create the eyelid and paint the pupils with Ivory Black. Create highlights in the eyes with Chinese White.

**3** When completely dry, use a no. 000 round to paint her eyelashes, lifting the brush at the end of the stroke. Paint the eyebrows and outline the eye using a no. 000 round loaded with a mixture of Burnt Umber and Chinese Orange. Add a mixture of Cobalt Blue, Payne's Gray and Chinese White to the upper part of the eyeball for shadow.

**4** Mix a tiny bit of Indigo and Cerulean Blue and apply it between the petals. Paint the seeds as they turn from the light with Indigo. Paint the outer edge of the fairy's wings with a very strong concentration of Quinacridone Red. Blend inward with a no. 1 round loaded with clear water.

Using a no. 000 round, add Cadmium Yellow and Chinese Orange to the fairy's choker. Use a tiny bit of Vermilion Hue on the end of her nose and shade the side of her nose with Chinese Orange and Burnt Umber. Wet her cheek area with clear water. With a no. 00 round, charge in a bit of Vermilion Hue and blend outward very carefully. This can also be done before applying her skin tone.

*To define the fairy's lips, follow the technique demonstration on this page.*

**5** It's time for the final touches. Darken the pencil lines in the large flower center. Accentuate the seeds using a mixture of Burnt Umber and Chinese Orange around each seed. Outline the large sunflower petals with Chinese Orange and paint within the wing veins with a deeper concentration of Cadmium Yellow.

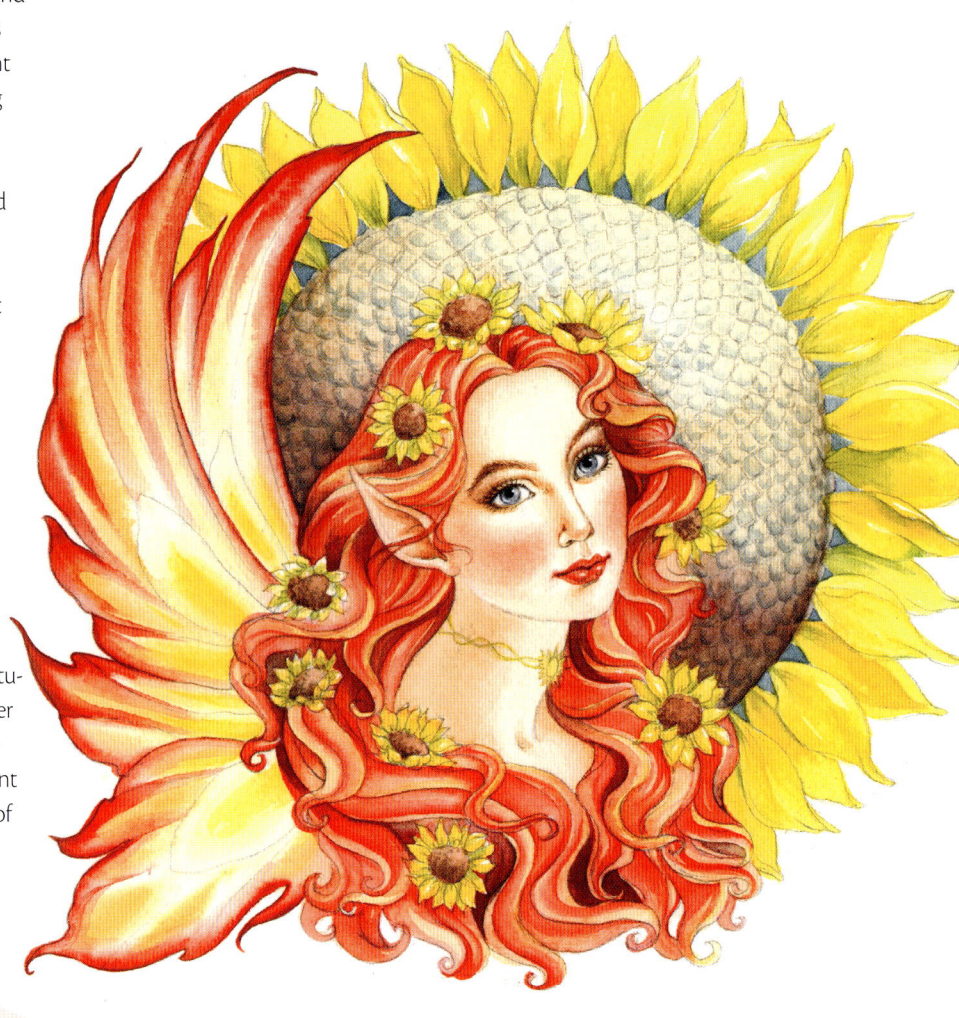

 **TECHNIQUE DEMONSTRATION** — *Defining Fairy Lips*

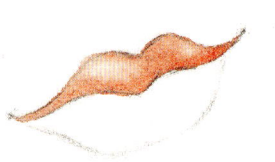

**1** Wet the upper lip with a no. 0 round loaded with water. When the shine has gone, use the same brush loaded with Cadmium Red to paint the top lip, beginning at the center and brushing towards the corners. Leave a white paper highlight on both sides of the lip.

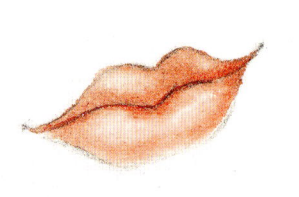

**2** Wet the lower lip with a no. 0 round. Apply Cadmium Red in the same manner as Step 1, leaving highlights on each side of the lip. Let dry.

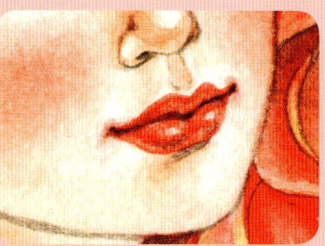

**3** Using a no. 0 round, apply a fine line with a mixture of Cadmium Red and Alizarin Crimson to the space between the upper and lower lips. Using a no. 0 round, outline the lower lip with a pale tint of Cadmium Red and Alizarin Crimson.

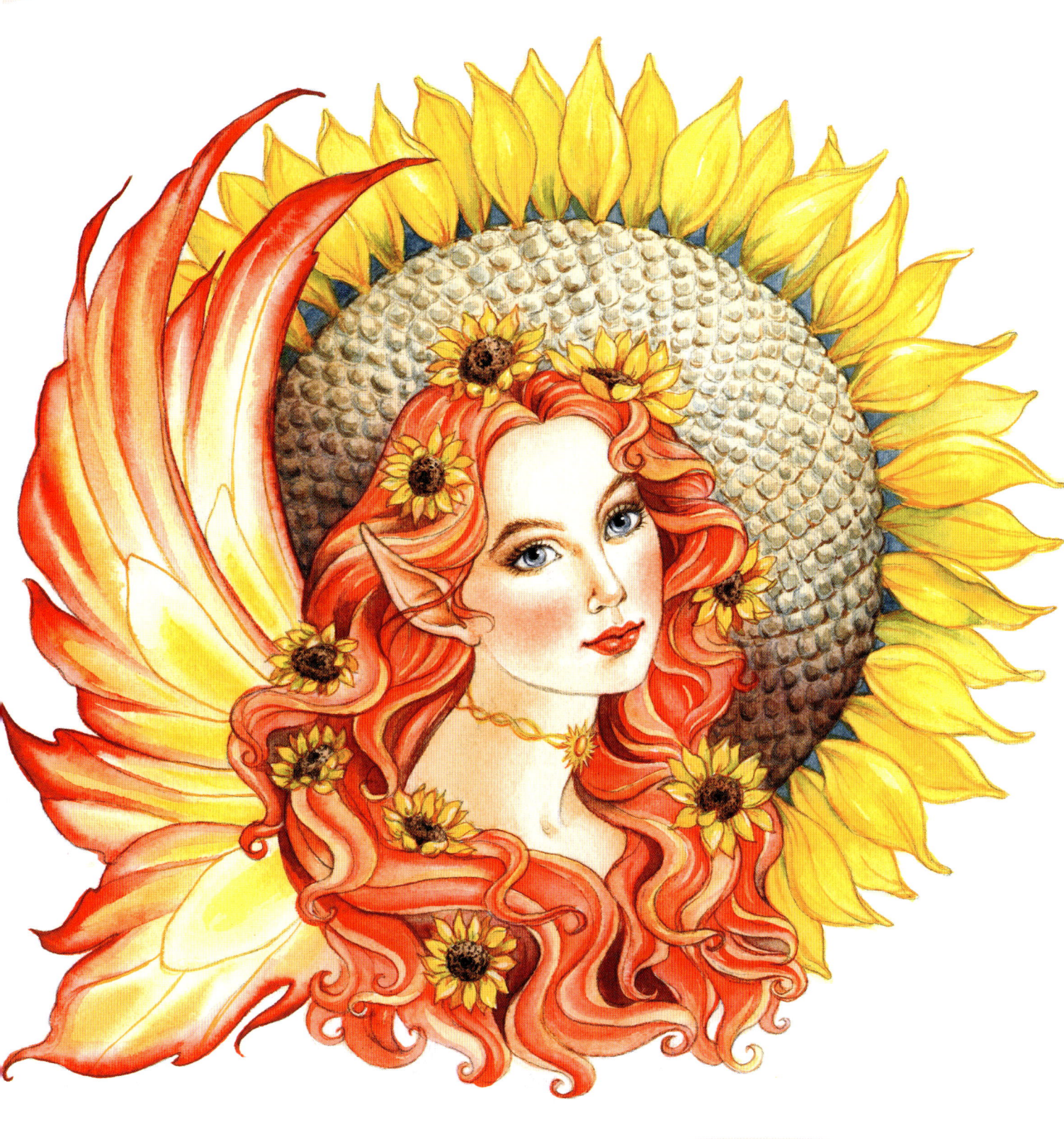

# DEMONSTRATION
# NIGHT FAIRY

*For the Night Fairy, I painted a moonflower to represent the moon, and I gave her long gloves and black hair to suggest an elegant evening. I took the color for her wings from those of the spectacular luna moth.*

### ~YOU WILL NEED~

#### MATERIALS

1½-inch (38mm) flat ✦ blue Saral transfer paper ✦ blue tape ✦ hard-leaded pencil or ballpoint pen that has run out of ink ✦ HB or 2B graphite pencil ✦ kneaded eraser ✦ masking fluid ✦ no. 00 acrylic round ✦ no. 2 miniature round ✦ nos. 00, 000, 1 and 2 rounds ✦ square masking fluid pickup ✦ stretched watercolor paper ✦ tracing paper

#### PIGMENTS

Alizarin Crimson ✦ Burnt Umber ✦ Cadmium Red ✦ Cadmium Yellow ✦ Chinese Orange ✦ Chinese White ✦ Cobalt Turquoise Light ✦ Indanthrene Blue ✦ Indigo ✦ Ivory Black ✦ Lemon Yellow ✦ New Gamboge ✦ Olive Green ✦ Payne's Gray ✦ Quinacridone Red ✦ Sepia ✦ Viridian ✦ Winsor Emerald

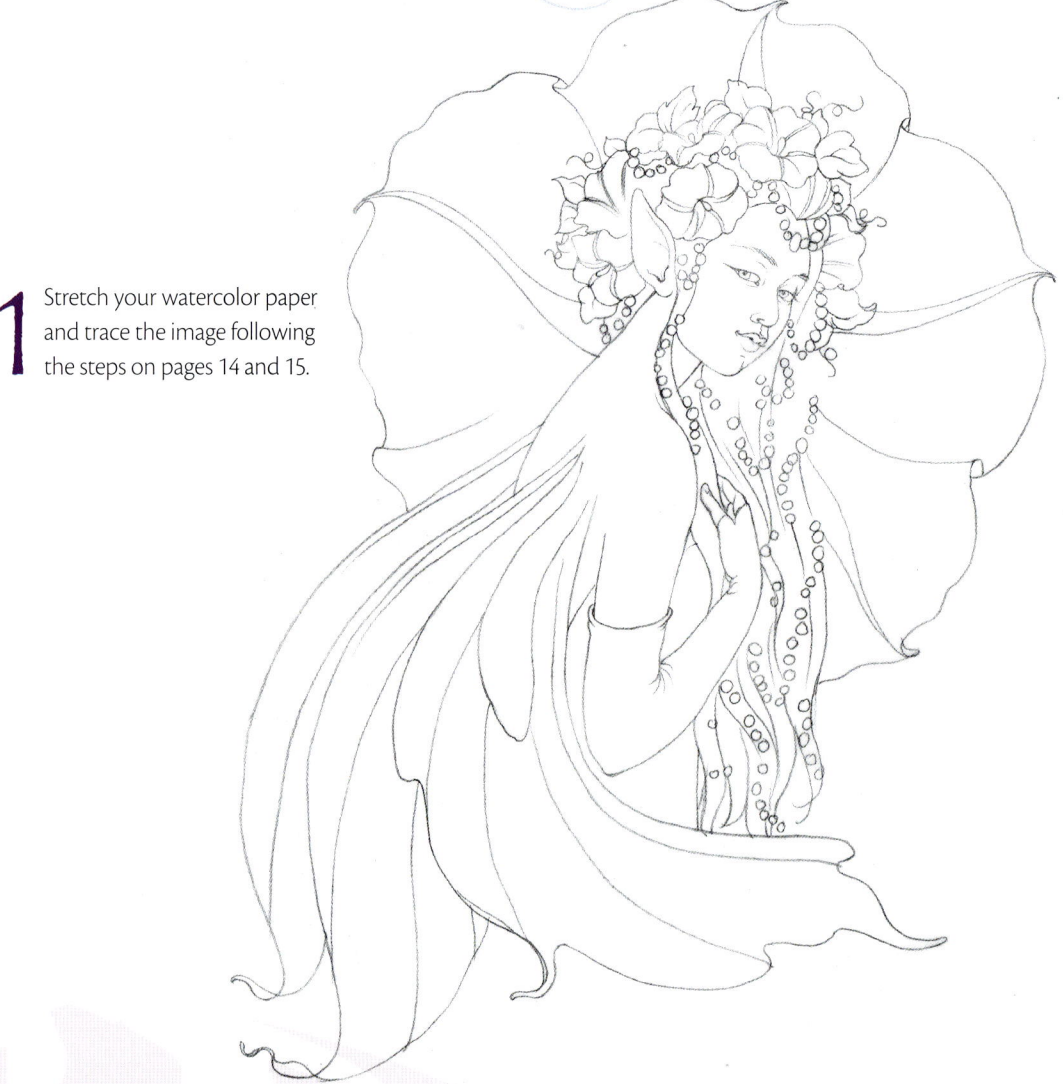

**1** Stretch your watercolor paper and trace the image following the steps on pages 14 and 15.

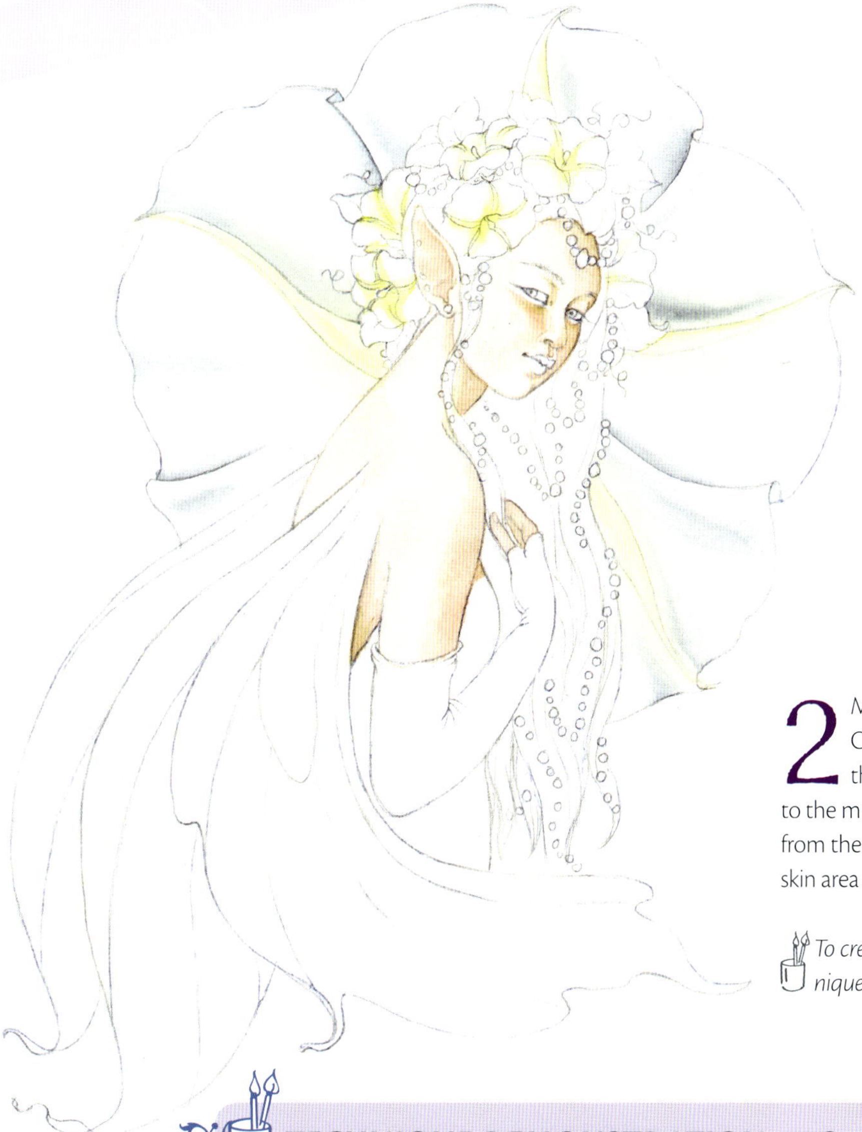

**2** Mix New Gamboge, Burnt Umber, Chinese Orange and Cadmium Red and apply this to the skin with a no. 1 round. Add Olive Green to the mixture and shade the fairy's skin where it turns from the light. When completely dry, cover the entire skin area with the initial skin tone mixture.

*To create the moonflower, follow the technique demonstration on this page.*

## TECHNIQUE DEMONSTRATION — Creating the Moonflower

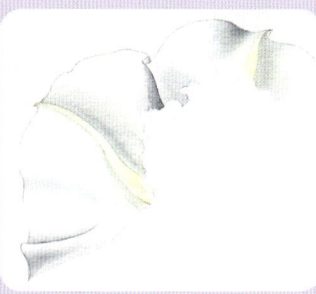

**1** Using a no. 1 round, apply a medium wash of Lemon Yellow in the folds of the moonflower behind the figure.

**2** Blend the color outward with the same size brush loaded with clear water.

**3** Apply a pale wash of Payne's Gray to the area of the folds turning from the light source. Make sure the outer edge of the wash diminishes gradually by blending with clear water.

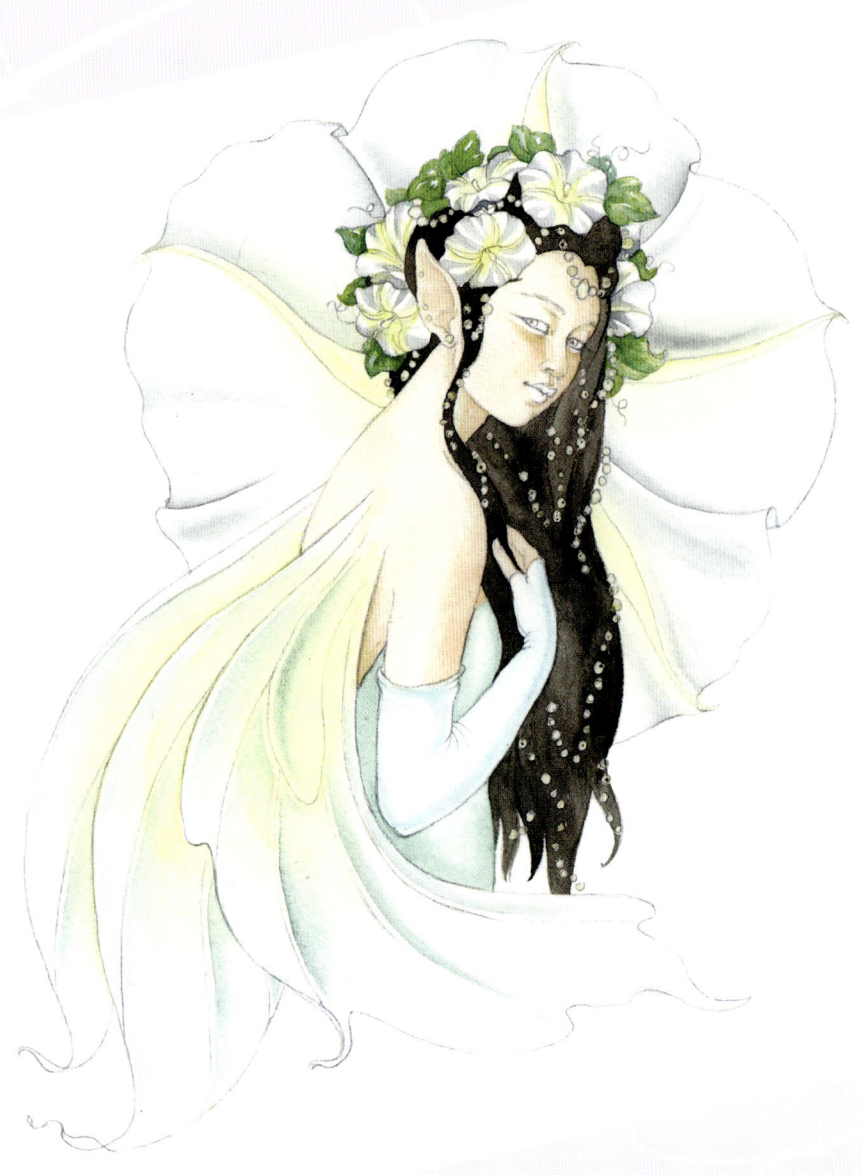

**3** Use a no. 00 acrylic round loaded with masking fluid to coat the pearls and jewels in the fairy's hair. On your palette, mix Lemon Yellow and Chinese White and apply it to the wing area closest to her body, blending outward using a no. 1 round loaded with clear water. When that has dried, add shading to the wings using a mixture of Viridian and Payne's Gray. With a no. 00 round, paint her gown using a pale shade of Viridian and let dry. Wet her entire glove with clear water. When the shine is gone, charge in a mixture of Cobalt Turquoise Light and Chinese White down the right side of the glove. Paint her hair following its curves using Ivory Black and a no. 1 round.

*To create the headdress, follow the detail demonstration on this page.*

## DETAIL DEMONSTRATION — Flower Headdress

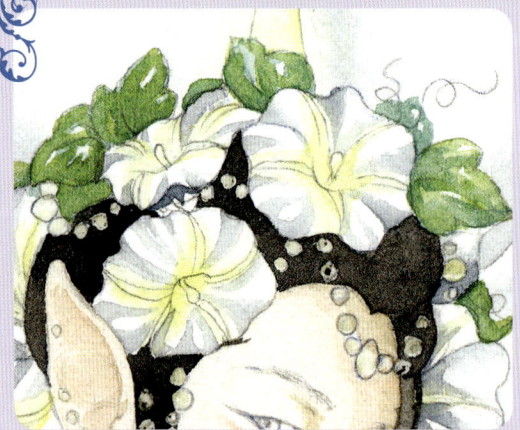

**1** With the no. 00 round, paint the centers of the headdress flowers with New Gamboge. Add Payne's Gray to the folds of the flowers. Shade the leaves with Viridian, leaving white for highlights.

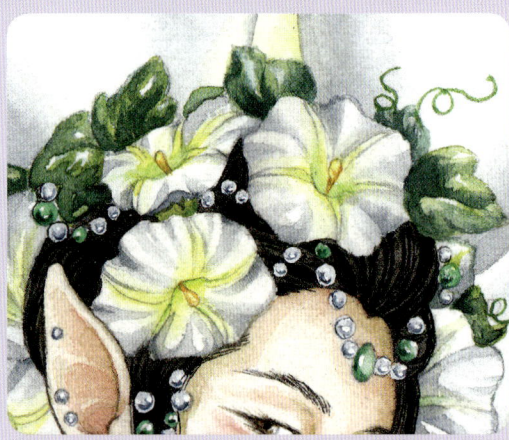

**2** When dry, use a no. 00 round to add Olive Green to the areas of the leaves facing the light, leaving a bit of pure Viridian here and there. Add Cadmium Yellow to the flower stamens.

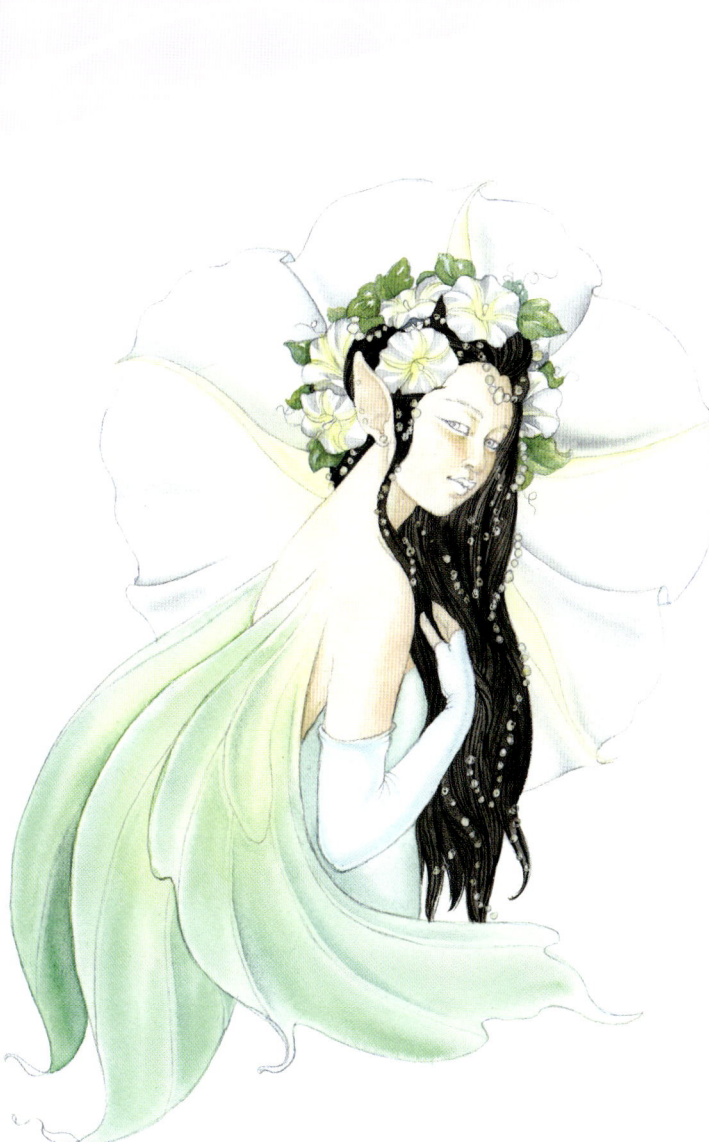

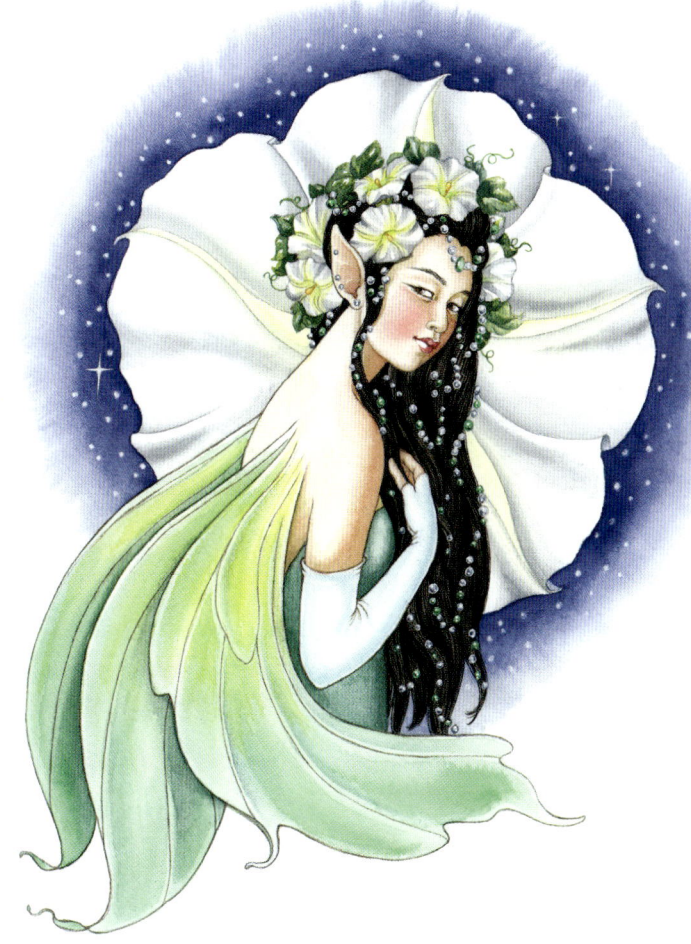

**4** Paint each wing separately beginning with the one in the background. Wet the entire background wing, and when it is no longer shiny, charge in Winsor Emerald using a no.1 round. When the paint is almost dry, use Winsor Emerald at the bottom of the wing and the area behind the foreground wing. Repeat with the wing in the foreground. Paint a wash of Sepia on the fairy's hair. When dry, use a no. 2 miniature loaded with a concentration of Ivory Black to define individual strands of her hair.

**5** With a no. 2 round, use Ivory Black to darken the hair where the strands overlap one another.

*To create the background color for this fairy, follow the technique demonstration on page 62.*

## TECHNIQUE DEMONSTRATION — *Creating a Night Sky*

 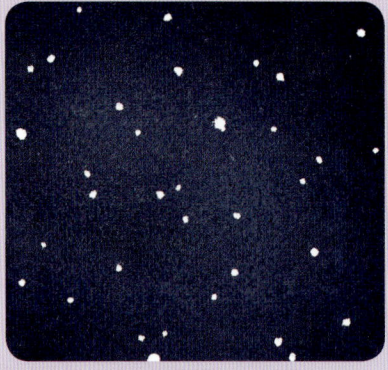 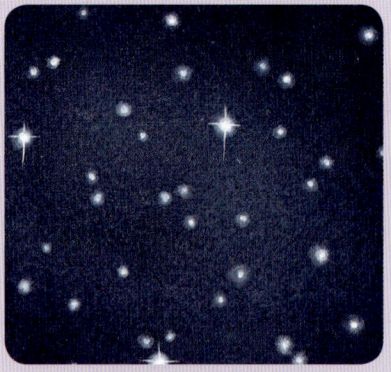

**1** Using a 1½-inch (38mm) flat, apply clean water to the paper. When the shine is gone, use the same brush to apply a deep tint of Indigo. Let dry.

**2** Using a no. 000 round, apply thick circles of Chinese White mixed with a little water. Create random patterns of circles, painting some in clusters and some larger for a realistic effect. Let the circles dry for a minute. Using a no. 000 round loaded with clean water, brush over the entire circle and soften the edges with your brush. Let dry.

**3** Using a no. 000 round loaded with Chinese White, apply paint to the center of the larger circles to give dimension to your sky. With the same brush, add vertical and horizontal lines to give the illusion of sparkle to a few stars.

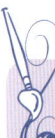

## DETAIL DEMONSTRATION — *Fairy Jewels*

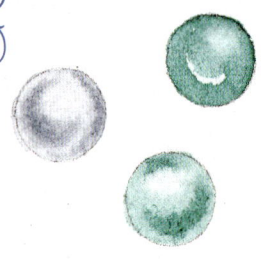 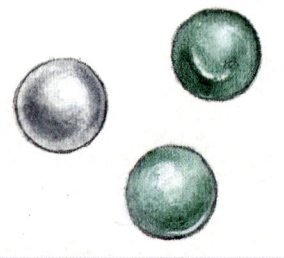 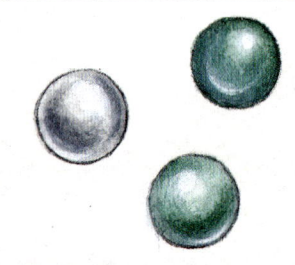

**1** Remove the masking fluid using your finger or a removal square. Paint the pearls and jewels using Indigo and Viridian by wetting the beads and carefully charging in the color, leaving white highlights as shown.

**2** Outline the beads and jewels with Indigo on a no. 000 round.

**3** When dry, add highlights to the jewels with Chinese White and a no. 000 round.

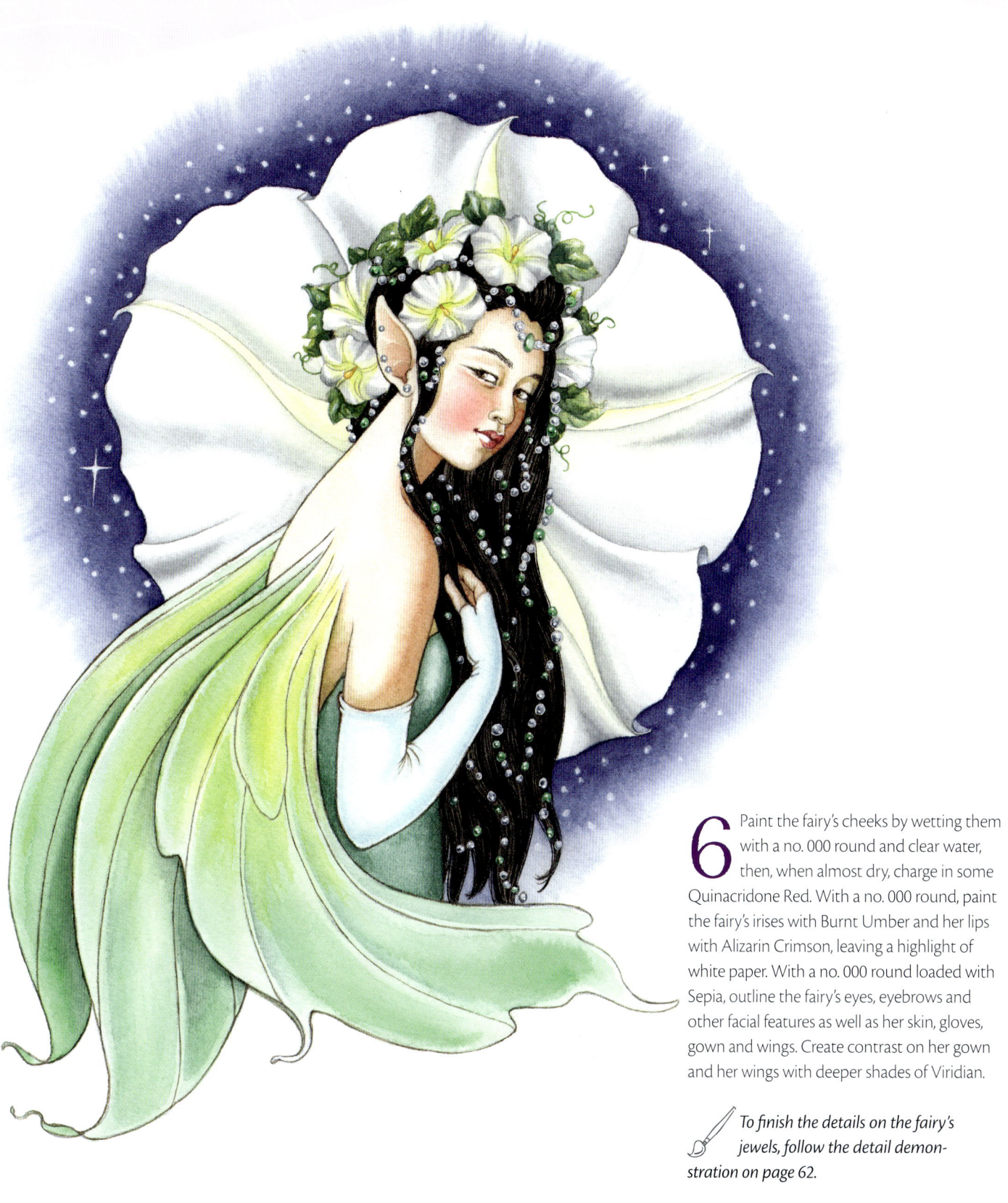

**6** Paint the fairy's cheeks by wetting them with a no. 000 round and clear water, then, when almost dry, charge in some Quinacridone Red. With a no. 000 round, paint the fairy's irises with Burnt Umber and her lips with Alizarin Crimson, leaving a highlight of white paper. With a no. 000 round loaded with Sepia, outline the fairy's eyes, eyebrows and other facial features as well as her skin, gloves, gown and wings. Create contrast on her gown and her wings with deeper shades of Viridian.

*To finish the details on the fairy's jewels, follow the detail demonstration on page 62.*

# DEMONSTRATION
# EARTH FAIRY

Earth Fairy stands tall and proud over her domain. Seeds fall from her hands to the nourishing soil from which a tender seedling emerges, and the folds of her earth-colored gown form a protective swirl over the ground. Her headdress of twigs and leaves frame her Native American features. The complementary colors of the figure and the background make this fairy stand out.

## ~ YOU WILL NEED ~

### MATERIALS
1½-inch (38mm) flat ～ blue tape ～ hard-leaded pencil or ballpoint pen that has run out of ink ～ HB or 2B graphite pencil ～ kneaded eraser ～ masking fluid ～ no. 2 acrylic round ～ no. 2 miniature round ～ nos. 000, 00, 0, 1, 2 and 6 rounds ～ Saral transfer paper ～ square masking fluid pickup ～ stretched watercolor paper ～ tracing paper

### PIGMENTS
Alizarin Crimson ～ Burnt Umber ～ Cadmium Red ～ Cadmium Yellow Deep ～ Chinese Orange ～ Chinese White ～ Cobalt Turquoise Light ～ Lemon Yellow ～ New Gamboge ～ Olive Green ～ Permanent Mauve ～ Chinese White ～ Sepia ～ Ultramarine Blue (Green Shade) ～ Winsor Violet (Dioxazine) ～ Yellow Ochre

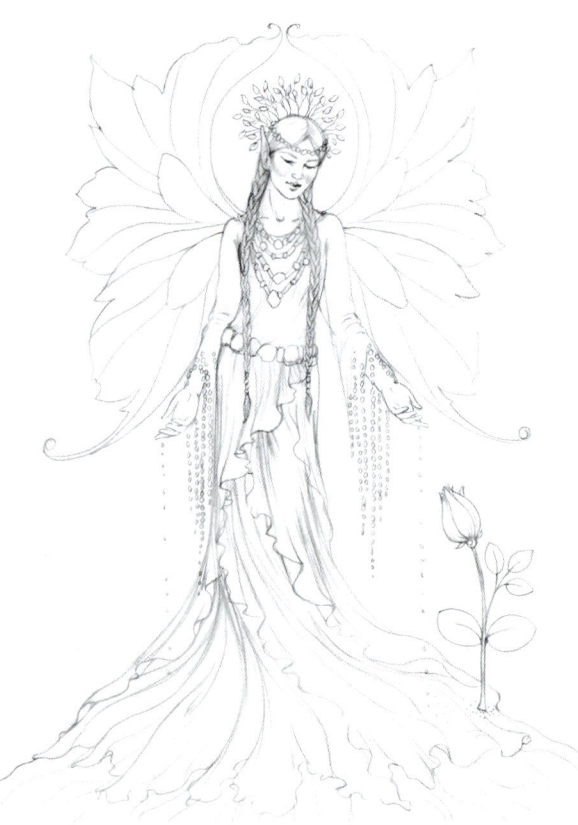

**1** Stretch your watercolor paper and trace the image following the steps on pages 14 and 15.

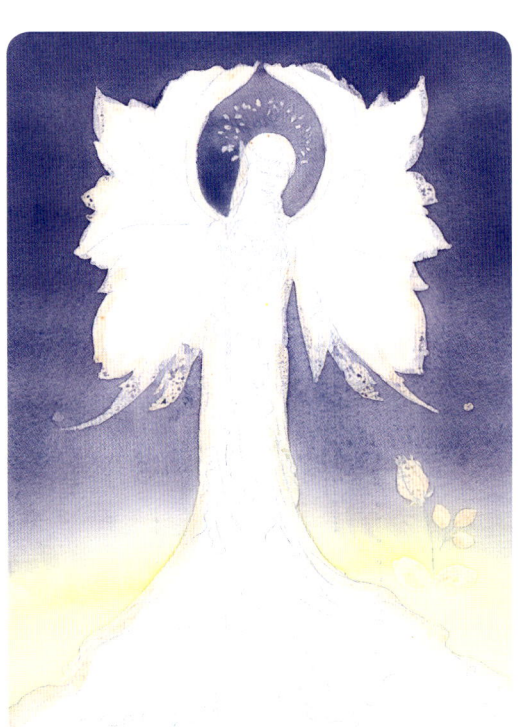

**2** Using a no. 2 acrylic round, mask the edges of the wings, figure, flower, earth, and the headdress. Dot the beads and seeds, covering them completely with masking fluid. Wet the background and when almost dry, charge Lemon Yellow into the horizon using a no. 6 round. Let dry.

*Follow the technique demonstration on page 65 to create the blue portion of the background.*

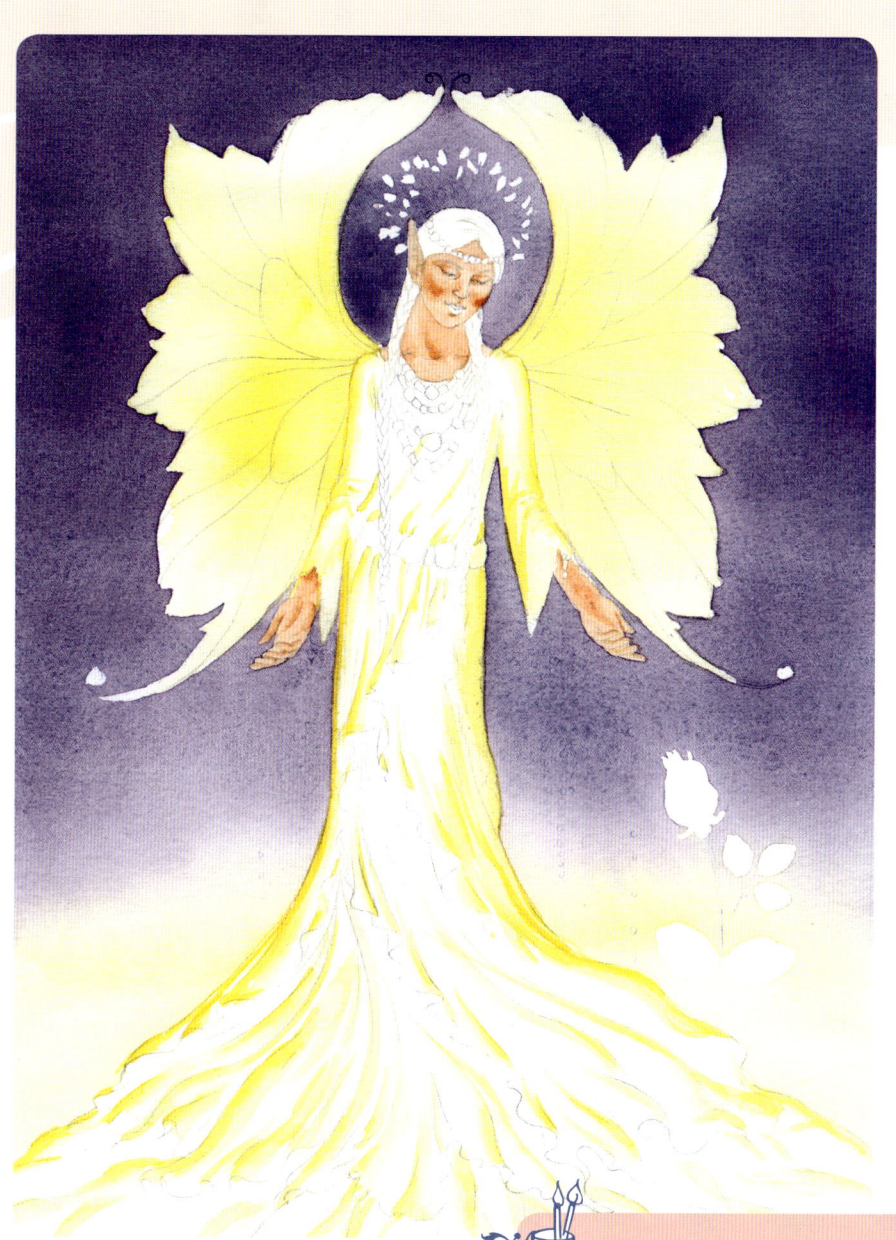

**3** Remove the masking fluid using your fingers or a removal square. Using a no. 2 round, add a strong tint of New Gamboge evenly over both wings, on the edges of the gown, and on the highlights on the earth ridges. While still wet, add a strong concentration of New Gamboge on the area of the wing closest to the fairy's shoulder using a no. 2 round.

Using a no. 0 round, add a medium tint of Burnt Umber to the fairy's throat, collarbone, eyelids, and hands. Paint her cheeks using a no. 00 round loaded with a mixture of Burnt Umber and Cadmium Red. Using a medium mixture of Chinese Orange and Burnt Umber and a no. 1 round, paint the fairy's head and hands.

## TECHNIQUE DEMONSTRATION — Creating a Gradated Background

**1** With a 1½-inch (38mm) flat, wet the sky area again and charge in a mixture of Ultramarine Blue (Green Shade) and Winsor Violet (Dioxazine), stopping three quarters of the way down and tilting the board to let the pigment flow into the Lemon Yellow.

**2** Turn the board upside down and allow the pigment to become more concentrated at the top of picture. Tilt the board if needed to ensure an even flow. With a dry brush, lift the pigment where it collects along the edges of the masking fluid.

**4** With a no. 1 round, add Chinese Orange between the wings' veins, letting the color pool in the center so that the area between the wings' veins has the darkest color. Add a mixture of Chinese Orange and Burnt Umber to the folds of the fairy's gown. Add Burnt Umber to the valleys in the earth.

🖌 *Paint the flower bud by following the detail demonstration on this page.*

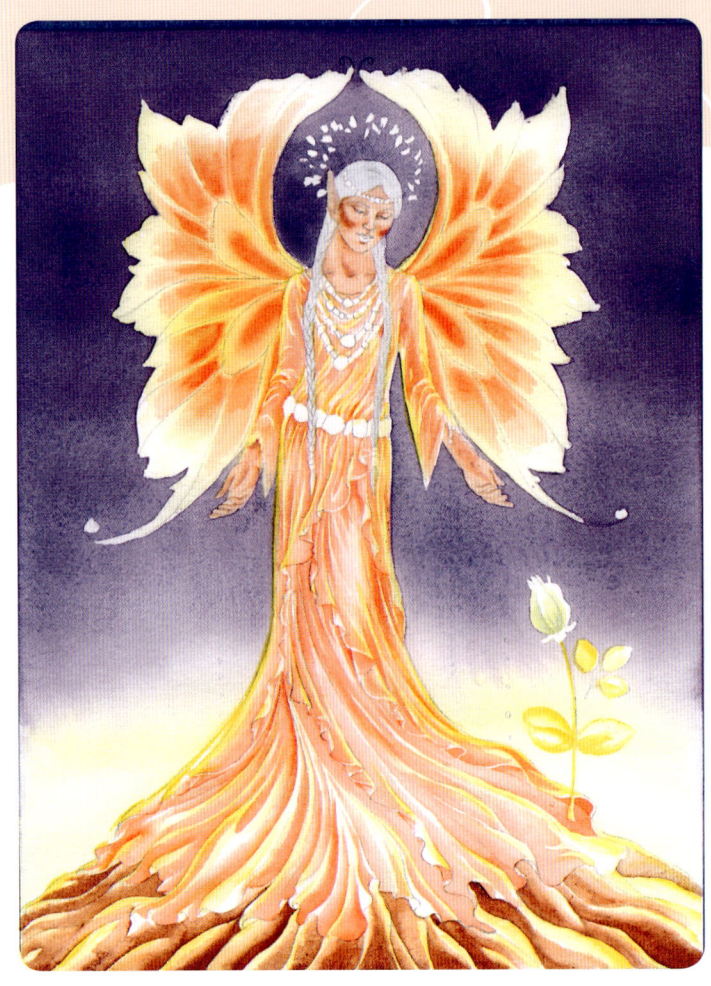

## DETAIL DEMONSTRATION — *Flower Bud*

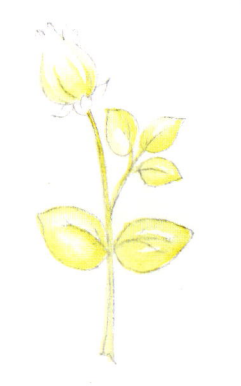
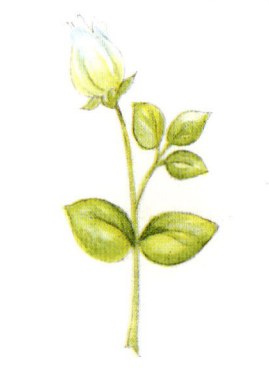
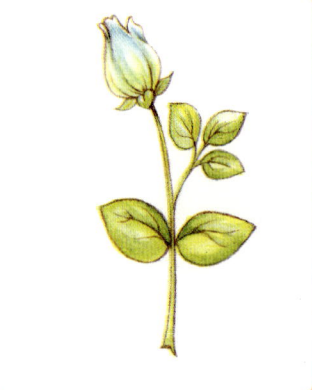

**1** Using a no. 0 round loaded with New Gamboge, paint the flower bud, the stem, and the leaves, leaving white paper for highlights.

**2** Apply Cobalt Turquoise Light to the tip of the bud using a no. 0 round. Using Olive Green on a no. 0 round, paint the shaded parts of the leaves, following the contours, and the tiny petals at the base of the bud and the stem.

**3** Using a no. 0 round, apply another coat of Cobalt Turquoise Light to the bud, dragging the color down to the base. Darken the base of the leaves with another coat of Olive Green. Outline the bud, stem, and leaves using a no. 000 round and Burnt Umber.

66

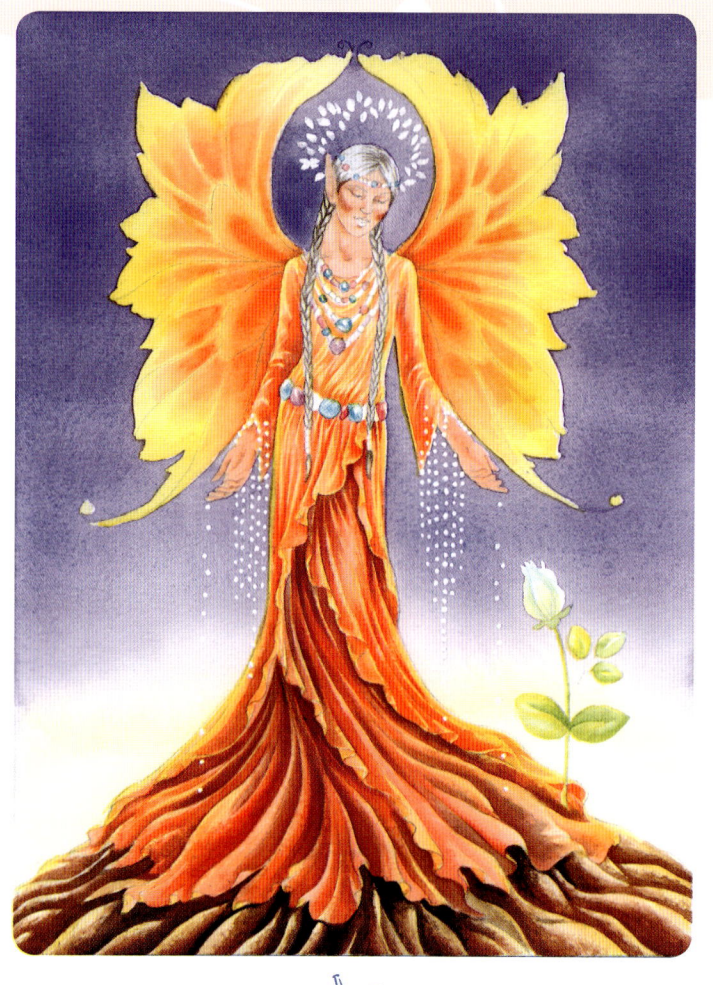

**5** With a no. 2 round, add a stronger shade of New Gamboge to the wings and the dress highlights. Strengthen the color in the valleys of the earth and the lower folds of her gown using Sepia. Paint the falling seeds with a mixture of Burnt Umber and Chinese Orange, adding a mixture of New Gamboge and Chinese White for highlights. Paint the fairy's hair with Sepia.

*To create the fairy's jewelry and belt, follow the steps in the detail demonstration on this page.*

## DETAIL DEMONSTRATION — Fairy Jewelry

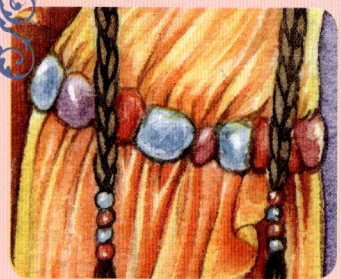

**1** Using a no. 000 round, wet the stones in the belt and charge in Cobalt Turquoise Light, Cadmium Red, Yellow Ochre and Permanent Mauve.

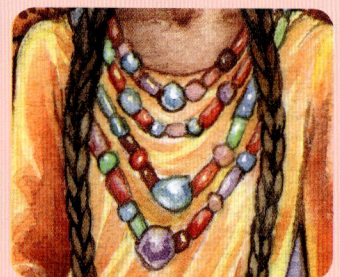

**2** Do the same for the necklace and the headband using the same brush.

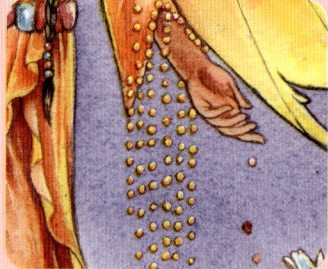

**3** Paint the beads on the fairy's sleeves with a mixture of Burnt Umber and Chinese Orange with a no. 000 round, adding a mixture of New Gamboge and Chinese White for highlights.

67

## DETAIL DEMONSTRATION — *Earth Fairy Headdress*

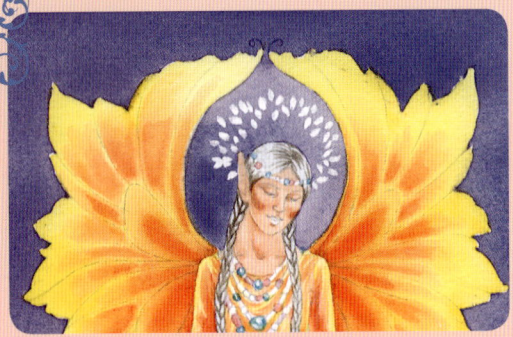

**1** Paint the headdress stems with a mixture of Chinese Orange and Cadmium Yellow Deep using a no. 000 round.

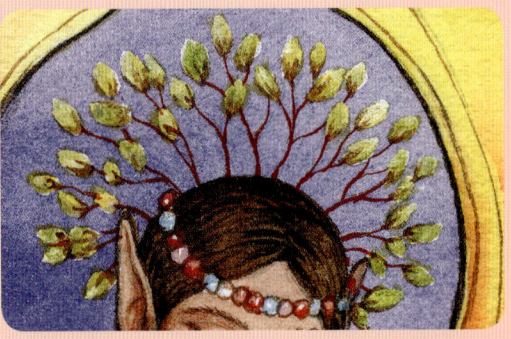

**2** Create the headdress leaves using a mixture of Olive Green and Yellow Ochre loaded on a no. 0 round.

## DETAIL DEMONSTRATION — *Earth Fairy Face*

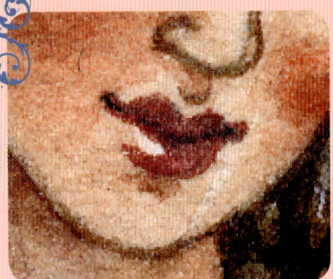

**1** To create the lips, apply a dark tint of Alizarin Crimson with a no. 000 round, leaving white highlights. When dry, use the same brush and a mixture of Alizarin Crimson and Sepia for the line between her upper and lower lips.

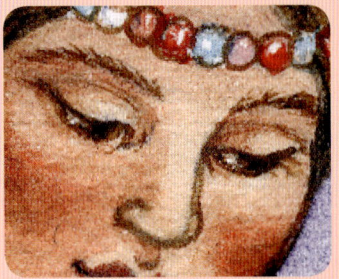

**2** Using a no. 000 round dipped in a medium dark tint of Sepia, outline her eyes. Paint the eyebrows using short strokes. Next, use Sepia and a no. 000 round to define her irises, nose and nostrils.

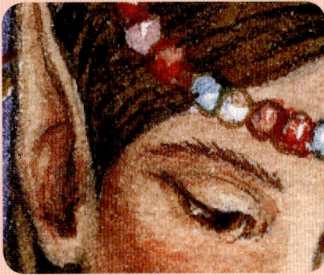

**3** Apply Burnt Umber to the inside of her ear using a no. 0 round.

**6** With a no. 000 round, add Cadmium Red to the circular tips of the wings. With a no. 2 miniature, add dots to indicate soil on the lower gown and earth as well as the fairy's wings where they meet the shoulder. Next, delicately outline the wings and the wing veins with a no. 000 round loaded with Sepia. Finally, use a no. 00 round to paint the fairy's braids with a dark tint of Burnt Umber, then outline the braid shapes with a no. 000 round dipped in Sepia.

 *To complete the fairy's face and headdress, follow the steps in the detail demonstrations on this page.*

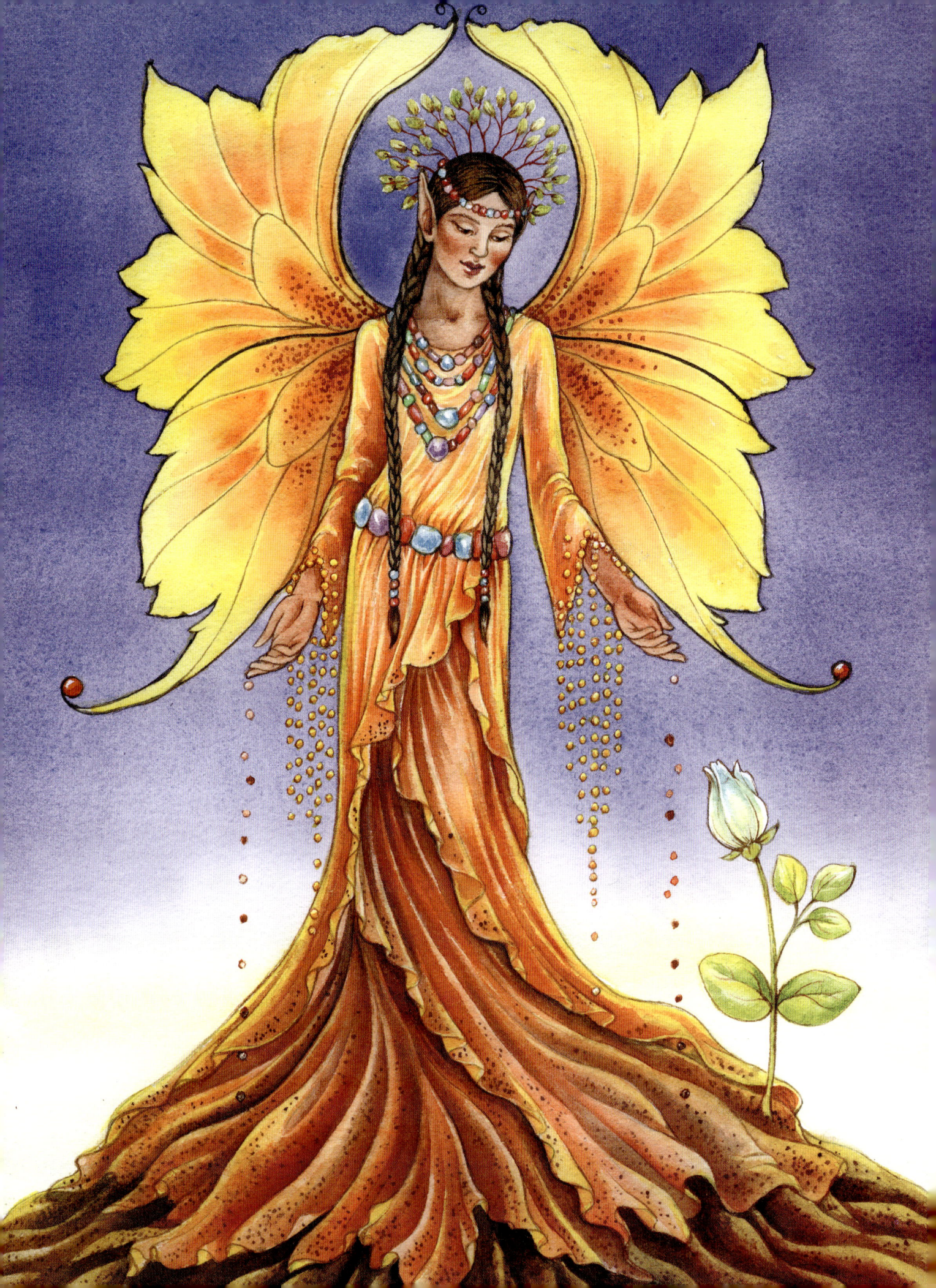

# DEMONSTRATION
# WIND FAIRY

*The wild dandelion was the flower that popped into mind as I considered a good way to show the Wind Fairy at work. She seems to enjoy, as do humans of all ages, blowing apart the seedhead and watching the seeds float away in the air. A strong diagonal composition follows the direction of the wind. The challenge in this picture is showing the volume and detail of the seedhead while retaining its delicacy.*

## ~ YOU WILL NEED ~

### MATERIALS

1½-inch (38mm) flat ◦ blue Saral transfer paper ◦ blue tape ◦ hard-leaded pencil or ballpoint pen that has run out of ink ◦ HB or 2B graphite pencil ◦ kneaded eraser ◦ masking fluid ◦ no. 2 miniature round ◦ nos. 000, 00, 0, 1, 2, 4 and 6 rounds ◦ square masking fluid pickup ◦ stretched watercolor paper ◦ tracing paper

### PIGMENTS

Alizarin Crimson ◦ Burnt Umber ◦ Cadmium Red ◦ Cadmium Yellow ◦ Chinese Orange ◦ Chinese White ◦ Cobalt Blue ◦ Cobalt Turquoise Light ◦ Indanthrene Blue ◦ Ivory Black ◦ Lemon Yellow ◦ Olive Green ◦ Payne's Gray ◦ Permanent Sap Green ◦ Sepia ◦ Vermilion Hue ◦ Winsor Violet (Dioxazine) ◦ Yellow Ochre

**1** Stretch your watercolor paper and trace the image following the steps on pages 14 and 15.

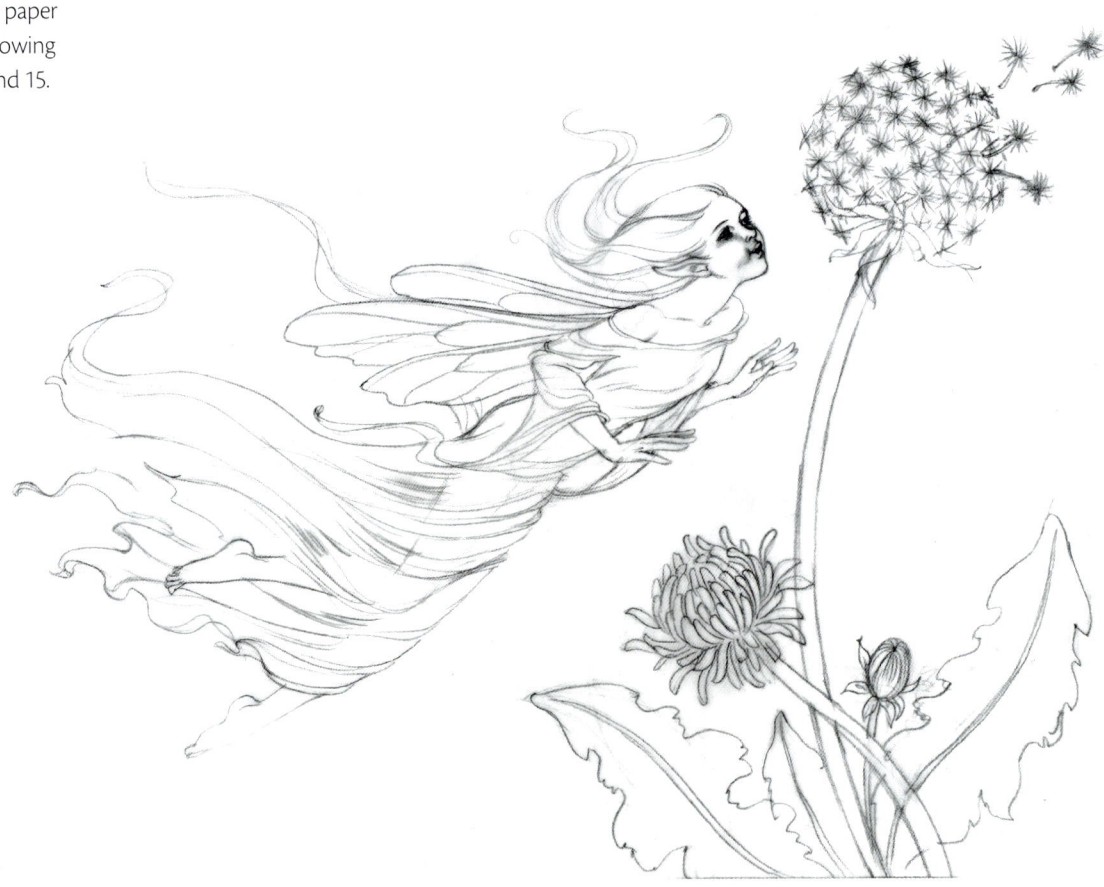

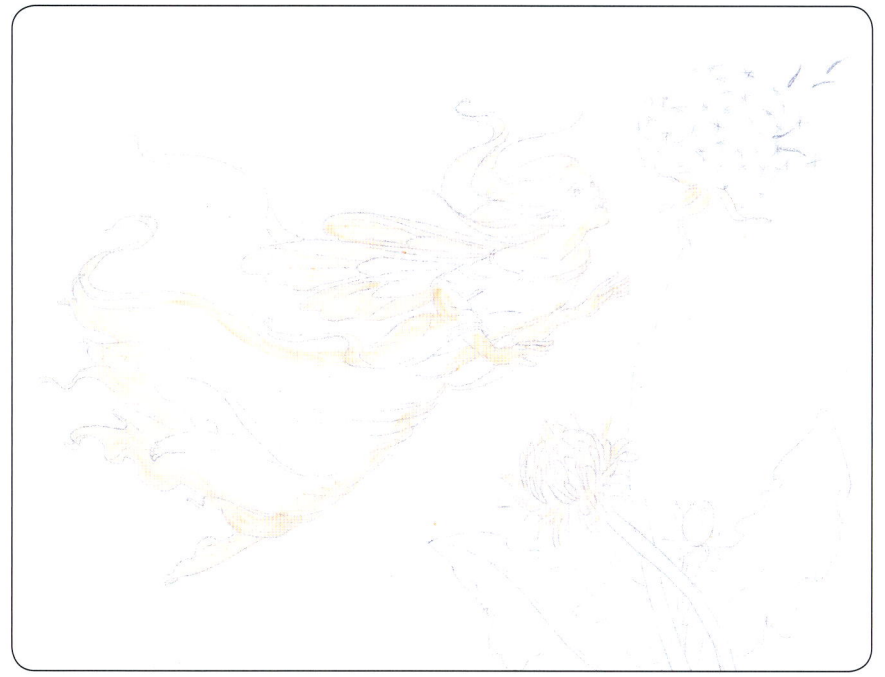

**2** Apply masking fluid to the fairy figure, dandelion flower and leaves using a no. 1 round for the tight spaces, such as along the fingers and toes, and a no. 4 round for the larger areas. Mask the entire figure so the background wash will not intrude. Also mask the dandelion head and the leaves at the base of the seedhead. Let the masking fluid dry.

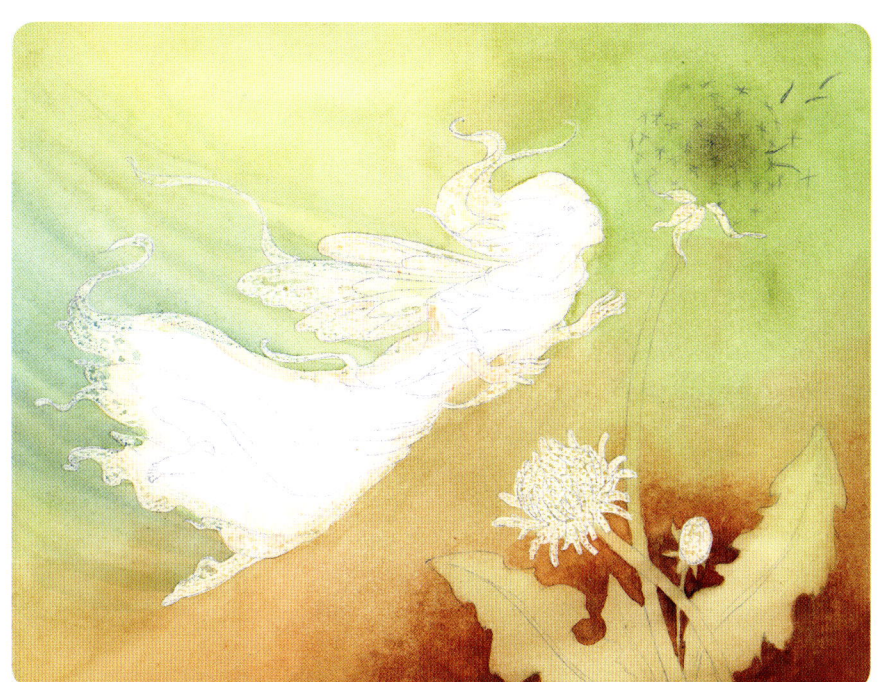

**3** For the background, mix Lemon Yellow, Olive Green, and a small amount of a Burnt Umber and Chinese Orange mixture in a palette well. Wet the entire background and, beginning at the top, use a 1½-inch (38mm) flat to apply the mixture, letting the color fade towards the bottom of the painting. While still wet, charge in a mixture of Burnt Umber and Chinese Orange to the lower right of the page.

Working quickly, and making sure that the background is still wet but not shiny, sweep Cobalt Turquoise Light up and away from the fairy with a no. 6 round to give the painting a feeling of motion.

*To finish the background and to paint the seedhead, follow the steps in the detail and technique demonstrations on page 72.*

71

## DETAIL DEMONSTRATION — *The Dandelion Seedhead*

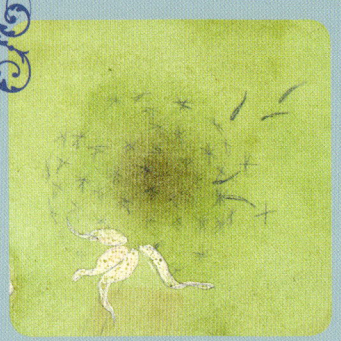 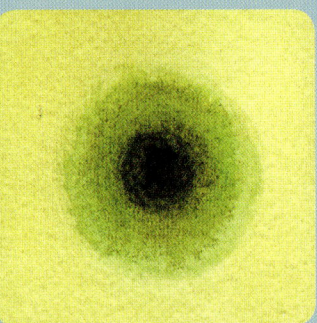 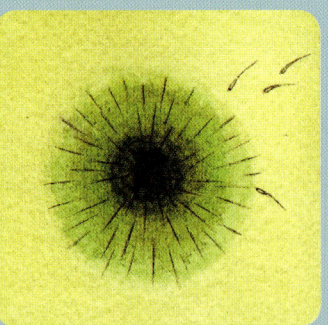 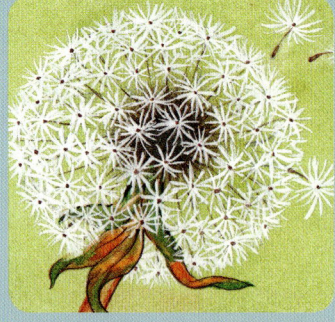

**1** If the background has not dried by this time, add some Olive Green to upper right portion of painting behind where the seedhead will go with a no. 2 round. If the paint has dried, re-wet the area, being careful not to lift color, then add Olive Green.

**2** While that area is still wet, add Payne's Gray to the center of the seedhead. When the background has dried, remove the masking fluid.

**3** With a no. 000 round loaded with a mixture of Sepia and Ivory Black, paint the delicate seed stems, including the ones that are floating away.

**4** When completely dry, use Chinese White on a no. 000 round to begin painting starlike seeds at the outer end of the stems, maintaining the spherical shape of the seedhead. Using a no. 000 round, dot the centers of the seeds and the floating seed stems with Burnt Umber.

## TECHNIQUE DEMONSTRATION — *Creating the Leaves and Stem*

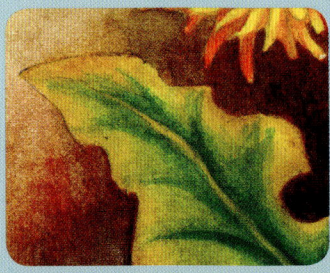 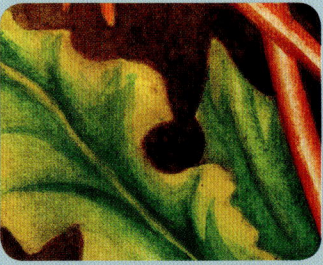 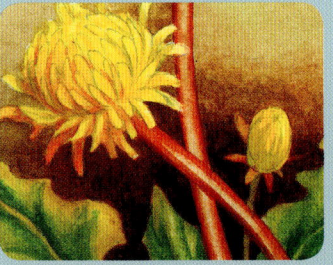 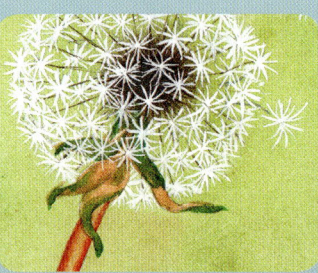

**1** With the no. 2 round, begin painting the leaf edges with Cadmium Yellow.

**2** While wet, add Permanent Sap Green to the shaded parts of the leaves and Olive Green to the parts facing the light source at the upper right.

**3** Paint the outer edges of the stems with Chinese Orange, blending the center of the stem with clear water.

**4** Wet the leaves at the base of the seedhead and charge in Olive Green and Chinese Orange.

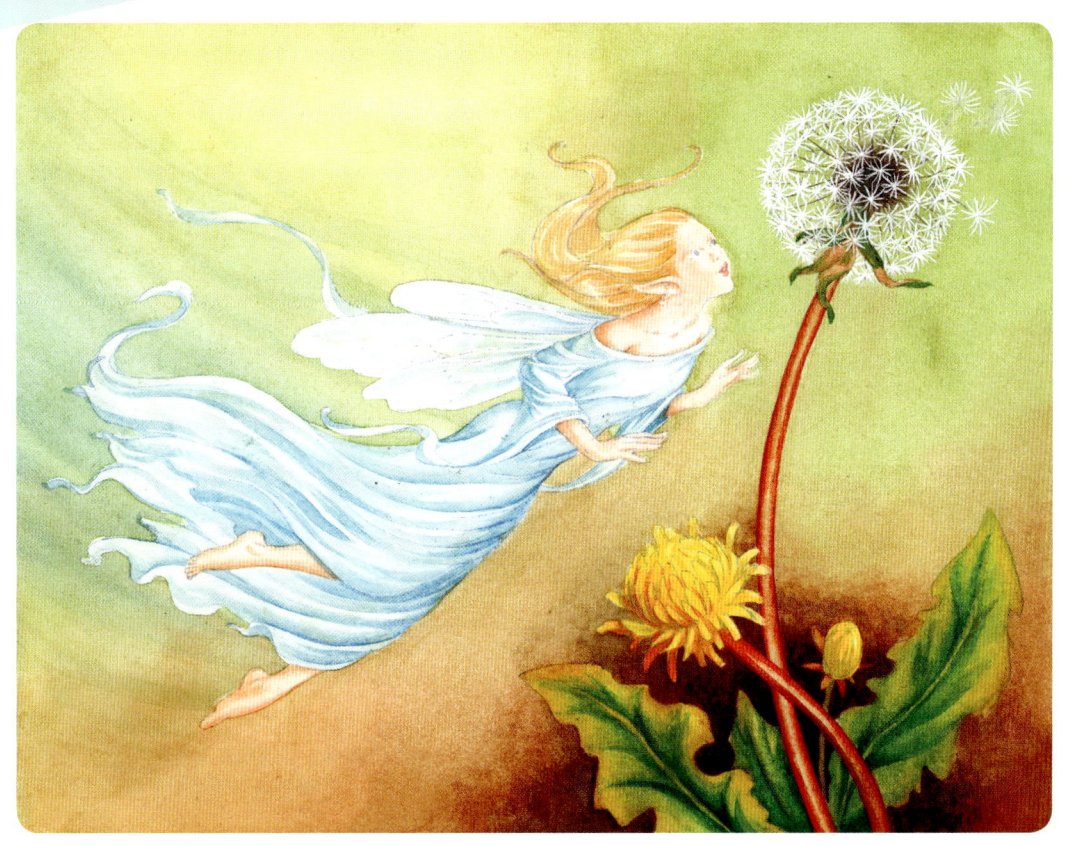

**4** With a no. 2 miniature, paint the shaded area of the fairy's skin with a combination of Burnt Umber, Chinese Orange and a tiny bit of Vermilion Hue. When dry, add a medium mixture of Burnt Umber, Chinese Orange and Cadmium Red to the lighter areas of the fairy's skin. Paint her mouth with Alizarin Crimson. Carefully paint the irises with a no. 000 round loaded with Cobalt Blue.

Next, use Yellow Ochre to paint individual strands of the fairy's hair. Paint the folds of her gown with Cobalt Turquoise Light, blending color into the white areas of the paper with clear water.

To create the rest of the flower, follow the detail and technique demonstrations on pages 72 and 73.

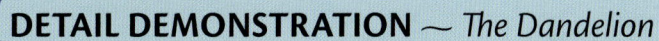

## DETAIL DEMONSTRATION — *The Dandelion*

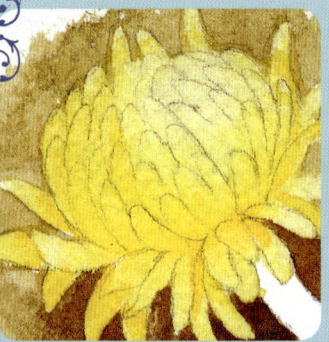
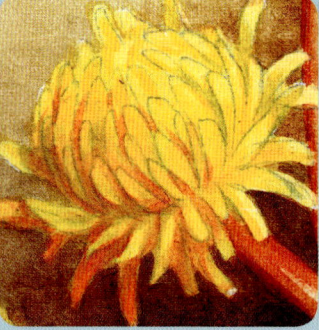

**1** Using a no. 2 round, paint the dandelion with Cadmium Yellow overall. With a clean, dry no. 1 round, lift color from the upper right of the flower for a highlight.

**2** With a no. 1 round, add a mixture Cadmium Yellow and Chinese Orange to the spaces between the petals on the left side of the flower. When dry, apply a mixture of Yellow Ochre with a touch of Ivory Black where the petals meet the base of the flower.

73

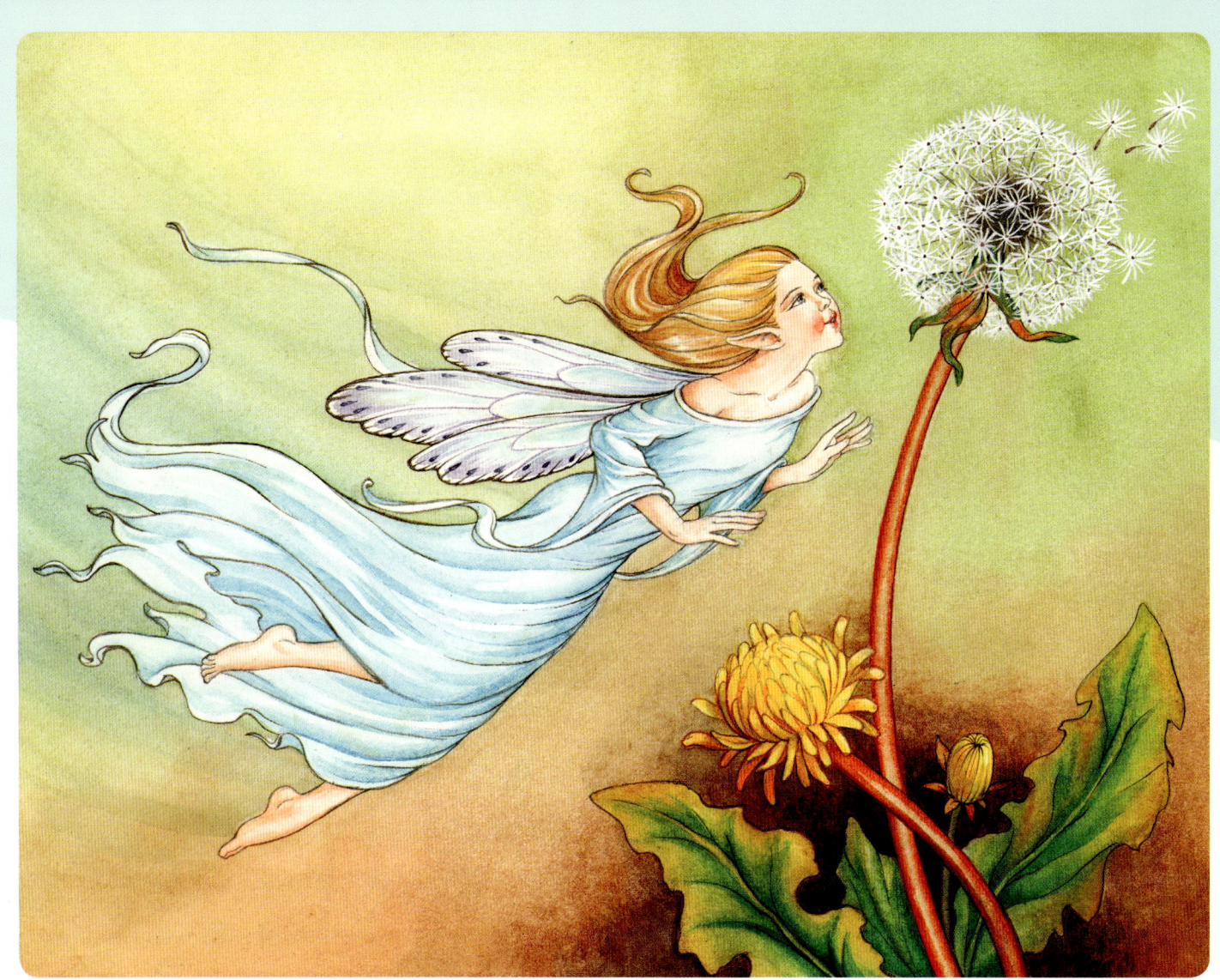

**5** With a no. 0 round, paint the fairy's wings between the veins with Winsor Violet (Dioxazine). Darken her hair behind the crown with a mixture of Burnt Umber and Chinese Orange, painting in the direction that her hair falls. When the wings are dry, accent the tips with teardrops of Indanthrene Blue, leaving a bit of white at the center. Use Sepia and a no. 000 round to outline her figure, dress and hair as well as the dandelion leaves and stems. Load Cadmium Red onto a no. 00 round for the fairy's cheeks and onto a no. 000 round for her lips, leaving white highlights. Next, use no. 000 round loaded with a mixture of Burnt Umber and Cadmium Orange to shade her eyelids and the left of her nose.

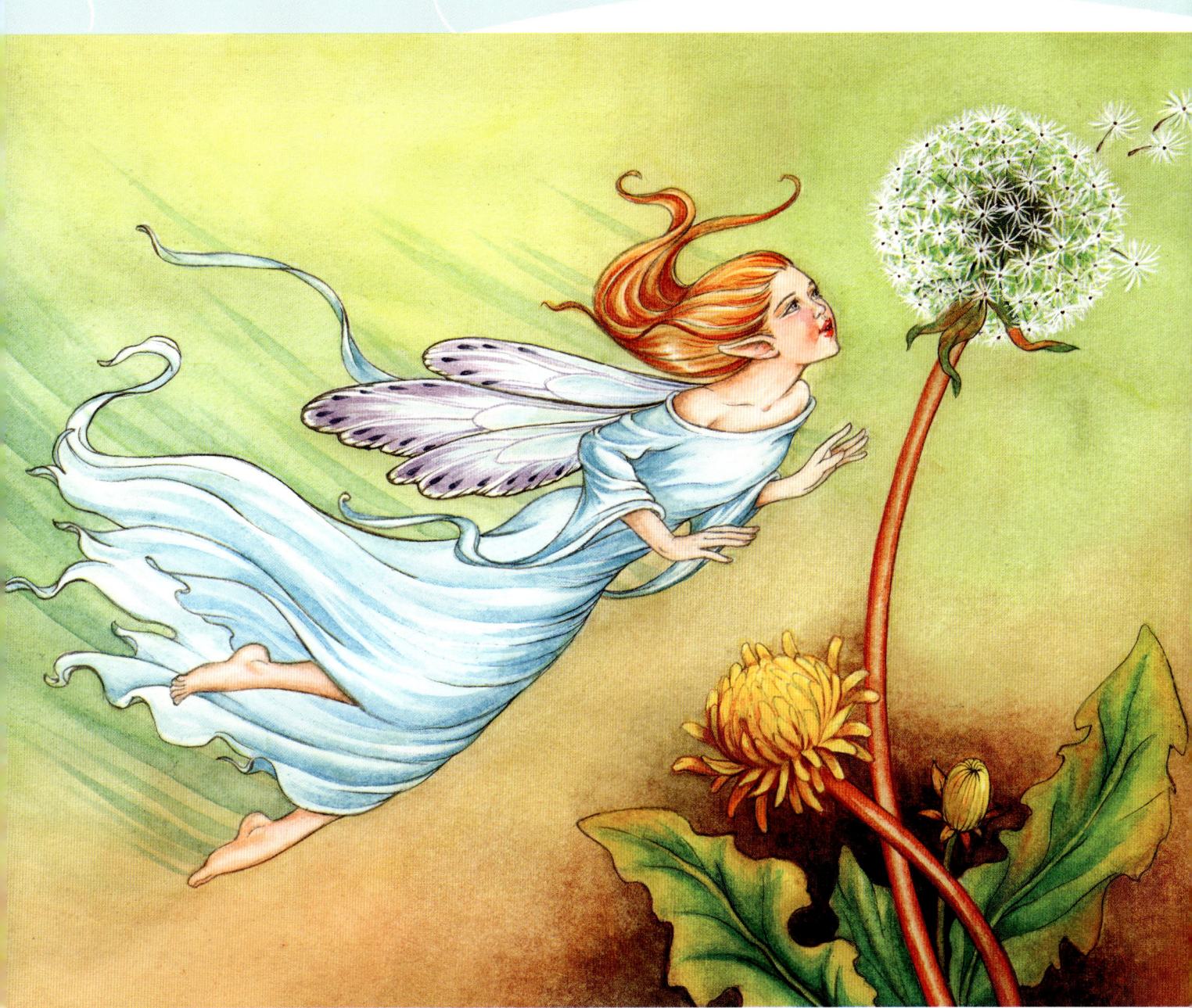

**6** Create more contrast and dimension by adding a darker tint of Indanthrene Blue to the curves and folds of the fairy's dress with a no. 1 round. Next, add a mixture of Burnt Umber and Chinese Orange to her neck and darken her wing at the shoulder. Add Cadmium Yellow to highlight her hair and then, using a no. 0 round loaded with a medium tint of a Cadmium Yellow and Chinese Orange mixture, define individual strands. Finally, darken the streaks of Cobalt Turquoise Light following the fairy using a no. 1 round, being careful to keep the same stroke direction.

## DEMONSTRATION
# WATER FAIRY

The graceful movements of underwater plant life influenced the pose of the Water Fairy. Her flaming hair flows out to her side and her fins and tail rise and fall with the current. Gentle waves behind her form strong horizontal shapes. Bubbles are fun to paint once you break down the steps. Have fun painting the Water Fairy in her peaceful world.

### ~ YOU WILL NEED ~
#### MATERIALS
1½-inch (38mm) flat ~ blue tape ~ hard-leaded pencil or ballpoint pen that has run out of ink ~ HB or 2B graphite pencil ~ facial tissue ~ kneaded eraser ~ masking fluid ~ no. 2 acrylic round ~ nos. 000, 00, 0, 1 and 2 rounds ~ Saral transfer paper ~ square masking fluid pickup ~ stretched watercolor paper ~ tracing paper

#### PIGMENTS
Alizarin Crimson ~ Burnt Umber ~ Cadmium Red ~ Cerulean Blue ~ Chinese Orange ~ Chinese White ~ Cobalt Turquoise Light ~ Indanthrene Blue ~ Ivory Black ~ Lemon Yellow ~ New Gamboge ~ Olive Green ~ Payne's Gray ~ Permanent Mauve ~ Sepia ~ Viridian ~ Winsor Emerald ~ Winsor Violet (Dioxazine)

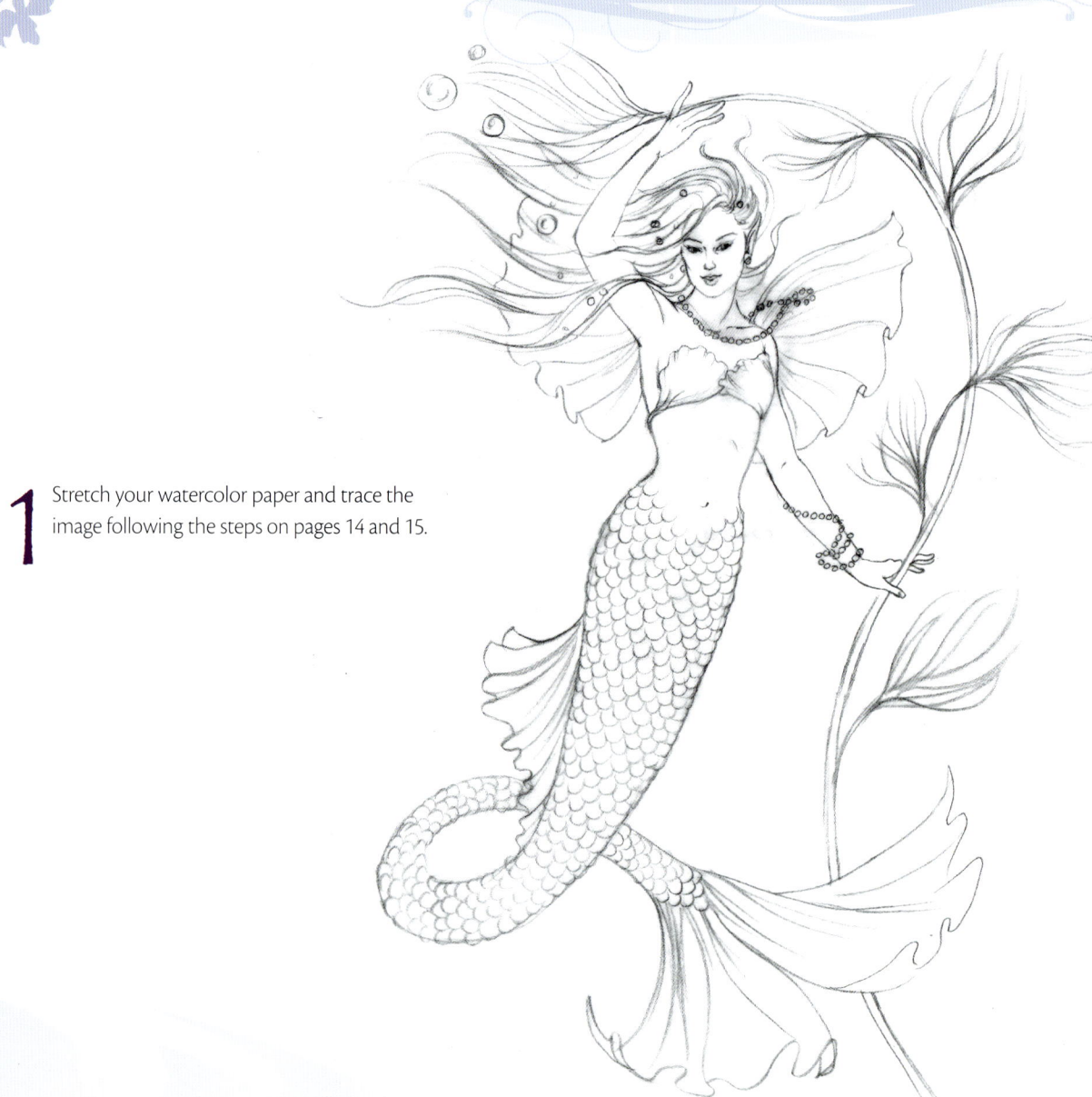

**1** Stretch your watercolor paper and trace the image following the steps on pages 14 and 15.

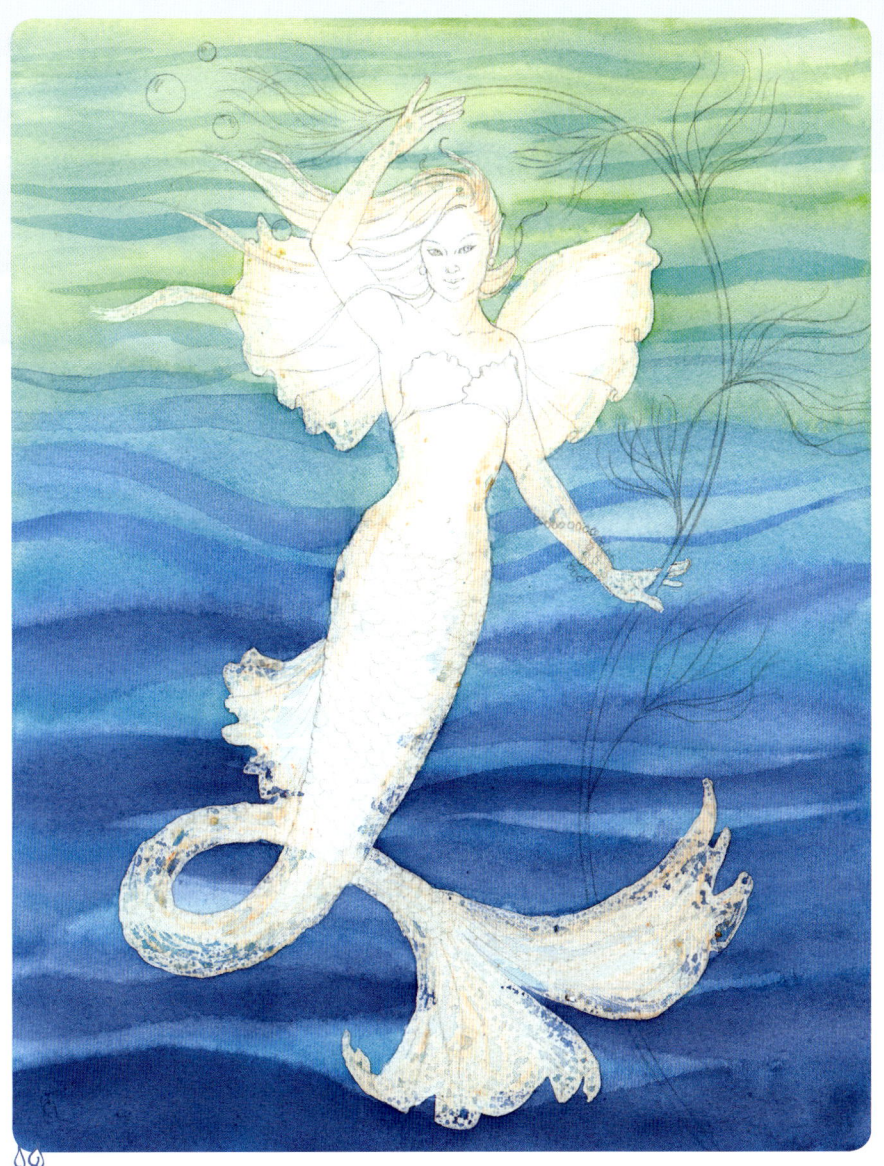

**2** Using a no. 2 acrylic round loaded with masking fluid, apply a thick coat along the inside edge of the fairy figure including her hair, wings, and tail. Let the masking fluid dry. Wet the entire background.

When most of the shine is gone, apply a thin wash of Cobalt Turquoise Light to the entire background and let dry. A more complicated wash follows so have ready on your palette little pools of Lemon Yellow, Cobalt Turquoise Light and Indanthrene Blue.

*To finish the background, follow the steps in the technique demonstration on this page.*

## TECHNIQUE DEMONSTRATION — *Creating Waves*

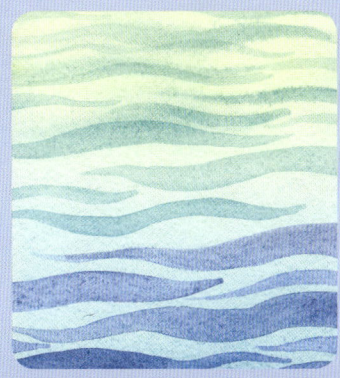

**1** Wet the background with a 1½-inch (38mm) flat. When the shine is gone, apply a wash of Lemon Yellow. Apply the strongest concentration of pigment at the top of the painting, letting the colors fade to a third of the way down. To merge the colors, tilt your board back and forth. Let this dry.

**2** Re-wet the painting using the 1½-inch (38mm) flat. When the shine has gone, use a no. 2 round to create horizontal waves with Cobalt Turquoise Light on the top half of the painting, a medium tint of Indanthrene Blue toward the middle, and a darker tint of Indanthrene Blue towards the bottom.

**3** Remove the masking using your fingers or a removal square. Using New Gamboge loaded on a no. 1 round, paint bands of color on the left side of the fairy's tail and in her hair.

*Follow the steps in the detail demonstration on this page to create the tail, wings, and top.*

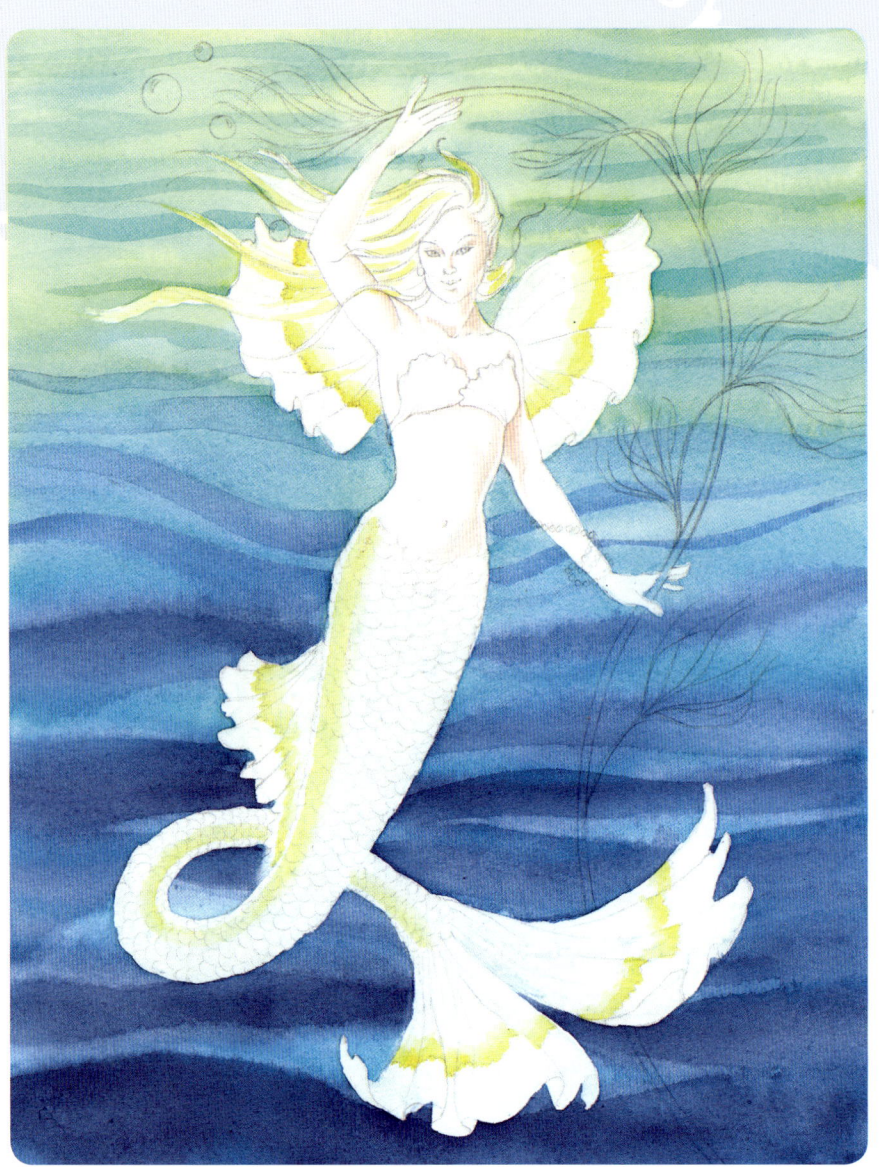

## DETAIL DEMONSTRATION — *Water Fairy Tail, Wings, and Top*

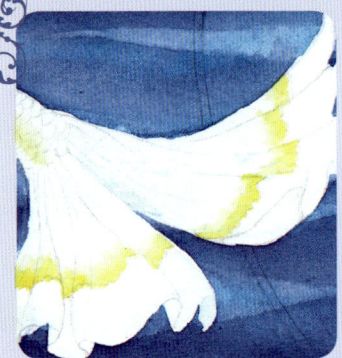

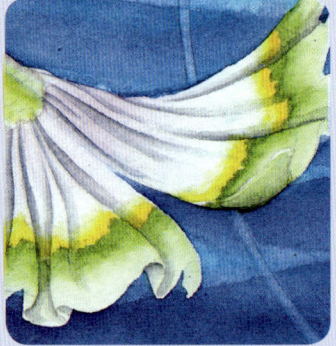

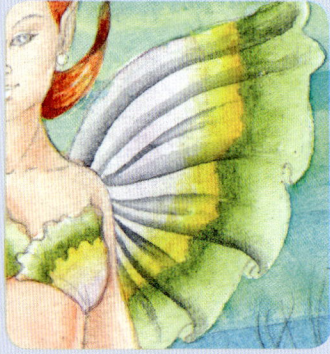

**1** Using a no. 1 round loaded with New Gamboge, paint bands of yellow on the underside of the fairy's top, about halfway on the length of her wings, and halfway to the tip of her main fin.

**2** Paint new bands of Olive Green next to the bands of New Gamboge, blending outward with water to the edges of the wings, tail, and top.

**3** With a mixture of Winsor Violet (Dioxazine) and Payne's Gray, paint the folds in the tail and the wings.

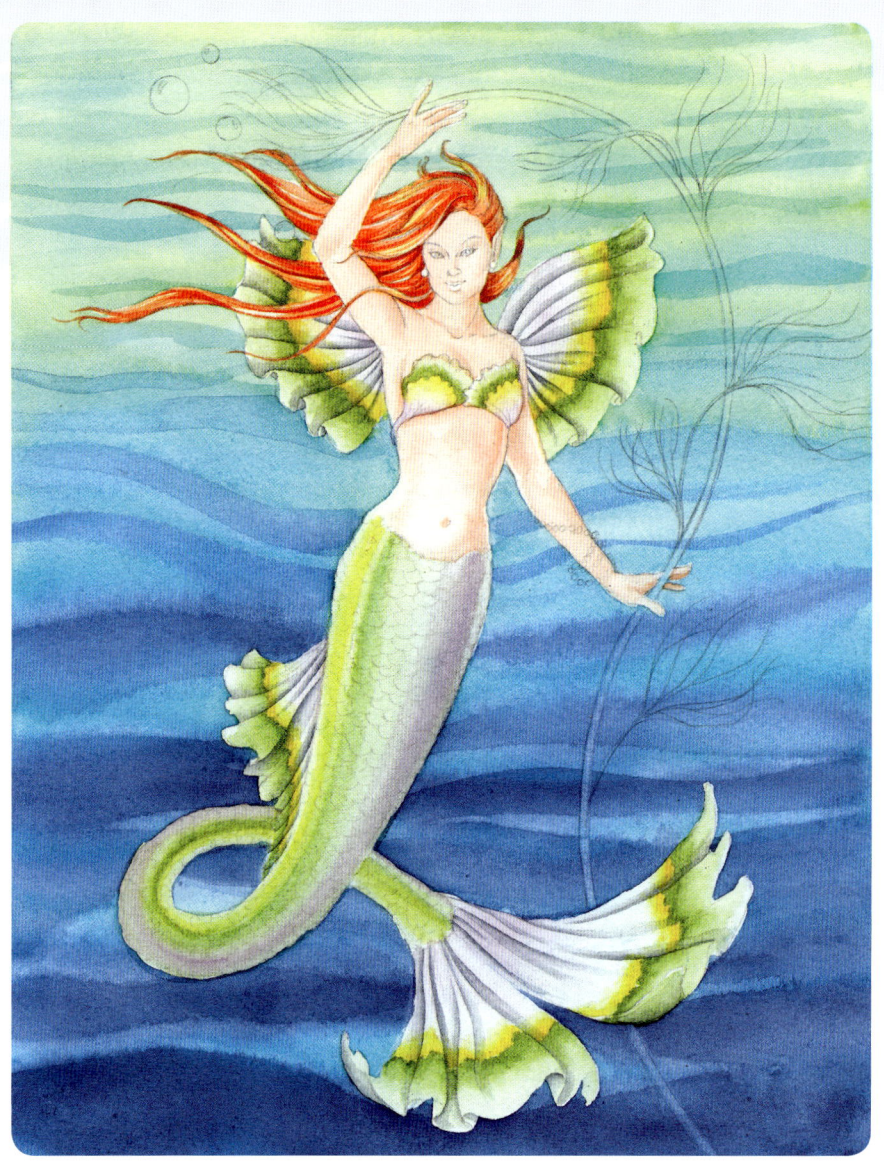

**4** With a no. 0 round, shade the contours of the fairy's skin using a mixture of Alizarin Crimson and Sepia, keeping in mind that the light source comes from the upper left. Add Chinese Orange to individual strands of the fairy's hair. To the right of the New Gamboge on the fairy's tail, add a band of Olive Green. Next, with a mixture of Winsor Violet (Dioxazine) and Payne's Gray, shade the right side of her tail.

*To create the seagrass, follow the steps in the technique demonstration on this page.*

## TECHNIQUE DEMONSTRATION — *Creating Seagrass*

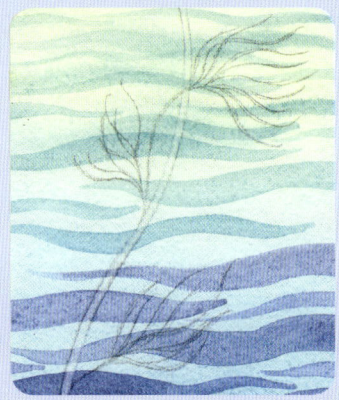

**1** Because the seagrass will be painted directly on top of the background, use a no. 00 round to apply clean water to the stem, and remove some of the background color by blotting with a tissue.

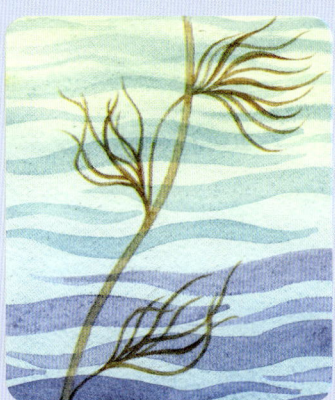

**2** Using a no. 00 round, apply a medium tint of a Burnt Umber and Chinese Orange mixture over all of the seagrass. When dry, remove any remaining transfer color or pencil marks with a kneaded eraser.

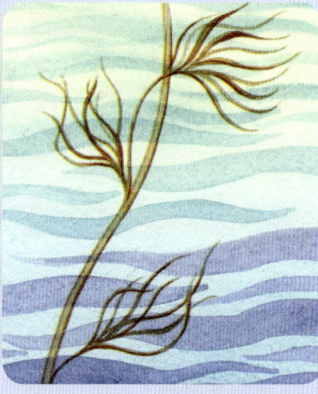

**3** Using a no. 0 round, apply a dark mixture of Burnt Umber and Chinese Orange to the right side of the seagrass stem. With the same brush, add touches of the mixture to every other blade in the seagrass clusters, being careful that the blades do not get too heavy looking.

## TECHNIQUE DEMONSTRATION — *Creating Mermaid Scales*

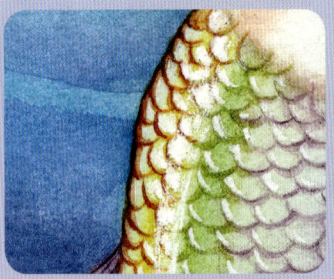 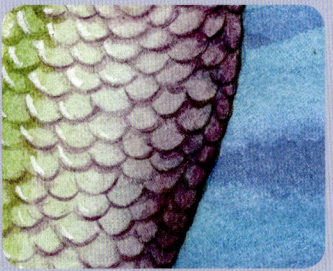 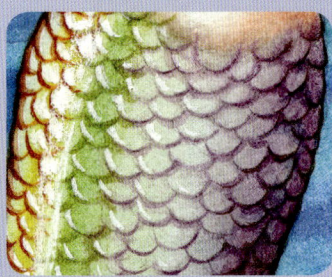

**1** Using a no. 000 round loaded with a tint of New Gamboge mixed with Chinese Orange, paint the edges of the overlapping scales on the left side of the tail.

**2** Use the same brush to define the scales in the middle of the tail using a darker tint of Olive Green. Outline the scales on the right side of the tail with a dark tint of Permanent Mauve.

**3** Use a no. 00 round to apply a highlight of Chinese White where the tail receives the most light. Highlight individual scales with crescents of Chinese White using a no. 000 round.

## TECHNIQUE DEMONSTRATION — *Creating Bubbles*

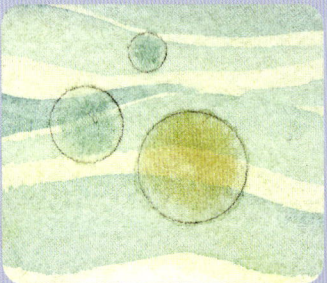 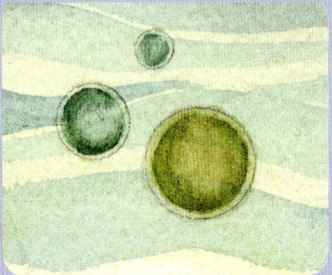 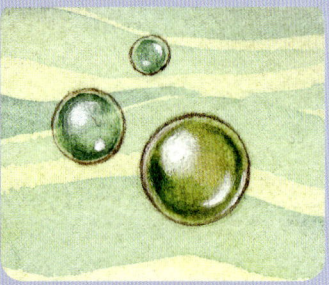

**1** Wet the circle and wait for the shine to disappear. Create the first bubble by painting the circle with a mixture of Olive Green and Payne's Gray using a no. 00 round, applying a thicker coat of the mixture on the left and right sides of the circle. Do the same thing for the smaller bubbles with Viridian.

**2** Using a no. 00 round, add an arc of a darker mixture of Olive Green and Payne's Gray just within the edge of the circle. Use Payne's Gray and Viridian for the smaller bubbles. At the center of each circle, blend in a tiny amount of a Burnt Umber and Chinese Orange mixture.

**3** When dry, add a highlight with Chinese White on the upper left, where the light source hits the bubble. Finally, outline the bubble using a no. 000 round loaded with Sepia. Follow this technique for the smaller bubbles.

**5** With a no. 1 round, paint all of the fairy's skin with a mixture of Cadmium Red, Burnt Umber, Chinese Orange and a touch of Olive Green. Use Winsor Emerald to paint her irises. Wet her cheeks and charge in Cadmium Red, blending outward with water. Using a no. 000 round, apply spots of Cerulean Blue on the right side of the pearls. Next, use Sepia on a no. 000 round to outline the pearls and the figure.

*To create the fairy mermaid's scales and the water bubbles, see the technique demonstrations on this page.*

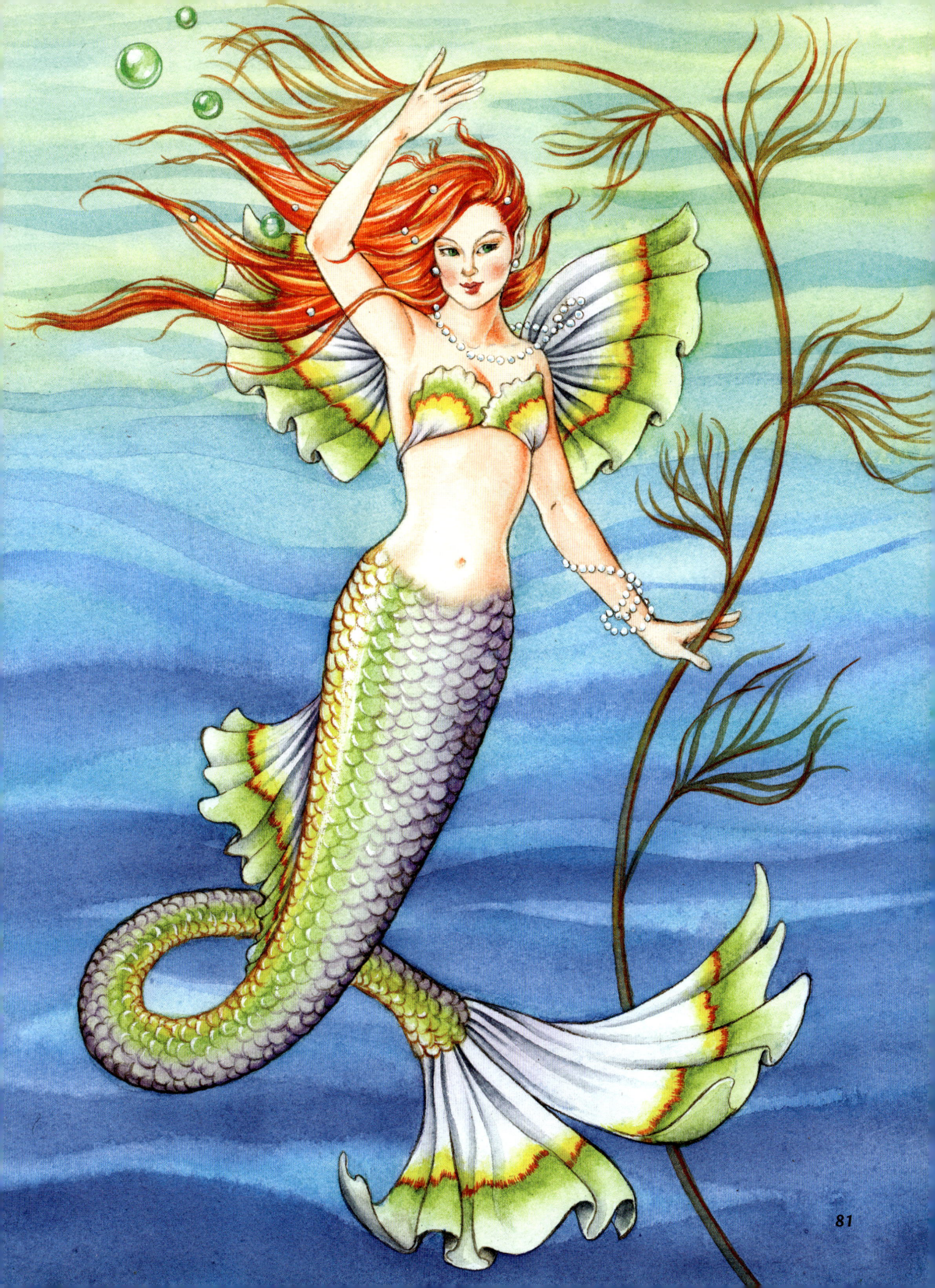

# DEMONSTRATION
## FIRE FAIRY

Fire Fairy carries her torch with strength, determination and grace. The vibrant colors of flames, which undulate through her hair, gown and wings, are set against a darkening background. Here's our chance to use our most powerful yellows and reds.

### ~YOU WILL NEED~

#### MATERIALS

1½-inch (38mm) flat • bar soap • blue tape • hard-leaded pencil or ballpoint pen that has run out of ink • HB or 2B graphite pencil • kneaded eraser • masking fluid • nos. 000 and 4 acrylic rounds • nos. 000, 00, 0, 1, 4 and 8 rounds • Saral transfer paper • square masking fluid pickup • stretched watercolor paper • tracing paper

#### PIGMENTS

Alizarin Crimson • Burnt Umber • Cadmium Red • Cadmium Yellow • Caput Mortuum Violet • Chinese Orange • Chinese White • Cobalt Turquoise Light • Indigo • Ivory Black • Payne's Gray • Raw Sienna • Vermilion Hue

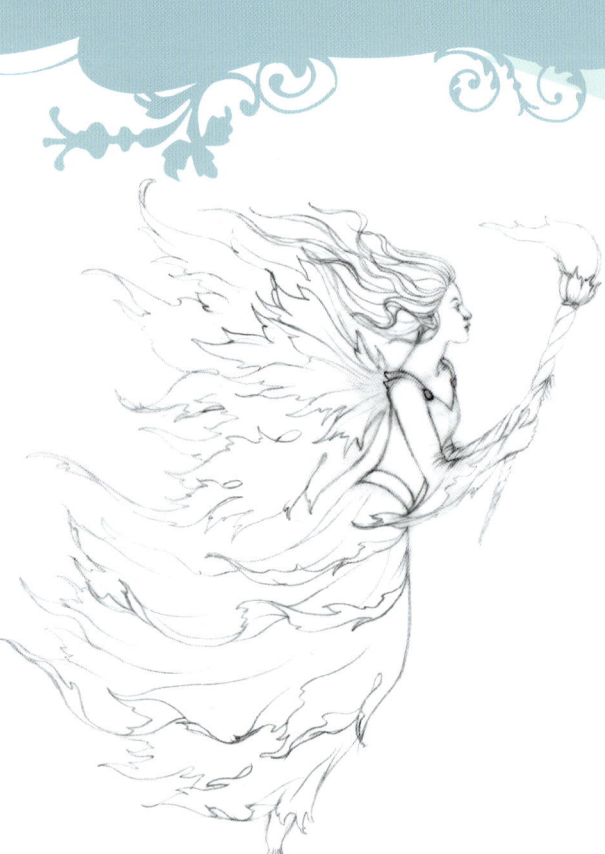

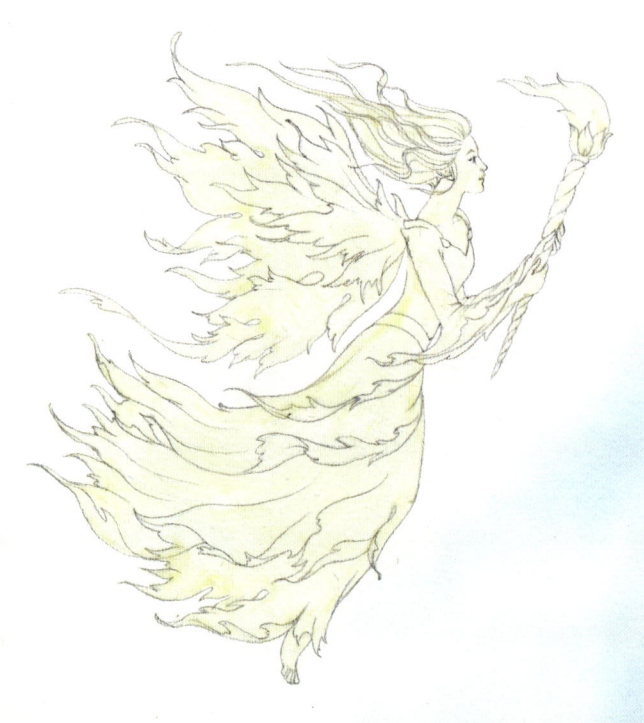

**1** Stretch your watercolor paper and trace the image following the steps on pages 14 and 15.

**2** Using a no. 000 acrylic round that has first been dipped in wet bar soap, apply masking fluid to the fine details of the outer edge of the fairy. Use a no. 4 acrylic round to mask the larger sections of the fairy.

Wet the background with a 1½-inch (38mm) flat. When the shine is gone, use a no. 8 round to apply two diagonal strokes of a medium tint of Cobalt Turquoise Light, tilting your board to spread the color. Next, add a few darker strokes of Cobalt Turquoise Light.

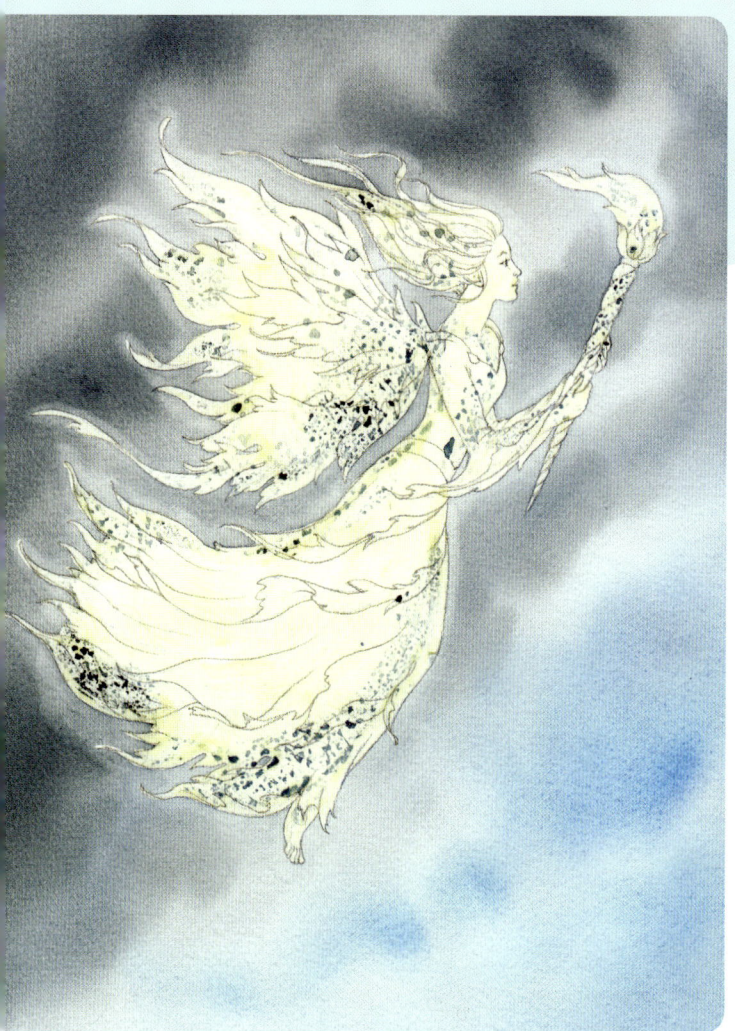

**3** When the Cobalt Turquoise Light has dried, re-wet the background. Using a no. 8 round, apply Indigo above the Cobalt Turquoise Light in two wavy diagonal strokes. Above that, apply Payne's Gray in two wavy diagonal strokes, working until you reach the upper left corner of the page. Tilt your board back and forth and side to side to blend the colors. Let this dry thoroughly.

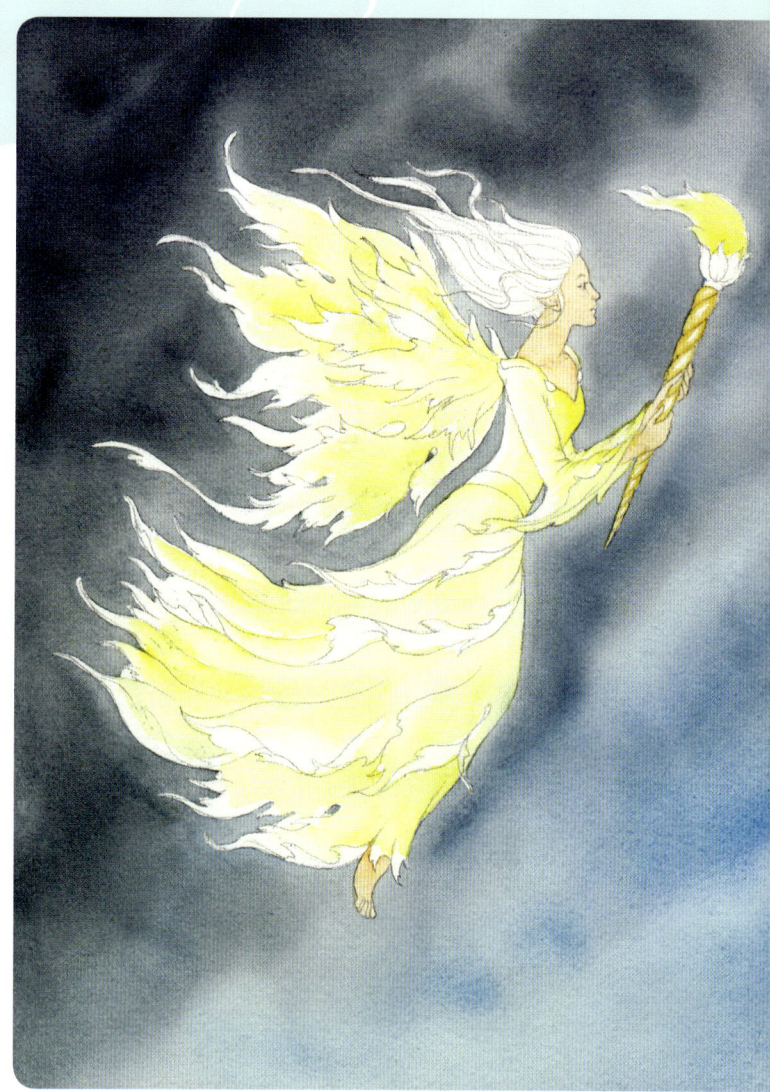

**4** Re-wet the background and, using your no. 8 round, apply strokes of a dark tint of Payne's Gray at the upper left and a dark tint of Cobalt Turquoise Light at the lower left of the page. Tilt your board again. After the wash is completely dry, remove the mask with a square masking fluid pickup or your fingers.

Mix a small amount of Burnt Umber, Chinese Orange and Cadmium Red to make a flesh tone. Using a no. 1 round, apply a medium tint of the flesh color to her face, neck, hands and foot. Using a no. 4 round, apply a mixture of Cadmium Yellow and Chinese White to the wings and dress.

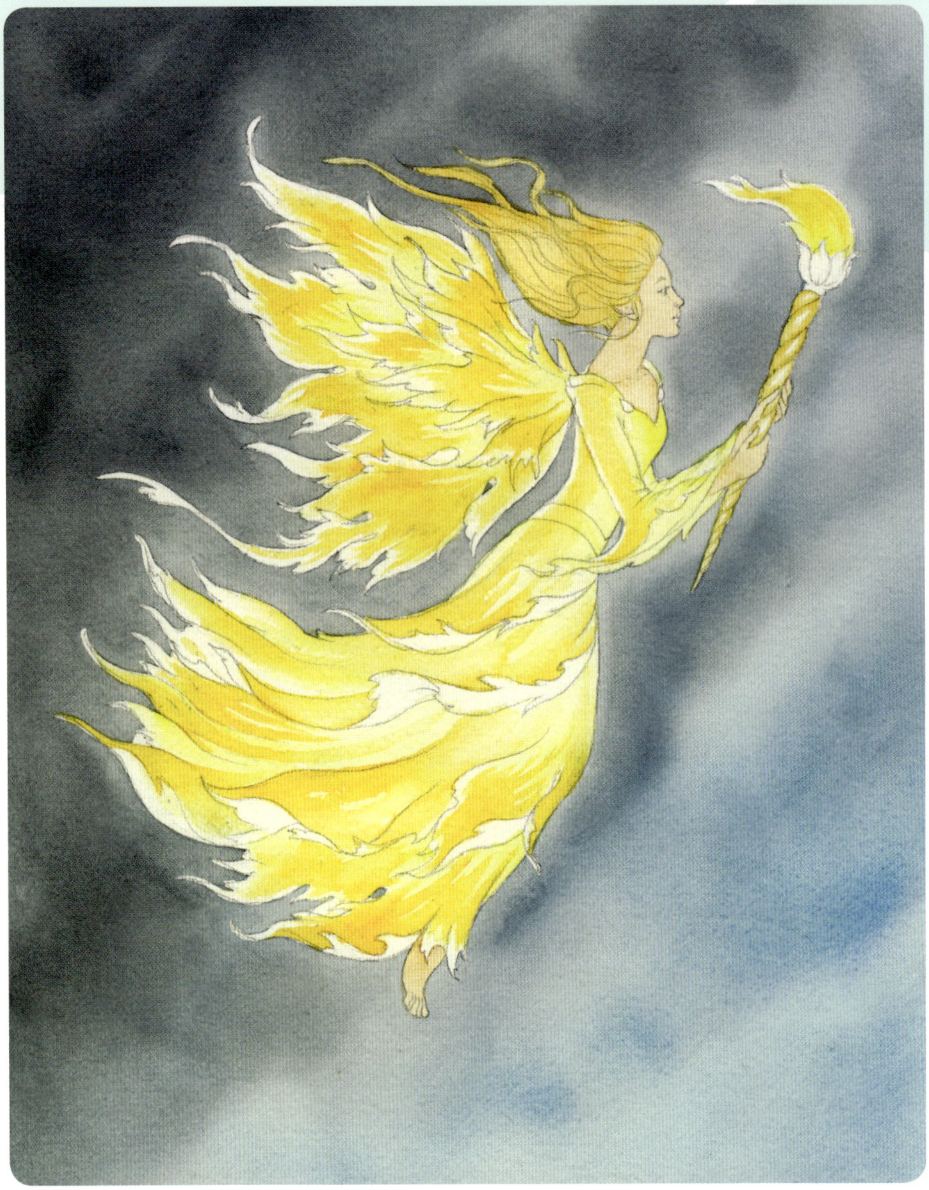

**5** Using a no. 1 round, apply a medium tint of a Cadmium Yellow and Chinese Orange mixture to her dress and to the outer edges of her wings, following the contours of each element.

*To create the torch, follow the detail demonstration on this page.*

## DETAIL DEMONSTRATION — *Fire Fairy's Torch*

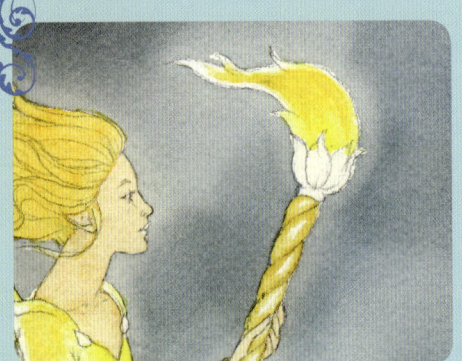

**1** Use a no.1 round to apply a medium tint of a Cadmium Yellow and Chinese White mixture to the base of the flame, blending to the outer edge with clean water. Apply Raw Sienna to the spirals of the torch.

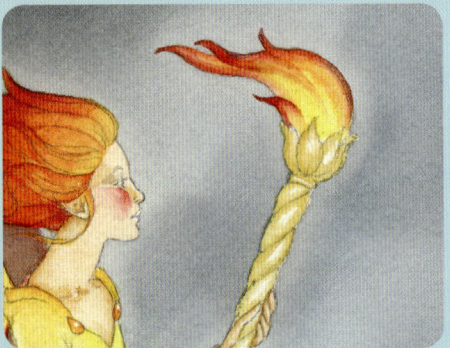

**2** Using a no. 0 round and a mixture of Cadmium Yellow and Chinese Orange, add this to the base of the flame, then define the outer edge using Cadmium Red. Paint the top of the torch using a no. 0 round and Raw Sienna. Let it dry.

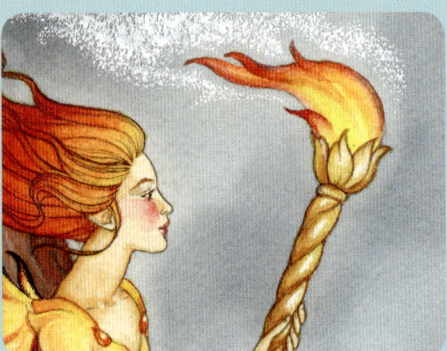

**3** Apply Alizarin Crimson to the tip of the flame with a no. 000 round. Using a no. 00 round, apply a dark tint of Raw Sienna to the left side curves of the torch.

84

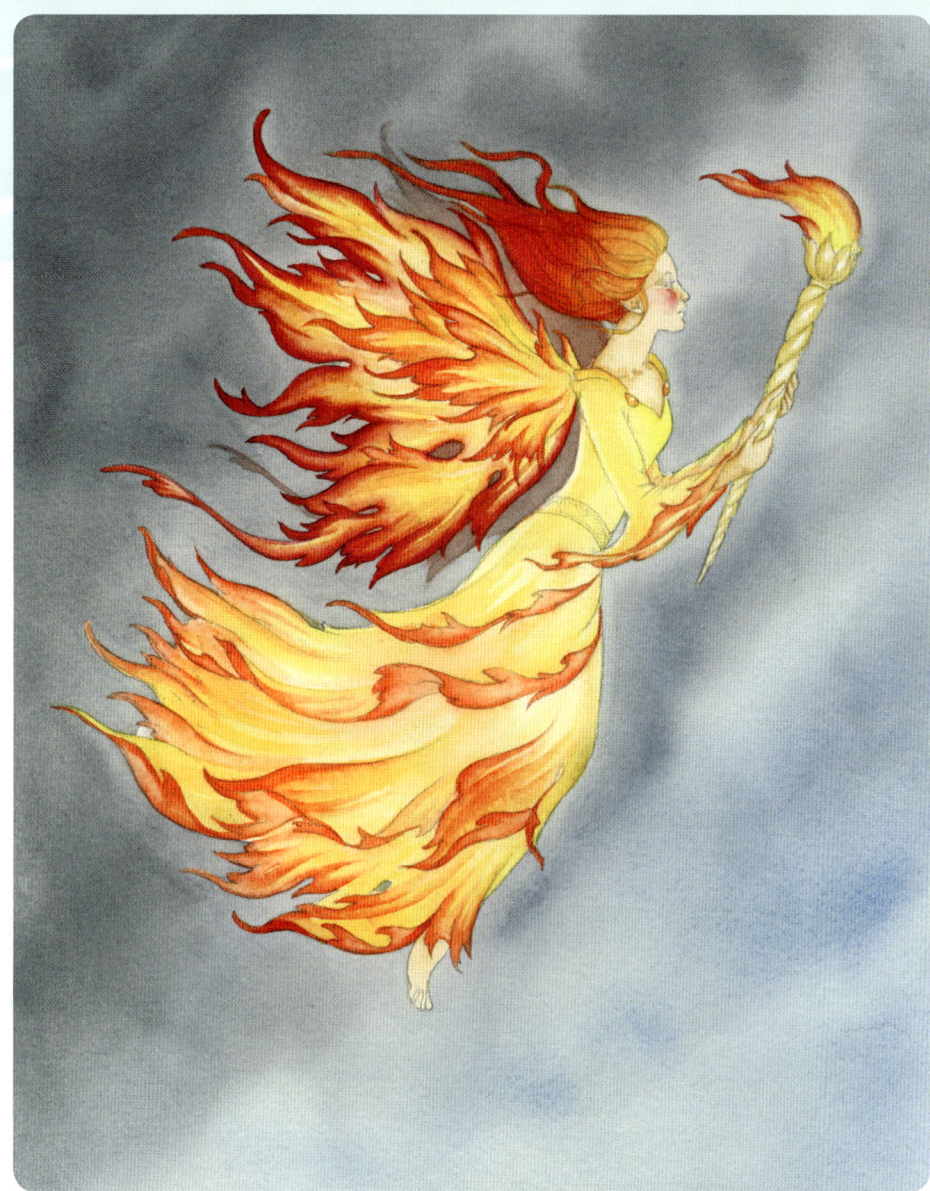

**6** Using a no. 0 round, apply Cadmium Red to the edges and folds of the fairy's dress. Begin by applying color to the outer edge, then dragging inward. Using a no. 00 round, apply a medium dark tint of Alizarin Crimson to the outer edges of the wings. With a no. 1 round, draw the background wing following the shape of the foreground wing. With a no. 00 round, apply a light tint of Alizarin Crimson to the second wing. Then, using a no. 4 round, apply a light tint of Cadmium Yellow to the fairy's dress.

Wet the cheek with a no. 00 round. Apply a medium tint of Quinacridone Red in an arc next to her nose. Blend outward with the same brush dipped in clean water. Add a shadow above the eye lid using a no. 00 round loaded with a mixture of Sepia and Caput Mortum Violet. Let dry. Shade to the side of her nose with a no. 000 round dipped in the same mixture.

*To paint the fairy's hair, follow the steps in the technique demonstration on this page.*

## TECHNIQUE DEMONSTRATION — *Painting Fairy Hair*

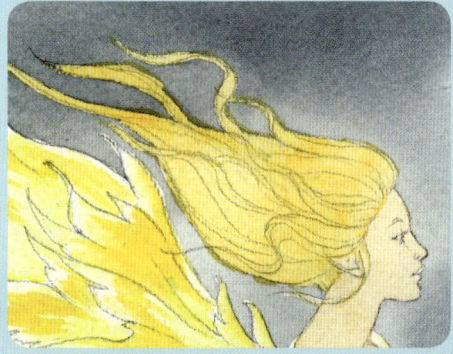

**1** Apply a medium tint of Cadmium Yellow and Chinese White with a no. 1 round to the fairy's hair.

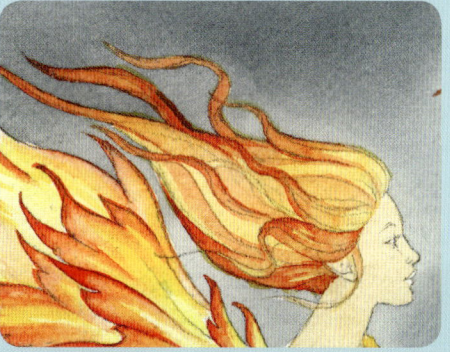

**2** Using a no. 0 round, paint Cadmium Red streaks in her hair. Using a no. 1 round, apply a medium tint Cadmium Yellow to the hair nearest her face and a medium tint of Chinese Orange to the rest of her hair.

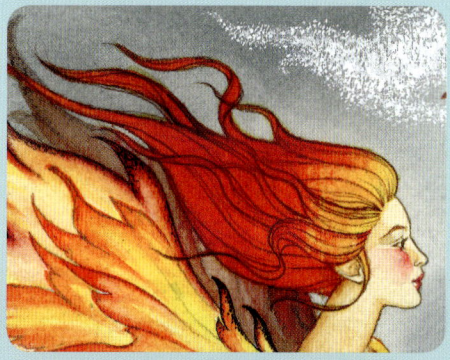

**3** Use a no. 000 round to outline strands of the fairy's hair with Caput Mortum Violet.

**7** Using a no. 000 round, apply Ivory Black to the outer edge of the wings. Holding your brush perpendicular to the paper, add tiny dots of Ivory Black just inside the edge. Deepen the shadows and folds at the gown's bottom with Alizarin Crimson. Using a no. 0 round, add a pale tint of Cadmium Red to the left side of her body and her sleeve to add volume to her figure. Using a no. 00 round, apply a medium light tint of Cadmium Red to the shaded part of her bosom, the folds of her sleeves and the details on the second wing.

**8** Using a no. 000 round, apply a medium dark tint of Quinacridone Red to the lips, leaving a spot of white paper for a highlight. Rinse the round in clean water, apply a dark tint of Burnt Umber to outline the eye and iris.

Use a no. 000 round loaded with a medium tint of Cadmium Red to outline the dress and the waistband. Use the same size brush and a medium tint of Burnt Umber to outline the fairy's skin. Using a no. 00 round, apply a dark tint of Alizarin Crimson to the shaded areas of the dress's sleeves and folds. With a dark tint mixture of Burnt Umber, Chinese Orange and Cadmium Red, shade the back of the fairy's neck, hands and top of her foot. Finally, deepen the shadow along the left side of the fairy's body with a medium tint of Cadmium Red.

*To the finish the flame, follow the steps in the technique demonstration on this page.*

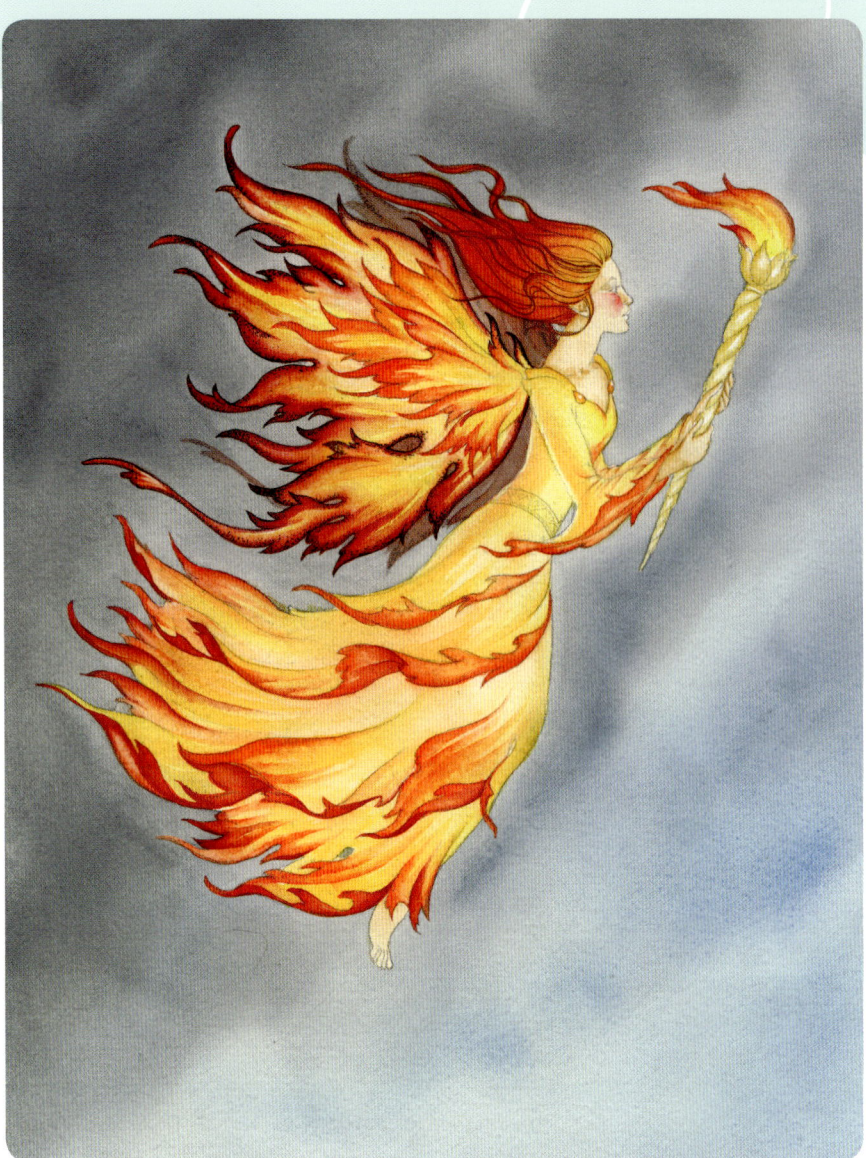

## TECHNIQUE DEMONSTRATION — *Creating Smoke*

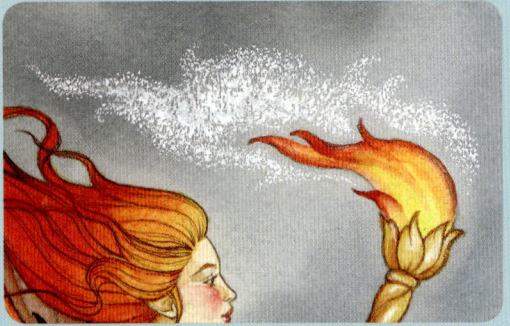
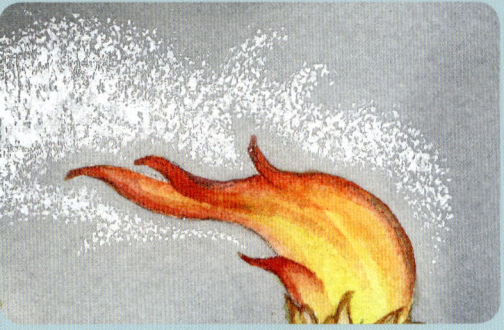

**1** Dip a no. 1 round in Chinese White and let it dry slightly. Next, drag the dry brush to the left of the flame, following its shape as shown.

**2** Using a no. 000 round, apply tiny dots of white to the outer edge to create the curls of smoke.

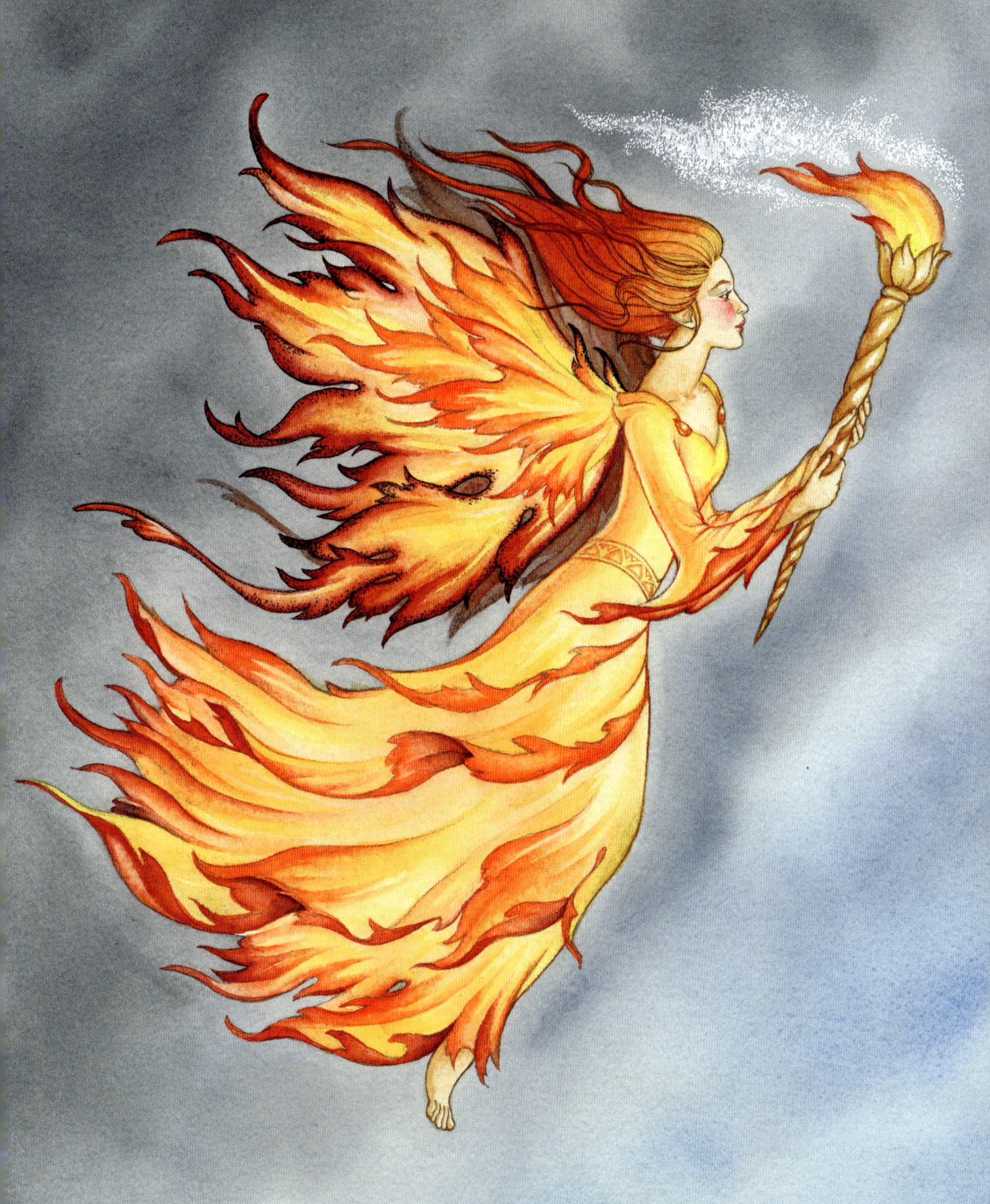

# DEMONSTRATION
# SPRING FAIRY

One of the most welcome sights in early spring is the crocus. They startle us with a vibrant array of violets, purples and yellows, which fade to white at the flower's base. Cadmium Yellow stamens add richness to their centers. Here a crocus serves as a bassinet for the Spring Fairy.

## ~ YOU WILL NEED ~

### MATERIALS
Bar of soap ∞ blade ∞ blue Saral transfer paper ∞ blue tape ∞ hard-leaded pencil or ballpoint pen that has run out of ink ∞ HB or 2B graphite pencil ∞ kneaded eraser ∞ masking fluid ∞ no. 1 acrylic round ∞ nos. 000, 0, 1, 2, 3 and 5 rounds ∞ square masking fluid pickup ∞ stretched watercolor paper ∞ tracing paper

### PIGMENTS
Burnt Umber ∞ Cadmium Yellow ∞ Caput Mortum Violet ∞ Chinese Orange ∞ Cobalt Blue ∞ Cobalt Turquoise Light ∞ Hooker's Green ∞ Indigo ∞ Olive Green ∞ Oxide of Chromium ∞ Payne's Gray ∞ Permanent Magenta ∞ Permanent Mauve ∞ Permanent Sap Green ∞ Quinacridone Red ∞ Sepia ∞ Ultramarine Blue (Green Shade) ∞ Viridian ∞ Winsor Violet (Dioxazine)

**1** Stretch your watercolor paper and trace the image following the steps on pages 14 and 15.

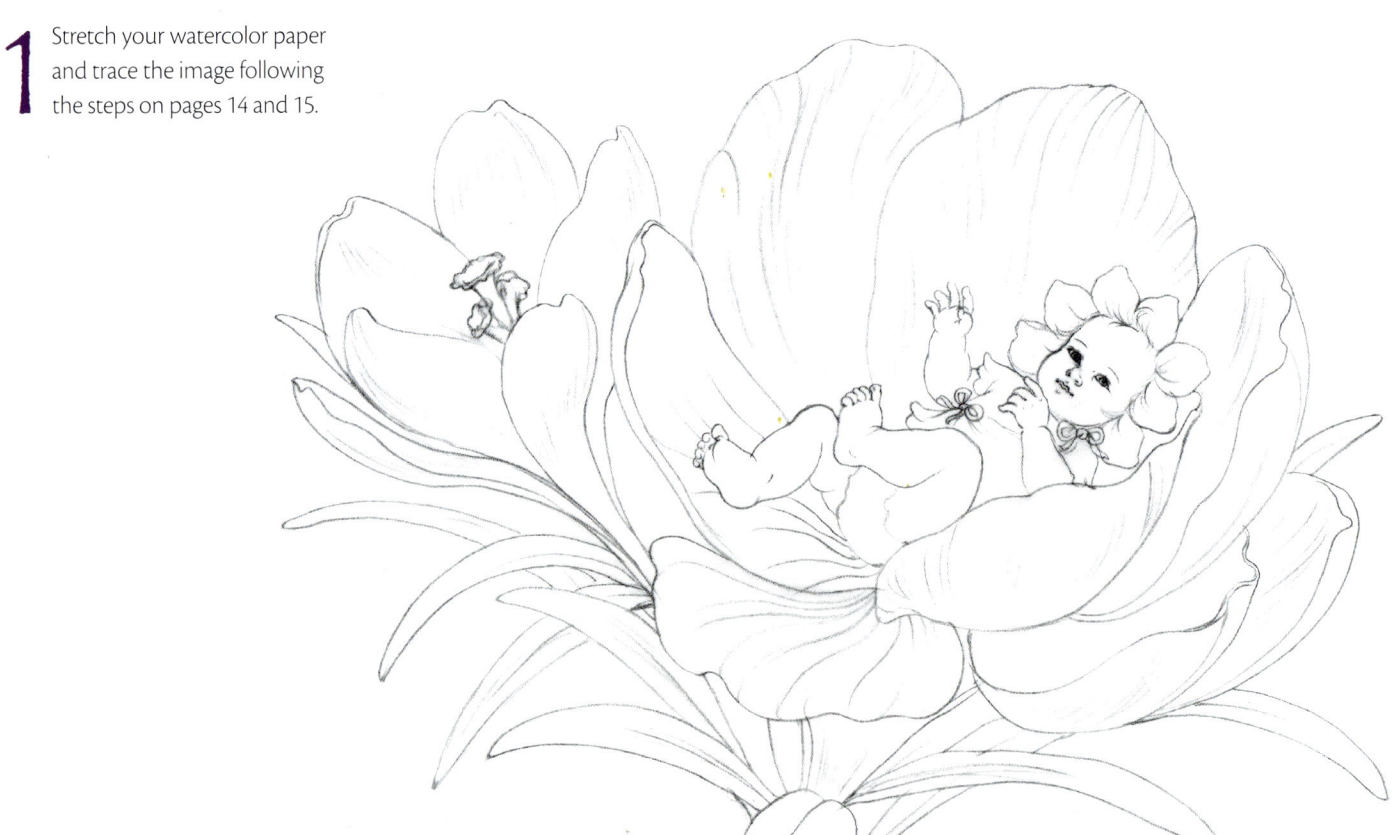

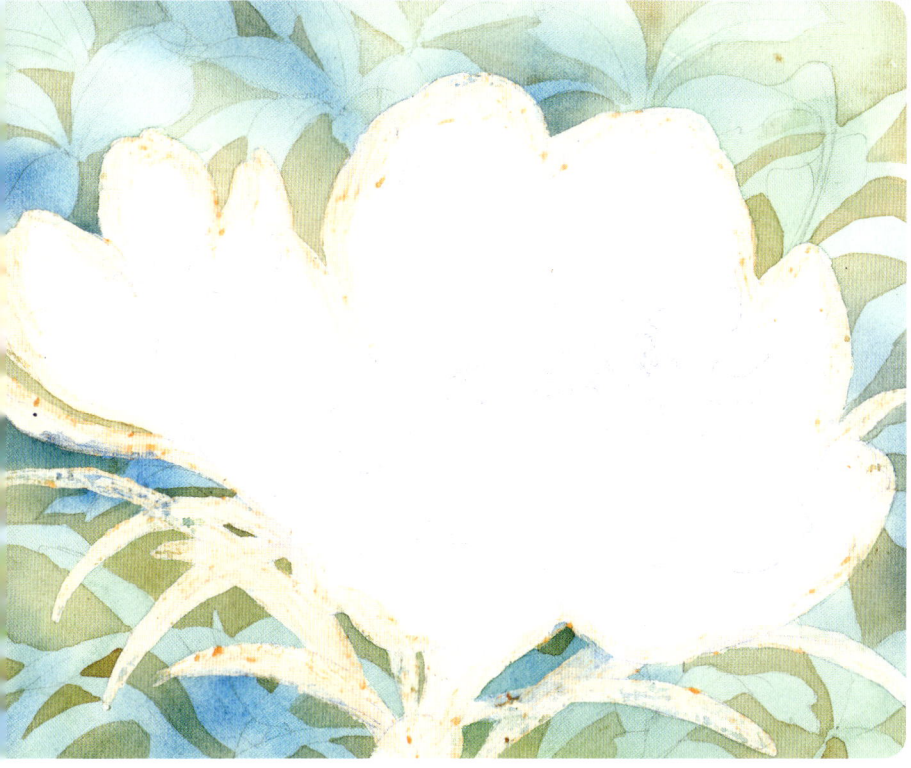

**2** Using a no. 1 acrylic round, which has first been rubbed in a wet bar of soap, then dipped in masking fluid, mask the flowers and the leaves attached to them. Pencil in additional shapes of leaves behind the flowers. With a no. 5 round, apply a cool wash of Cobalt Turquoise Light mixed with Viridian to the entire background. Create the leaf shapes by filling in the negative background space with a pale wash of Sepia and a no. 3 round.

**3** Using a wet-into-wet approach with Permanent Sap Green and a no. 1 round, paint the leaves at the top of the page, letting some of the Cobalt Turquoise Light show through for leaf veins and contours. Use Olive Green to paint the underside of the leaves. Continue to paint the leaves with Permanent Sap Green, Viridian and a mixture of Olive Green and Oxide of Chromium.

When you have achieved a good amount of depth, begin painting the most distant leaves using Indigo mixed with Sepia. Vary the value of this color to create depth. When dry, remove the mask and paint the leaves of both croci a pale shade of Viridian. Use Permanent Mauve to paint the base of foreground crocus.

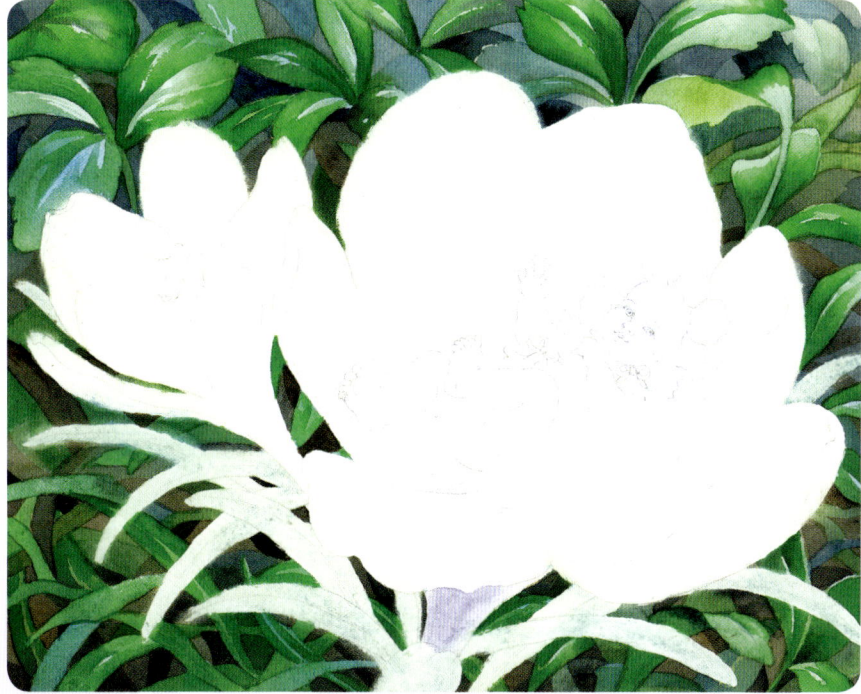

## TECHNIQUE DEMONSTRATION — *Creating Crocus Petals*

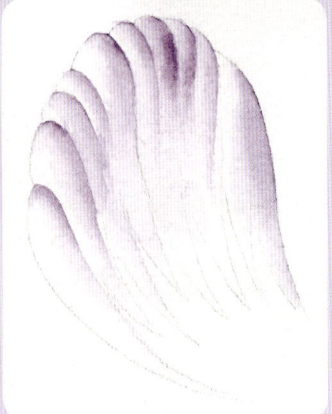
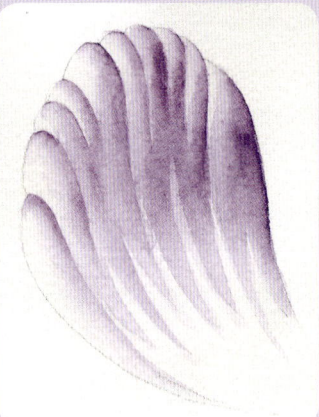
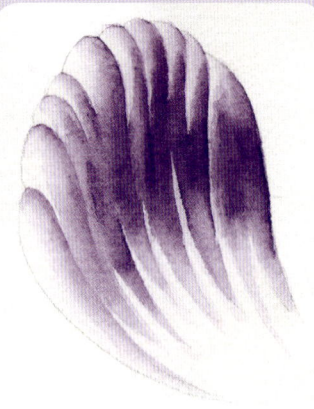
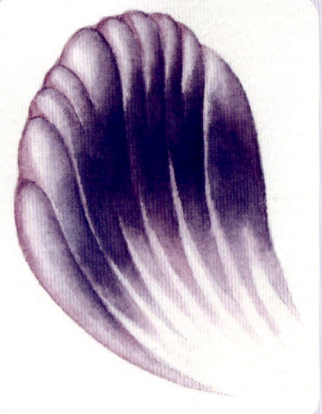

**1** Using a no. 3 round and working on one petal at a time, wet the entire petal with water. When the shine has gone, use a no. 2 round to apply Winsor Violet (Dioxazine) to the edges of the curves at the top of the petal.

**2** Dip the no. 2 round in clear water and drag the Winsor Violet (Dioxazine) down toward the center of the flower.

**3** When the shine has gone, work stronger bands of Winsor Violet (Dioxazine) into the petal using the wet-into-wet technique.

**4** With a no. 1 round, apply Permanent Mauve in the areas that face the light and Cobalt Blue where the petal becomes concave. Use a no. 1 round to apply a mixture of Winsor Violet (Dioxazine) and Permanent Magenta to the curve of the petal folds.

## DETAIL DEMONSTRATION — *Spring Fairy's Clothes*

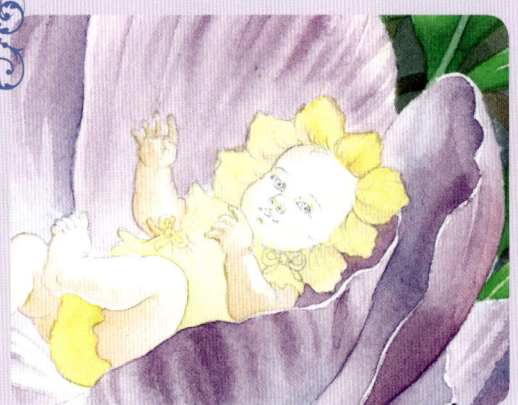
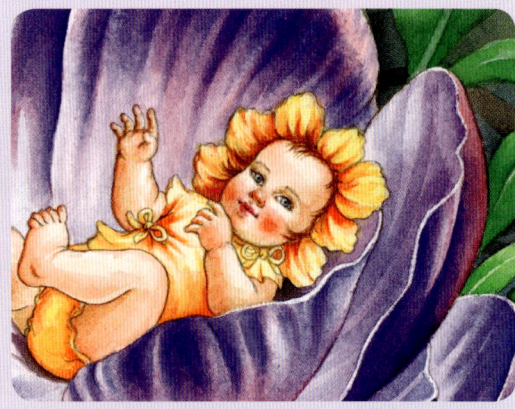

**1** With a no. 1 round, paint the fairy's clothing and hat with Cadmium Yellow, leaving lighter areas on the chest and hat by blending with clear water on a no. 1 round.

**2** Finish the baby fairy's clothes and hat by using a no. 1 round loaded with Chinese Orange to shade the folds and creases.

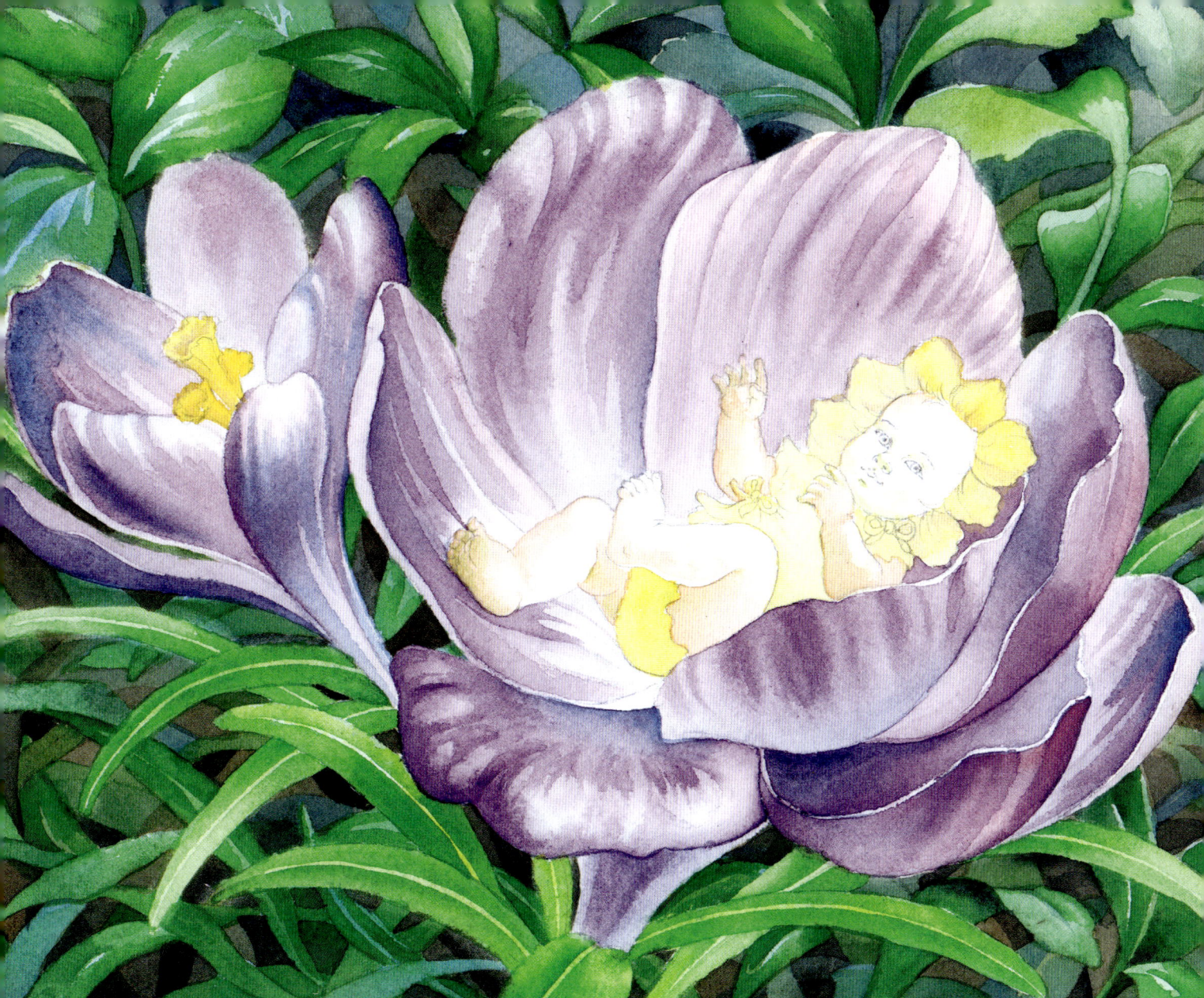

**4** Once you have completed the croci petals, paint the shaded areas of the fairy's skin using a mixture of Burnt Umber, Chinese Orange and Olive Green and a no. 00 round. Let dry. Paint the flower stamen and the fairy's clothing with Cadmium Yellow. Paint the foreground leaves attached to the crocus stem using Hooker's Green and Olive Green and a no. 0 round.

*To the paint the petals and the fairy's clothes, follow the technique and detail demonstrations on page 90.*

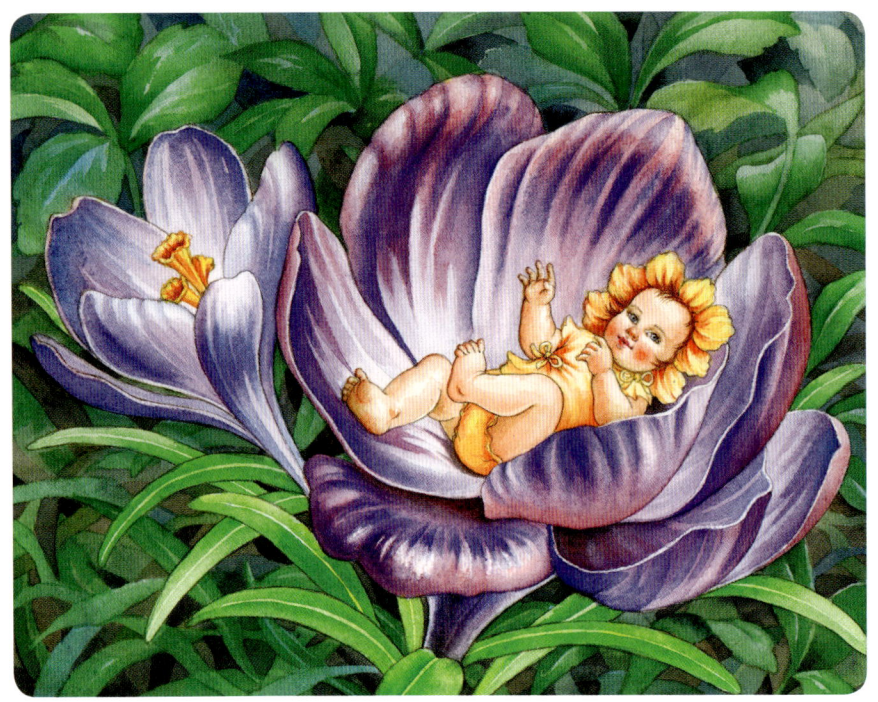

**5** Using a no. 0 round, apply a mixture of Burnt Umber, Chinese Orange and Olive Green to along right side of face. Let dry. Wet cheeks using a no. 00 round. Add medium tint of Cadmium Red to center of her cheeks. Rinse the brush and use it to blend the color into the rest of the cheeks.

Apply Cadmium Red to the end of the nose with a no. 000 round, leaving a dot of white paper for a highlight. Rinse the brush and apply a medium tint of Quinacridone Red to the lips, leaving a white paper highlight. Rinse the brush again and apply a medium dark tint of Chinese Orange and Burnt Umber to her hair.

Paint her irises using a no. 000 round and Cobalt Blue. Leave a highlight of white paper. Using a no. 000 round and a dark shade of Sepia, paint the fine details of her eyes, nose and mouth. With a no. 5 round, apply a pale tint of Payne's Gray to the background behind the croci and their leaves. Define the flower stamen with Cadmium Yellow and Chinese Orange. Apply a little Caput Mortum Violet to the center of the stamen. When dry, outline the baby's figure with a no. 000 round loaded with Sepia. Outline the foreground leaves with Sepia.

*To the finish the crocus petals, follow the steps in the technique demonstration on this page.*

## TECHNIQUE DEMONSTRATION — Finishing Crocus Petals

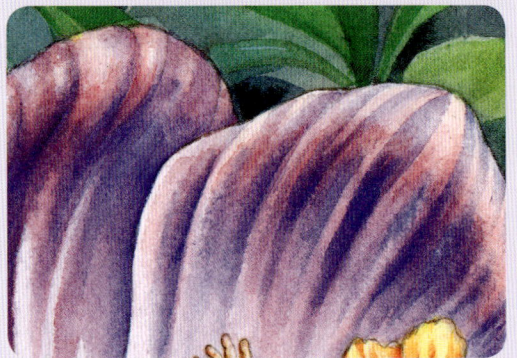

**1** With a no. 1 round, begin building stronger bands of Permanent Mauve and Ultramarine Blue (Green Shade) on the crocus in the foreground.

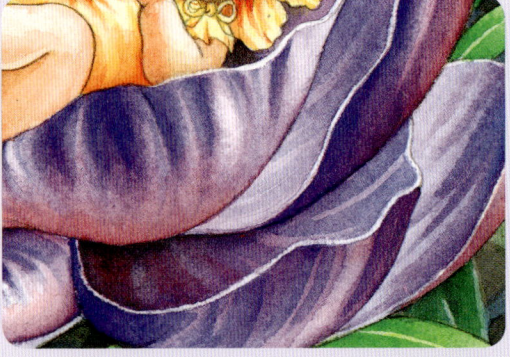

**2** Shade under the foreground petals with Caput Mortum Violet. When dry, use a blade to pull color from the edges of the petals as needed.

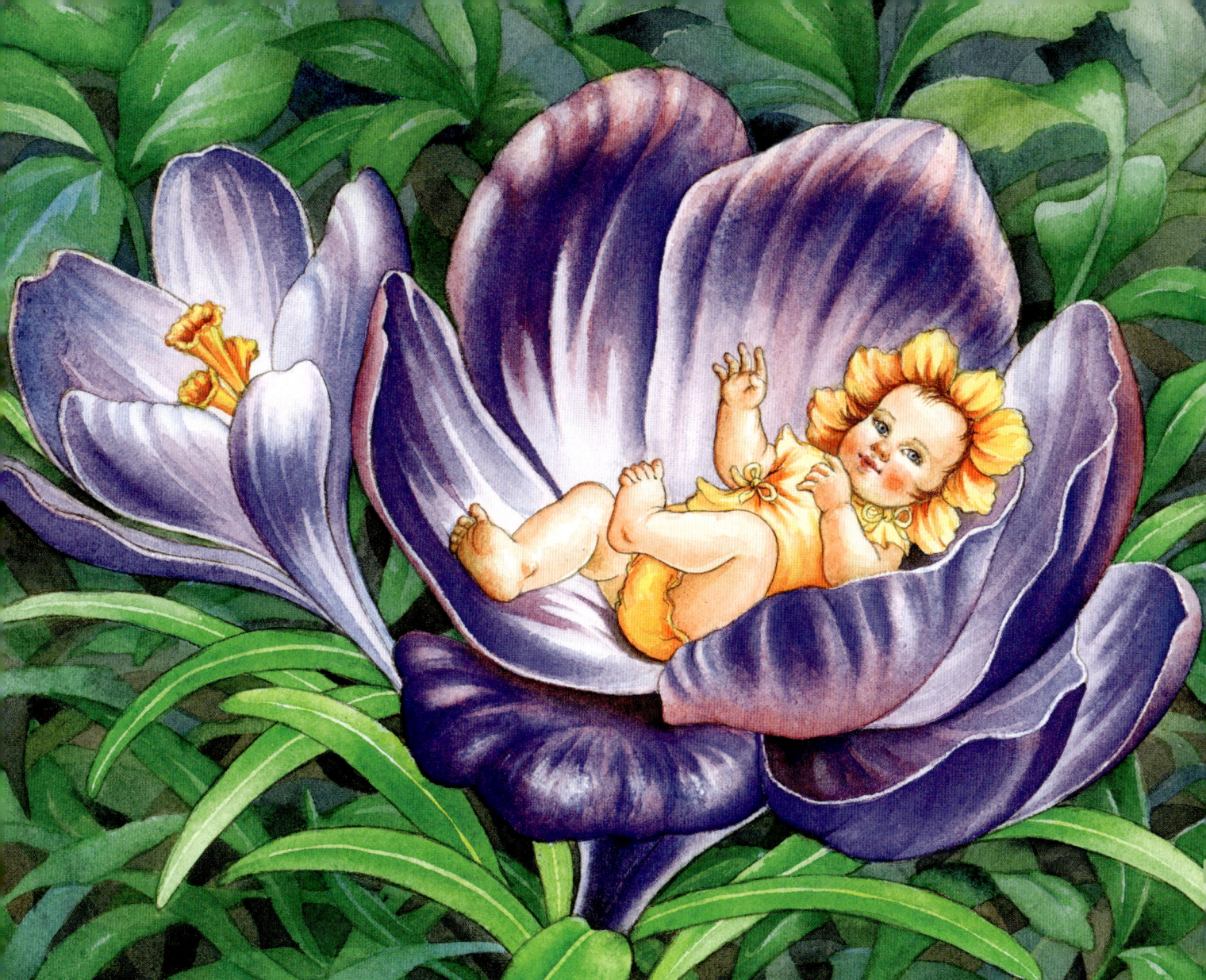

**6** Using Ultramarine Blue (Green Shade) loaded on a no. 1 round, paint the curves of the petals above the head, the curves of the petals in the foreground, and the inside of the petal under the foot, keeping the white areas to draw attention to the fairy. Using a no. 0 round, apply a mixture of Quinacridone Red and Permanent Mauve to the outside of the petals in the darkest shadows.

# DEMONSTRATION
# SUMMER FAIRY

*There are so many flowers that could represent summer. I chose the rose for this demonstration because scent is key to the enjoyment of a summer garden. Summer Fairy expresses that pleasure.*

## YOU WILL NEED

### MATERIALS

Bar of soap ◦ blue Saral transfer paper ◦ blue tape ◦ hard-leaded pencil or ballpoint pen that has run out of ink ◦ HB or 2B graphite pencil ◦ kneaded eraser ◦ masking fluid (optional) ◦ nos. 000, 0, 1 and 6 rounds ◦ stretched watercolor paper ◦ tracing paper

### PIGMENTS

Alizarin Crimson ◦ Burnt Umber ◦ Cadmium Yellow ◦ Cerulean Blue ◦ Chinese Orange ◦ Chinese White ◦ Cobalt Turquoise Light ◦ Hooker's Green ◦ Indigo ◦ Ivory Black ◦ New Gamboge ◦ Olive Green ◦ Oxide of Chromium ◦ Permanent Magenta ◦ Raw Sienna ◦ Sepia ◦ Vermilion Hue ◦ Viridian ◦ Winsor Violet (Dioxazine) ◦ Yellow Ochre

**1** Stretch your watercolor paper and trace the image following the steps on pages 14 and 15.

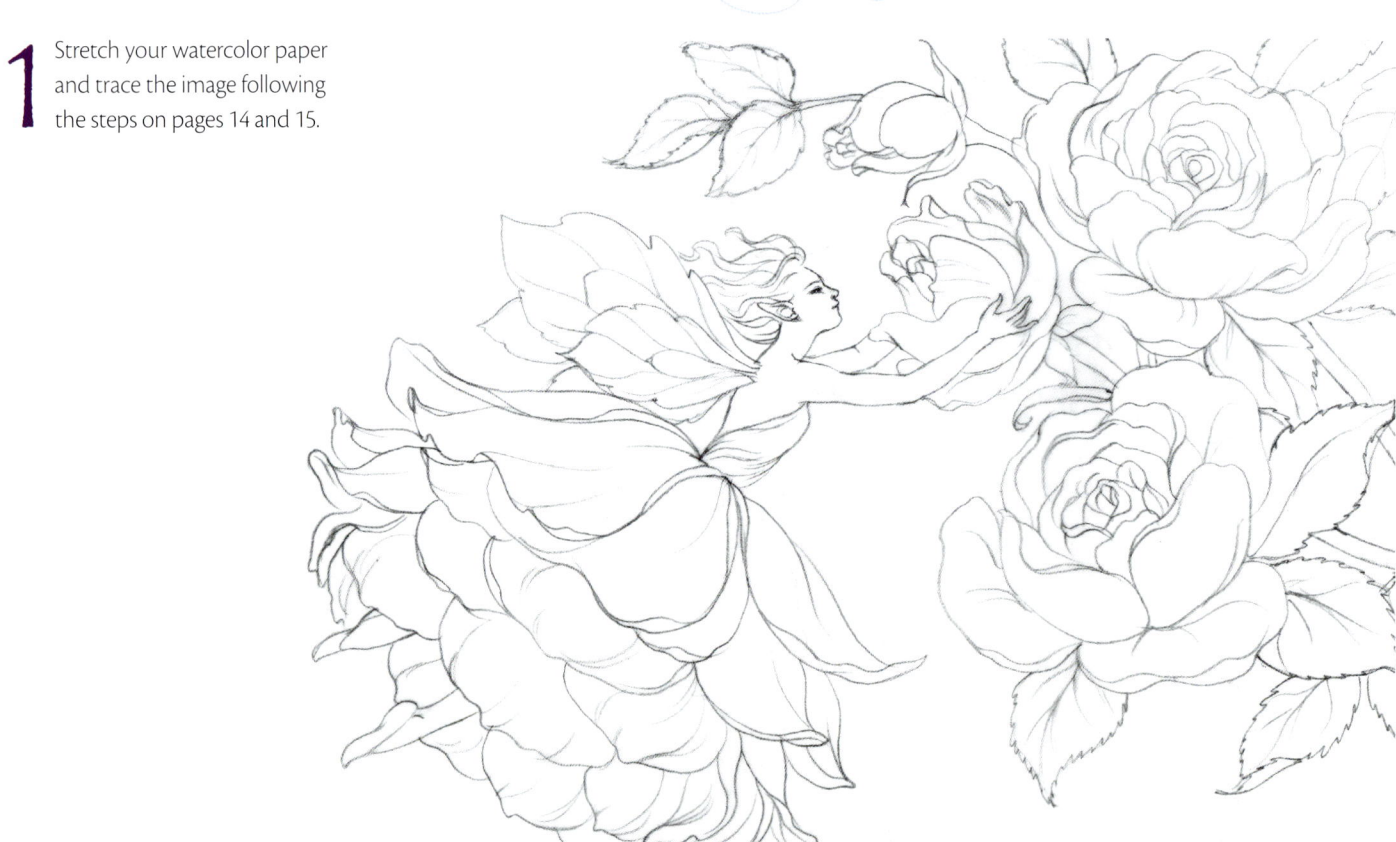

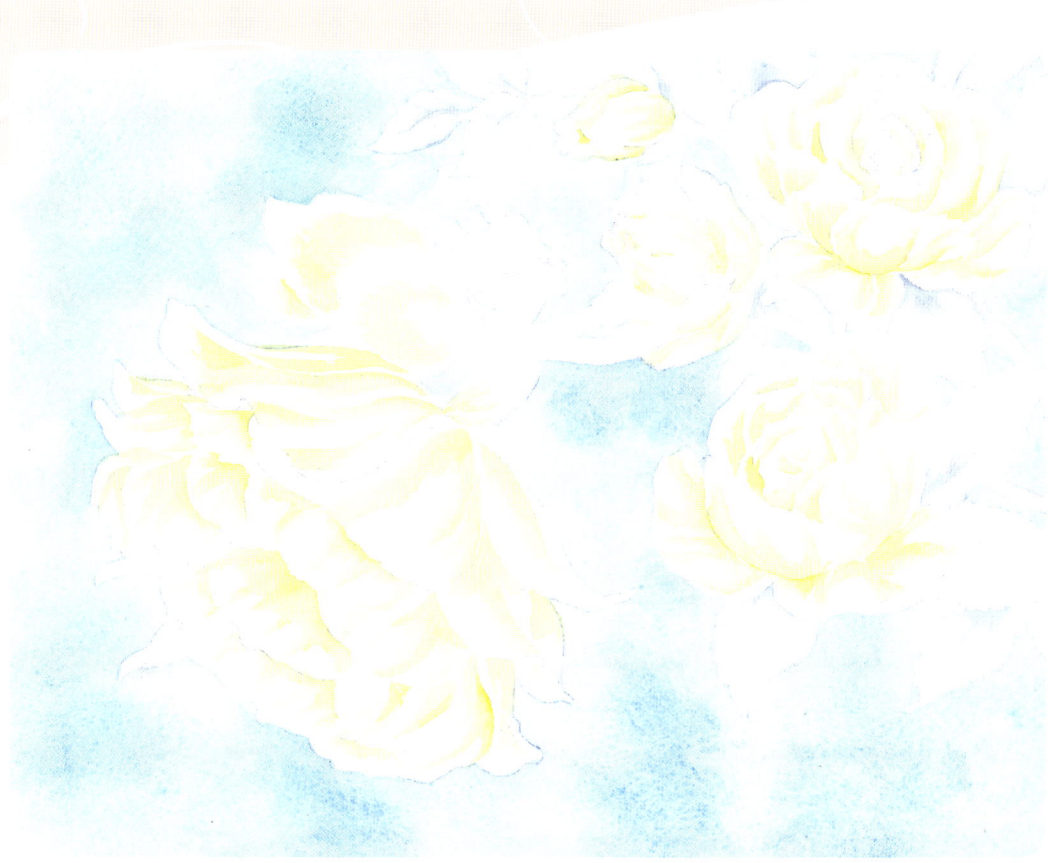

**2** Carefully apply clear water to the background and along the perimeter of the fairy and the roses with a no. 1 round. If you would like to use masking, apply it before wetting the paper. Working quickly using a no. 1 round, charge a medium tint of Cerulean Blue into the background and, when dry, charge even stronger concentrations of Cerulean Blue and Cobalt Turquoise Light in various areas.

When dry, use New Gamboge and a no. 1 round to paint the petals, letting the color radiate from the base of the flower. Use the same color on the fairy's dress and wings. Apply a medium tint of Indigo to the shaded parts of the rose leaves, blending outward with clear water.

**3** Using a medium tint of Vermilion Hue and starting from the outer edge, use a no. 1 round to begin to paint the petals and the fairy's dress. Do not overlap the yellow at this point. Working wet-into-wet, add a darker tint of Vermilion Hue to the areas where the petals and the dress turn from the light source at the upper right. Next, evenly apply a pale flesh mixture of Burnt Umber, Chinese Orange and Vermilion Hue to the fairy's head, neck, arms, hands and feet.

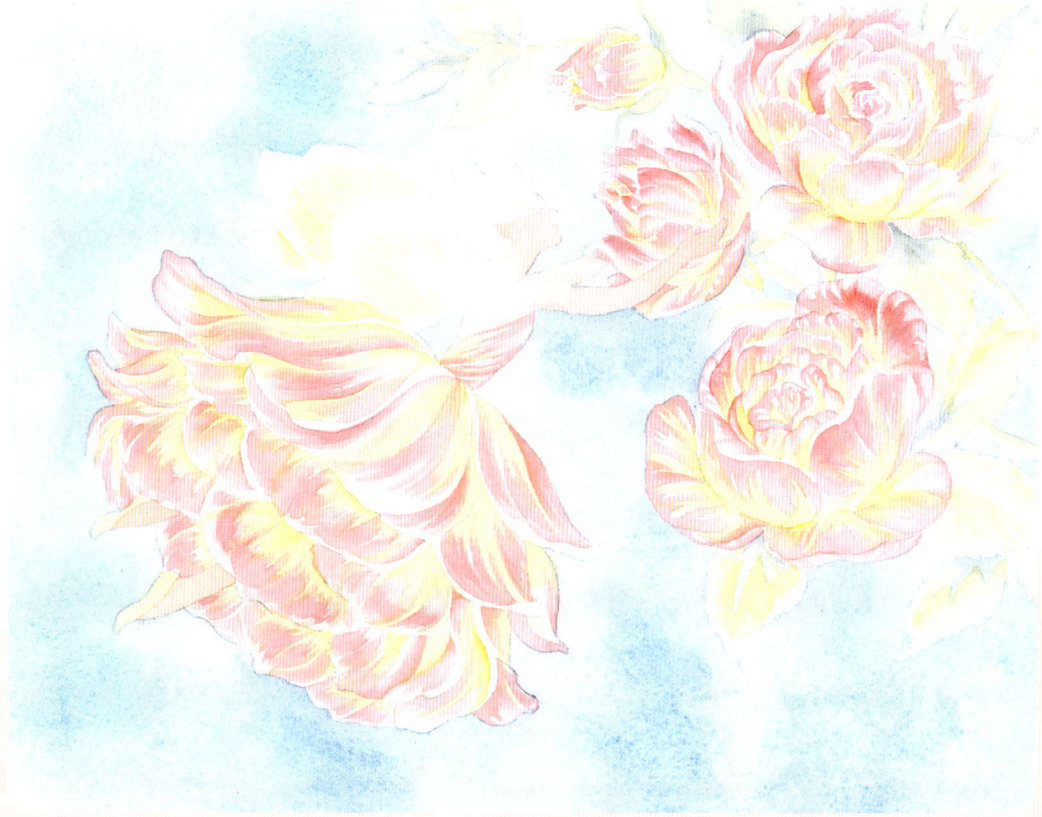

## DETAIL DEMONSTRATION — *Rose Leaves*

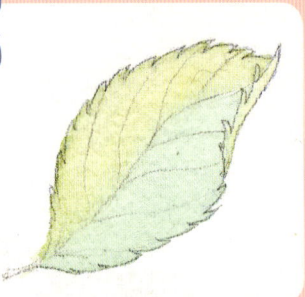
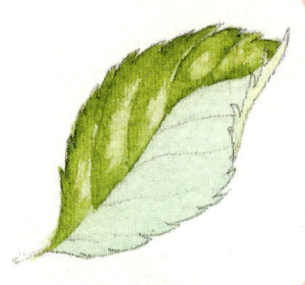
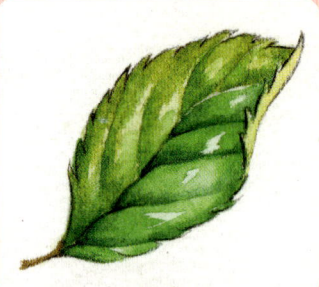

**1** With a no. 1 round, apply a medium mixture of Olive Green and Oxide of Chromium on the leaf contours that turn toward the sun. Add Viridian in areas where leaves are in shadow.

**2** Apply Hooker's Green with a no. 1 round to the left side of the leaf where the veins join the center.

**3** Using the same brush, apply a medium tint of Hooker's Green over the Viridian, leaving white highlights. With a no. 000 round, apply a light tint of Cadmium Yellow to the curled edge and a touch of Burnt Umber to the stem. Paint the rest of the leaves in the same manner.

## DETAIL DEMONSTRATION — *Summer Fairy's Wings*

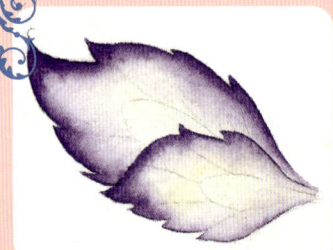
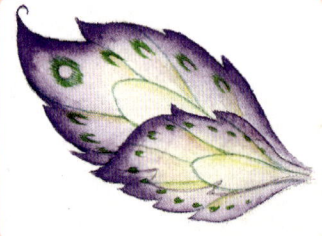
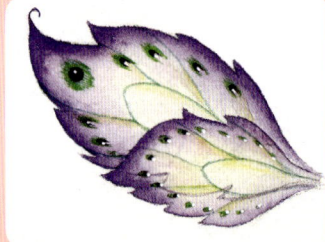

**1** Wet the wings and apply a pale tint of New Gamboge with a no. 0 round. When dry, wet the wings again and when the shine disappears, use a no. 0 round to apply Winsor Violet (Dioxazine) to the edge of the wings, blending inward.

**2** Use a no. 1 round to apply a very pale tint of Permanent Magenta between the wing veins. Once dry, use Viridian loaded on a no. 000 round to paint the delicate veins of the wings. Using the same size brush, paint circles of Hooker's Green along the inside edge of the wings.

**3** Add a dot of Ivory Black inside the circles with a no. 000 round and let dry. Rinse your brush and use it to add a dot of Chinese White over the black for a highlight.

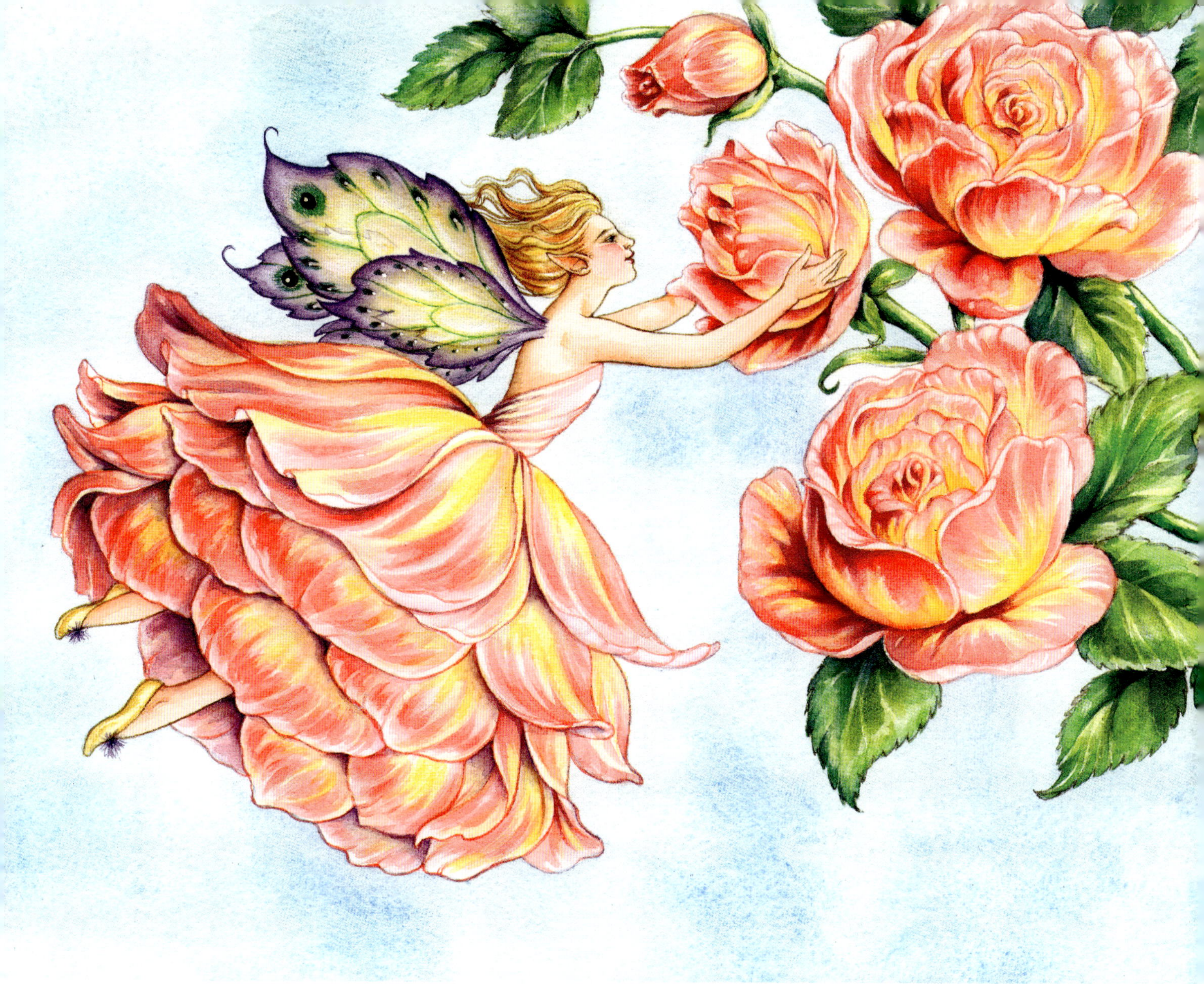

**4** Using a no. 0 round loaded with Raw Sienna, paint the fairy's hair where it turns from the light source. Add deeper values of Vermilion Hue to the rose petals, following the contours and blending with clear water. Apply a mixture of Winsor Violet (Dioxazine) and Vermilion Hue to the darkest areas of the roses on the upper right and to the Summer Fairy's gown where the petals overlap. Use Yellow Ochre to paint her hair, adding a mixture of Chinese Orange and Cadmium Yellow to the strands that are in partial shade. Add New Gamboge and Yellow Ochre to her slippers, and paint the pom-poms with Winsor Violet (Dioxazine).

Use Alizarin Crimson to paint the fairy's cheeks and lips, leaving a white highlight on lips. Outline the eyes, figure, roses, petals and stems with Sepia on a no. 000 round. Next, outline the roses with a diluted shade of Vermilion Hue.

 *To complete the fairy's wings and the rose leaves, follow the steps in the detail demonstrations on page 96.*

97

# DEMONSTRATION
# AUTUMN FAIRY

A gown suggesting the shape of a popular fall item, the pumpkin, seemed in order for this Autumn Fairy. Against a strong blue background, she dances upon another seasonal woodland object, a mushroom. Chinese Lanterns and fallen leaves add scale and color to the scene.

## ~YOU WILL NEED~

### MATERIALS

1½-inch (38mm) flat ~ bar of soap ~ bathroom tissue ~ blue tape ~ hard-leaded pencil or ballpoint pen that has run out of ink ~ HB or 2B graphite pencil ~ kneaded eraser ~ masking fluid ~ no. 1 acrylic round ~ nos. 000, 00, 1, 2 and 3 rounds ~ Saral transfer paper ~ square masking fluid pickup ~ stretched watercolor paper ~ tracing paper

### PIGMENTS

Alizarin Crimson ~ Burnt Umber ~ Cadmium Red ~ Cadmium Yellow ~ Caput Mortum Violet ~ Chinese Orange ~ Chinese White ~ Cobalt Blue ~ Indigo ~ Ivory Black ~ Lemon Yellow ~ Olive Green ~ Permanent Sap Green ~ Sepia ~ Viridian ~ Vermilion ~ Winsor Emerald ~ Winsor Violet (Dioxazine) ~ Yellow Ochre

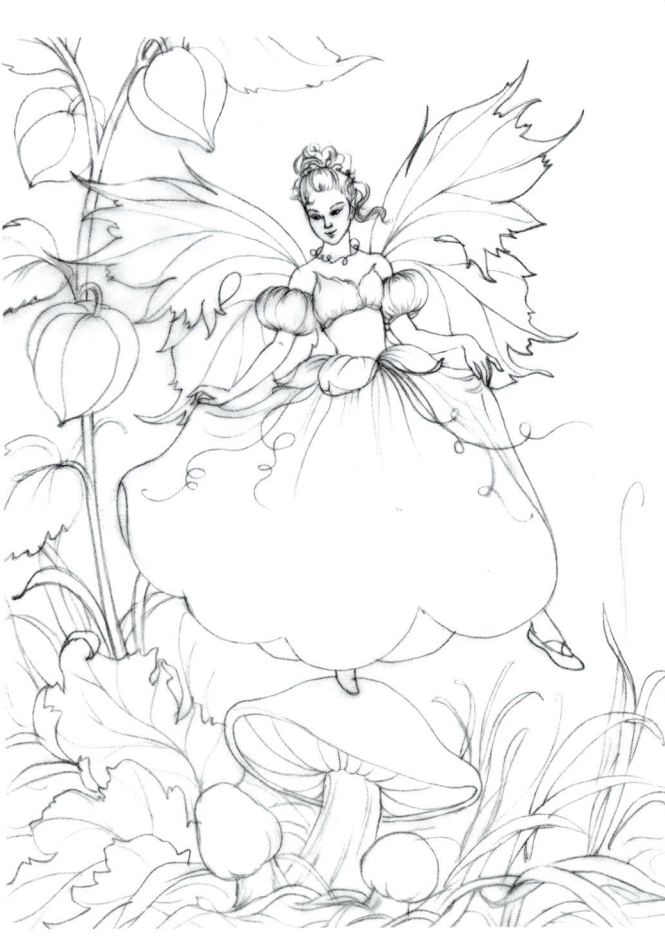

**1** Stretch your watercolor paper and trace the image following the steps on pages 14 and 15.

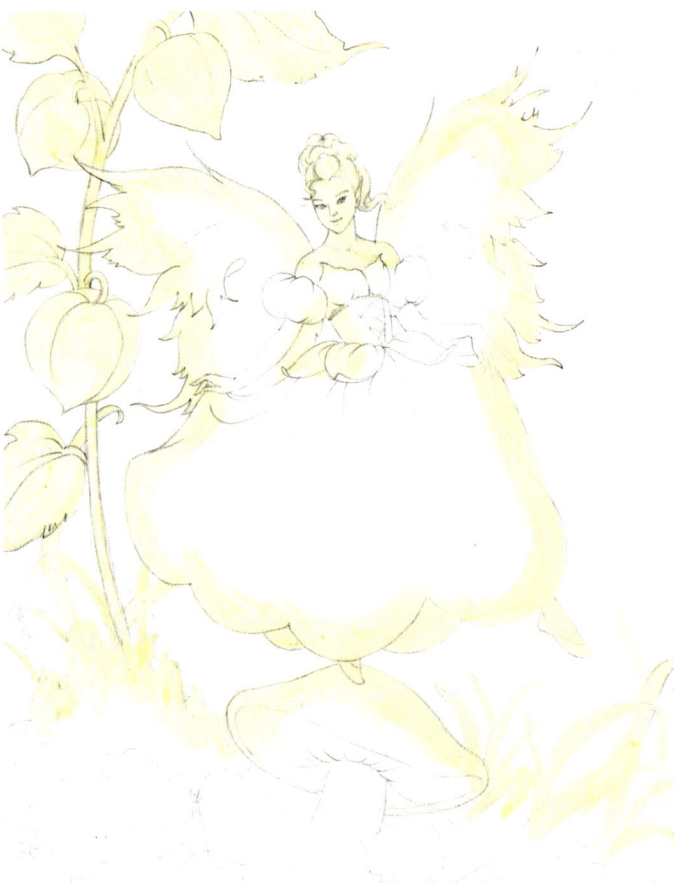

**2** Use a 1½-inch (38mm) flat to apply a light tint of Yellow Ochre over the entire page. When dry, use a worn no. 1 acrylic round that has first been dipped in wet soap to apply the masking fluid. Mask along the grass line including the top of the mushroom, the fairy figure, her wings, and the Chinese Lantern plant to her left. Let dry.

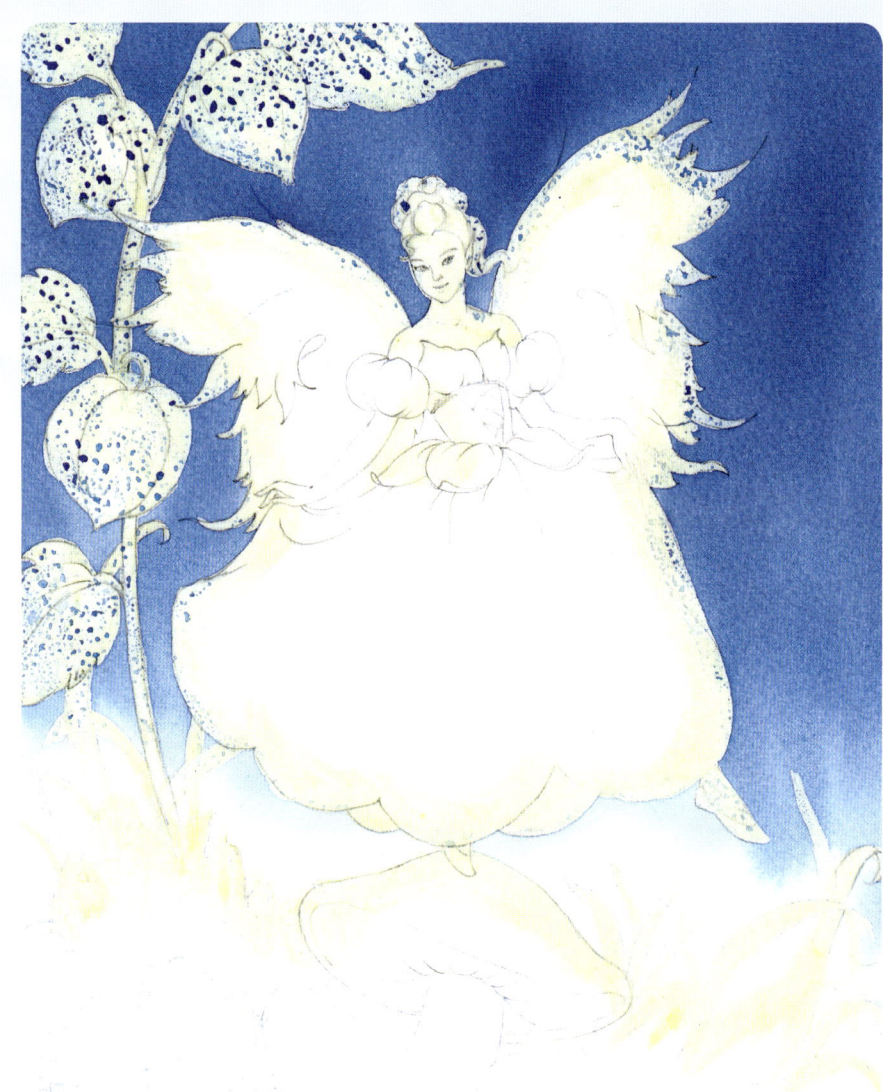

 **3** Create the background wash and let it dry completely. If the sky dries to a color you think is too light, don't worry. Gently apply another wash of clear water and add more concentrated color. Just make sure you tilt your board to allow even distribution of pigment. With a damp tissue, remove any pigment that may have collected on the mask. When the background has fully dried, remove the mask.

*Following the steps in the technique demonstration on this page, create the background color.*

## TECHNIQUE DEMONSTRATION — *Creating a Gradated Wash*

**1** With a 1½-inch (38mm) flat, wet the entire sky area and apply Lemon Yellow to the horizon. Turn your board upside down and back to allow the color to fade into the clear water. On your palette, prepare three different tints of Cobalt Blue by adding increasing amounts of water.

**2** Apply the medium tint of Cobalt Blue above the Lemon Yellow, brushing back and forth. Next, add a darker tint of Cobalt Blue above the medium tint, working as quickly as possible.

**3** Above the medium tint, add the darkest tint of Cobalt Blue. Turn your board upside down again, allowing the blue and the yellow to blend together. Tilt the board from left to right to even the coverage of the wash. Finally, use a dry brush to absorb any color that pools between the wing and the Chinese Lanterns.

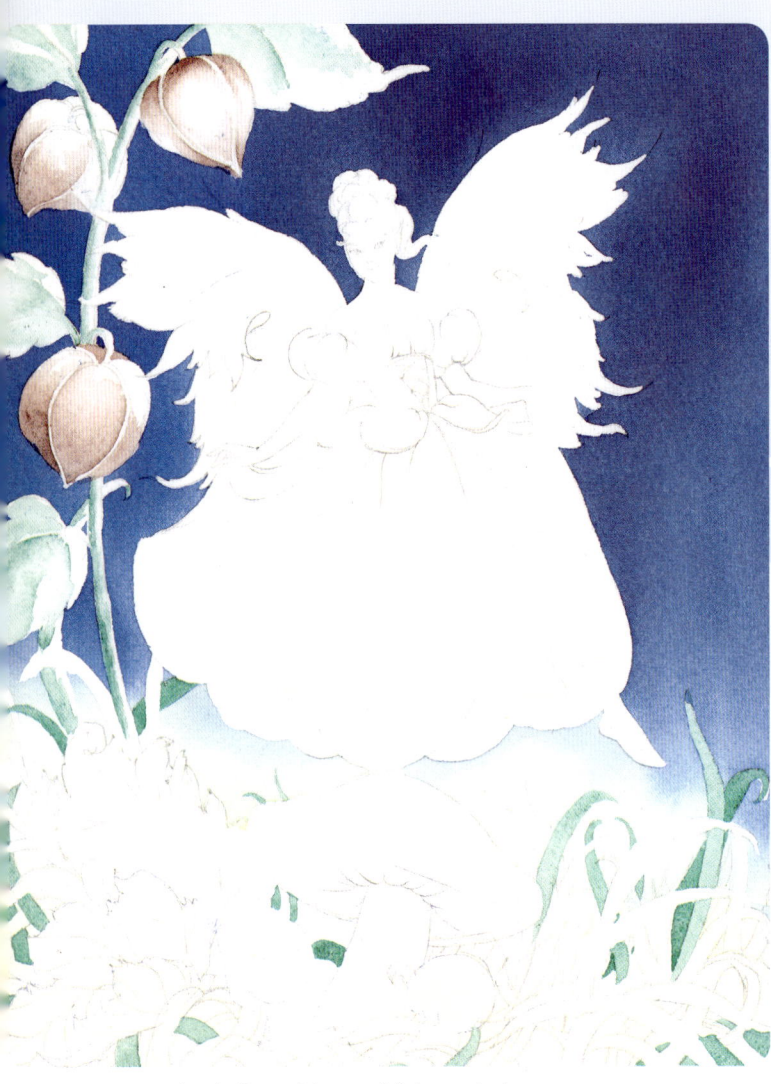

**4** Apply Caput Mortum Violet to the lanterns for shading. Use Viridian for the shaded side of the lantern's stem, the leaves, and the blades of grass in the background.

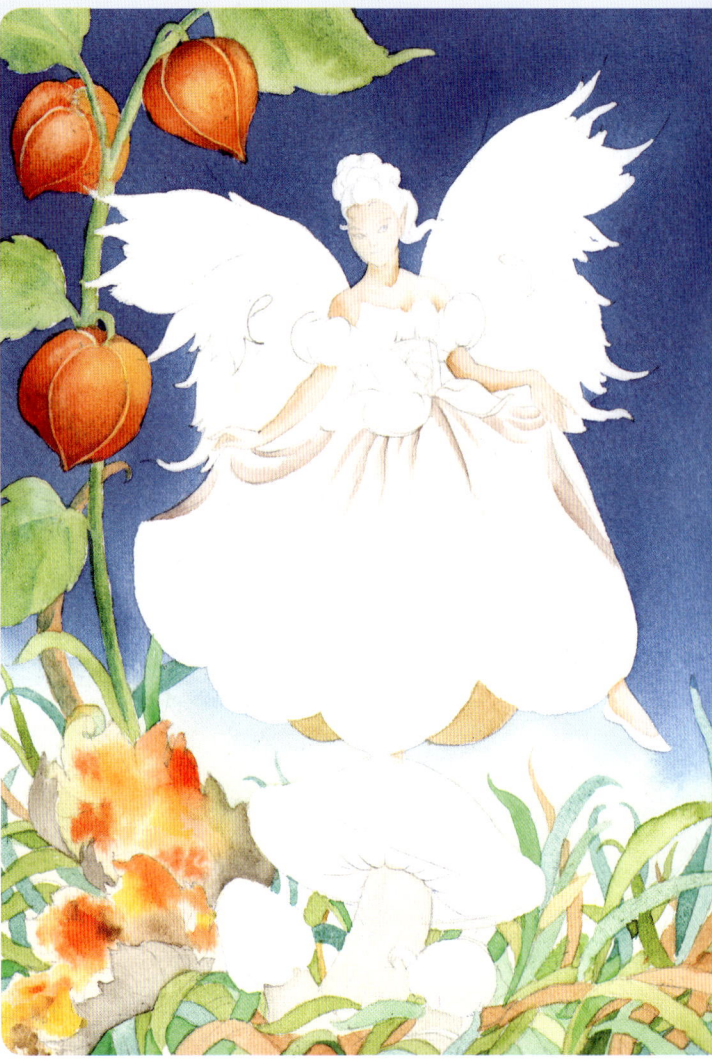

**5** With a no. 1 round, paint the lanterns with Chinese Orange, being careful to keep the color lighter where the lanterns face the light source coming from the right. Paint the grass in shades of Permanent Sap Green, Olive Green, Burnt Umber, Chinese Orange and Viridian, using Olive Green in the highlighted areas and Viridian in the shaded areas. Use lighter tints as the grass recedes. Use Olive Green to paint the lantern leaves. Wet the leaves on the lower left. When the area is no longer shiny, use a no. 0 round to drop in tints of Chinese Orange, Burnt Umber and Cadmium Yellow. Paint the underside of the leaf with Sepia. While still wet, charge in Indigo for shading. Shade the fairy's skin with a mixture of Burnt Umber, Chinese Orange and Olive Green. When dry, paint the skin with a mixture of Burnt Umber, Chinese Orange and Vermilion Hue.

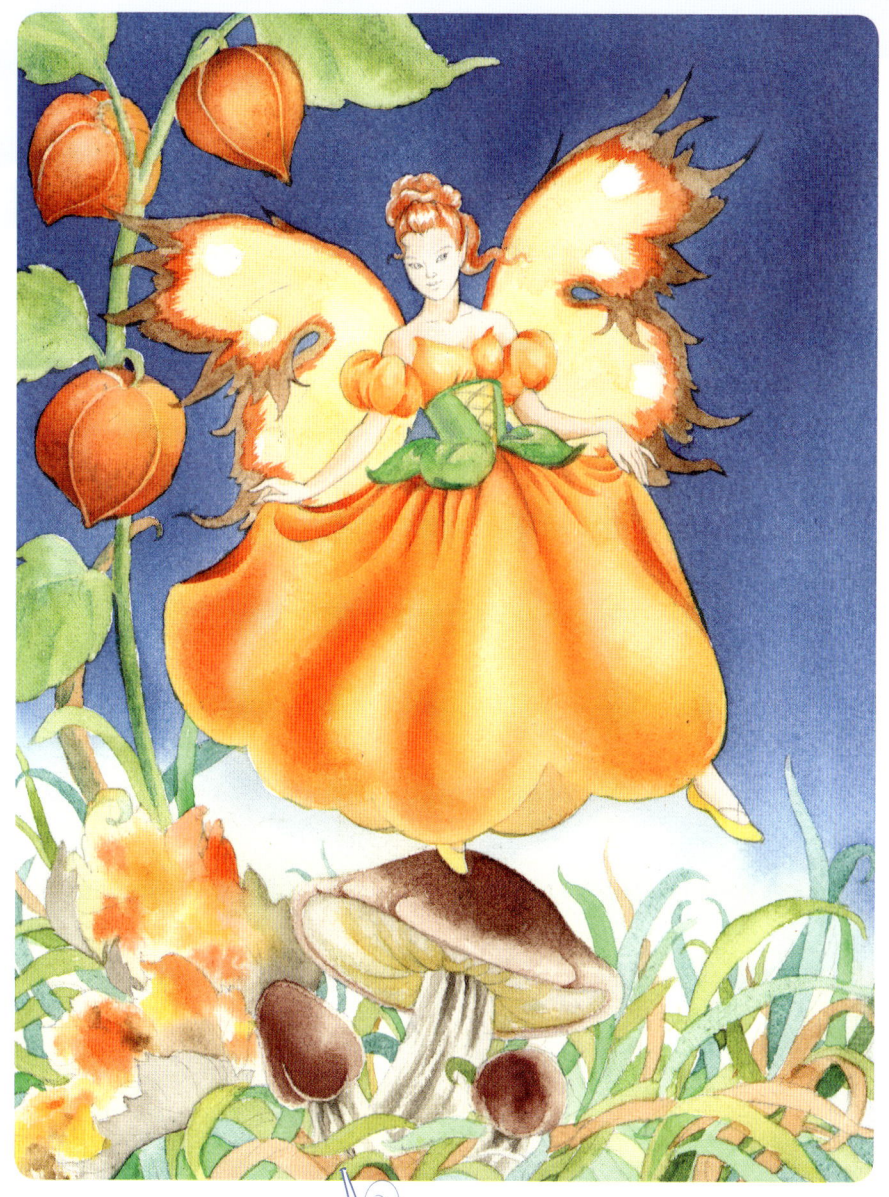

**6** Using a no. 0 round loaded with Lemon Yellow, paint the sky area between her wings and corset. Let this dry. Rinse the brush and apply Cobalt Blue over the Lemon Yellow. Paint the fairy's hair with Chinese Orange and a no. 00 round. When dry, shade her hair using Burnt Umber. Paint the underside of the large mushroom with Sepia. When dry, add a pale tint of Ivory Black mixed with Olive Green. Paint the mushroom top using Caput Mortum Violet, blending with clear water to the lower edge. When dry, add a darker shade to the topmost part of the mushroom.

🖌 *To finish Autumn Fairy's dress, follow the detail demonstration on this page.*

🖌 *To paint Autumn Fairy's wings, follow the detail demonstration on page 102.*

## DETAIL DEMONSTRATION — *Autumn Fairy's Dress*

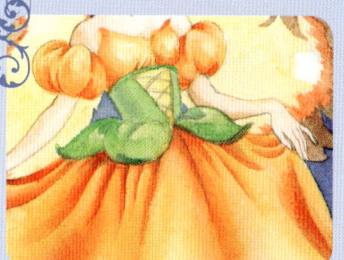

**1** Use Caput Mortum Violet to paint the folds of the bodice, the sleeves and the skirt with a no. 1 round. Mix a light shade of Cadmium Yellow and Chinese Orange and paint the bodice, the sleeves and the skirt with a no. 3 round.

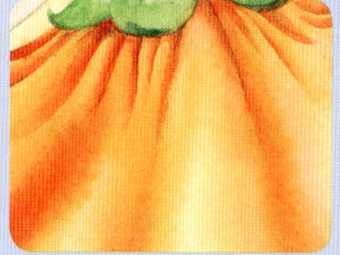

**2** When the sheen has gone, use a darker shade of Cadmium Yellow and Chinese Orange to paint the contours of the skirt. When dry, add Chinese Orange to the folds of the skirt. Repeat on the sleeves and bodice.

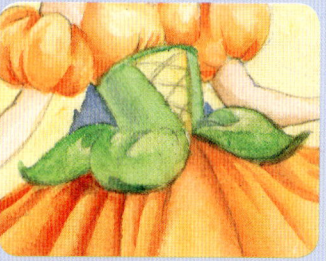

**3** Paint the shaded parts of the gown's petals and the corset using Indigo. When dry, add Olive Green, leaving highlights.

## DETAIL DEMONSTRATION — *Autumn Fairy's Wings*

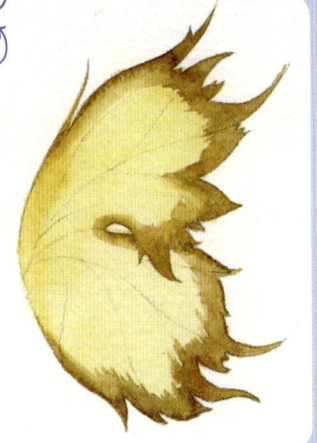

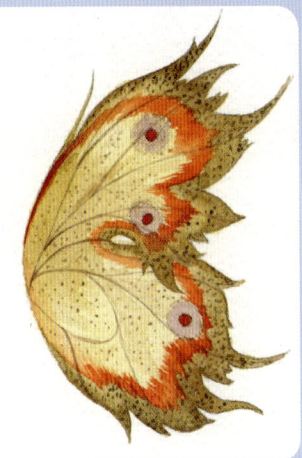

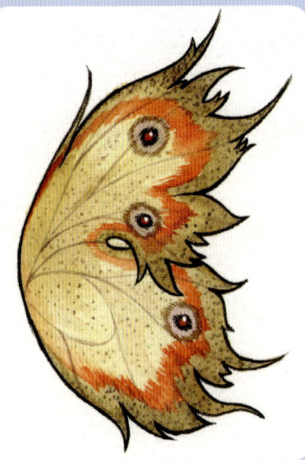

**1** Using a no. 2 round, apply a medium mixture of Yellow Ochre and Cadmium Yellow inside the entire wing. Paint the outer edge of the wing using a no. 1 round loaded with Burnt Umber.

**2** Using a no. 1 round, apply an irregular band of Chinese Orange next to the Burnt Umber. Next, apply a pale tint of Caput Mortum Violet to the veins and wing spots with a no. 000 round. With the same size brush, fill in the center of the wing spot using Chinese Orange. Using a dry no. 000 round loaded with a medium tint of Ivory Black, dab dots to the inside rim of the wings.

**3** Apply Burnt Umber in short strokes around the wing spot with a no. 000 round. Finally, outline the wings with the same brush loaded with Ivory Black.

**7** Using a no. 0 round, paint the fairy's skin using a mixture of Burnt Umber, Chinese Orange and Vermilion Hue. Use Burnt Umber to shade the hair and outline the figure. To define each mushroom, outline each with a dark shade of Caput Mortum Violet and paint the foreground edge with a little Winsor Violet (Dioxazine). Use an opaque line of Permanent Sap Green to paint the necklace and the vine detail on the gown, finishing the corset tie with Ivory Black. Still using the no. 0 round, apply a pale tint of Cadmium Yellow to the fairy's slippers, shading the left sides with Yellow Ochre.

In the foreground, outline the blades of grass and the smaller mushrooms using darker tints of Permanent Sap Green, Olive Green, Burnt Umber, Viridian and Chinese Orange.

*To create the fairy's wings and to finish her face, follow the steps on this page.*

*To create the stars in the background, follow the mini demonstration on page 62.*

## DETAIL DEMONSTRATION — *Autumn Fairy's Face*

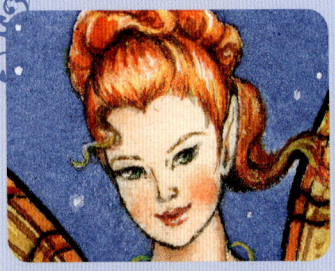

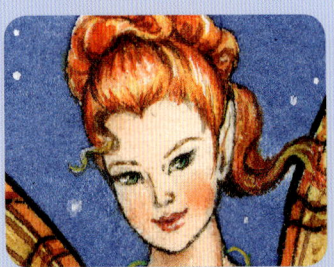

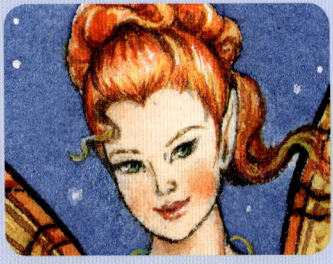

**1** Using a no. 000 round, paint the fairy's irises with Winsor Emerald. When dry, use the same size brush to add Ivory Black to the pupil and a dot of Chinese White for a highlight. Paint her eyebrows using a no. 000 round loaded with Sepia.

**2** Wet the cheeks and, with a no. 00 round loaded with Cadmium Red, charge color into the fairy's cheeks.

**3** Paint the mouth with Alizarin Crimson, leaving the white paper highlights. Add Caput Mortum Violet to the center of her mouth and outline her nose, ears and face using Sepia on a no. 000 round.

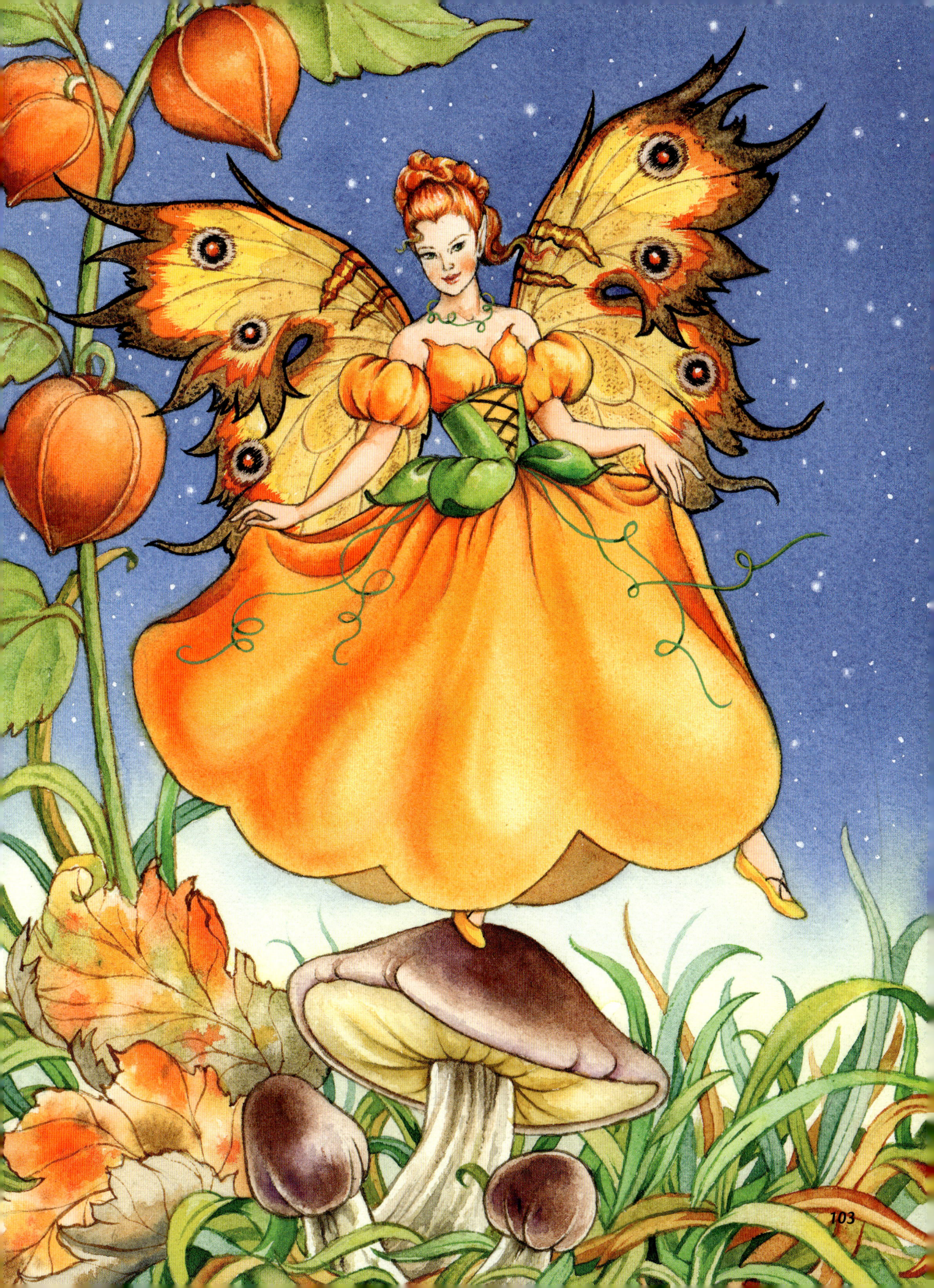

## DEMONSTRATION
# WINTER FAIRY

*Imagining different types of fairies can be a lot of fun. The possibilities are endless. Winter Fairy's white hair represents not only snow, but the last season of the year and of life itself.*

### ~ YOU WILL NEED ~

#### MATERIALS

1½-inch (38mm) flat ~ bar of soap ~ blue tape ~ hard-leaded pencil or ballpoint pen that has run out of ink ~ HB or 2B graphite pencil ~ kneaded eraser ~ masking fluid ~ no. 1 acrylic round ~ nos. 000, 0, 1 and 8 rounds ~ Saral transfer paper ~ scrap paper ~ square masking fluid pickup ~ stretched watercolor paper ~ tracing paper

#### PIGMENTS

Alizarin Crimson ~ Burnt Umber ~ Cadmium Red ~ Chinese Orange ~ Chinese White ~ Cobalt Blue ~ Cobalt Turquoise Light ~ Indanthrene Blue ~ Indigo ~ Ivory Black ~ Olive Green ~ Payne's Gray ~ Sepia ~ Winsor Violet (Dioxazine)

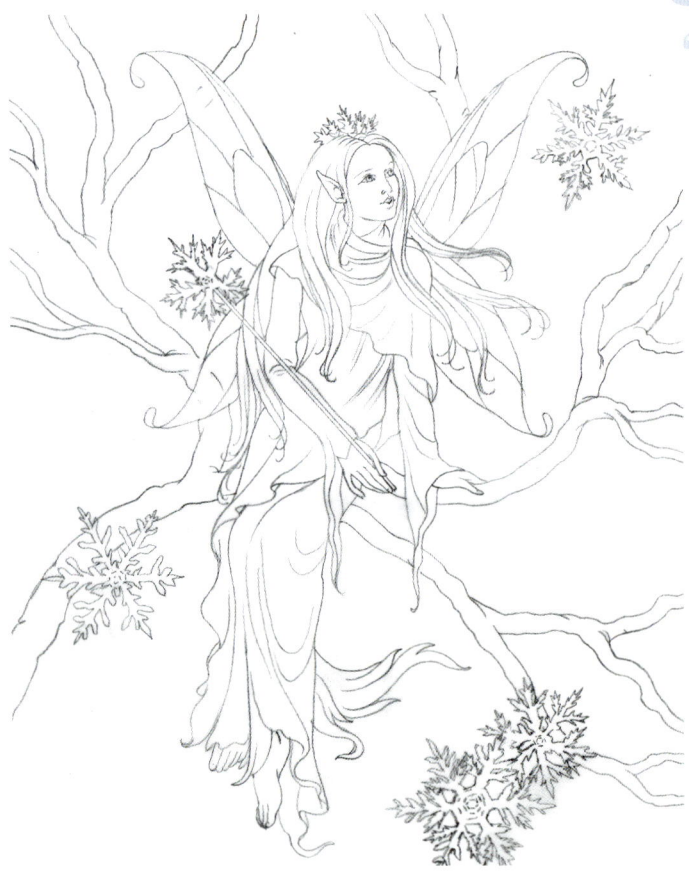

**1** Stretch your watercolor paper and trace the image following the steps on pages 14 and 15.

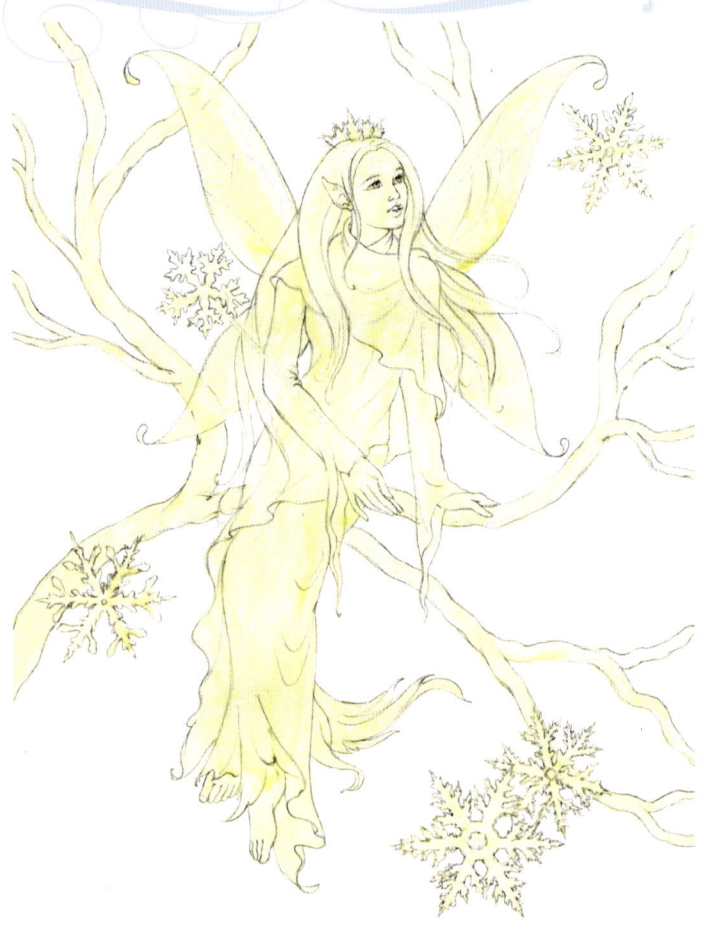

**2** Dip a no. 1 acrylic round in soap, then load it with masking fluid. Mask the entire figure, the branches and the snowflakes. Let dry.

104

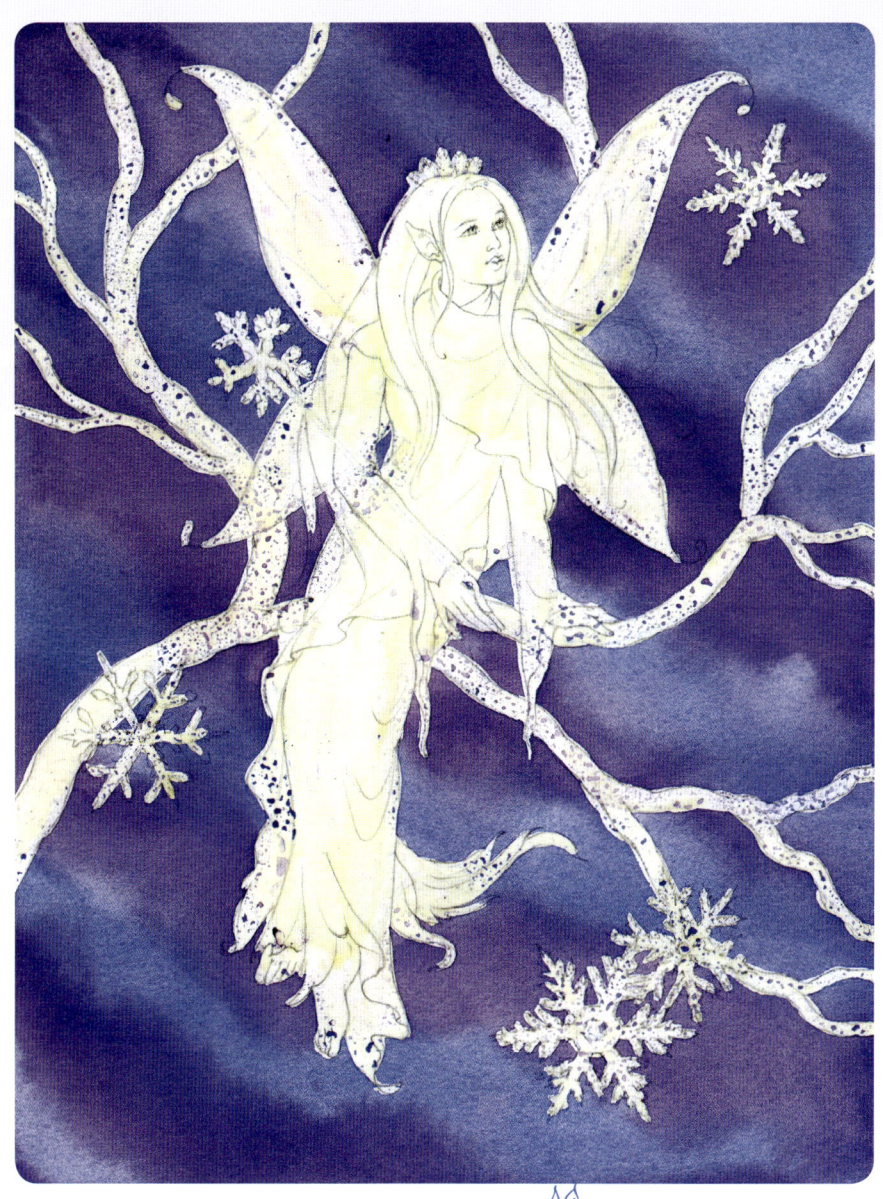

**3** In a pan, mix a small amount of water into Cobalt Blue to create a dark tint. Test the darkness on scrap paper and let it dry. In another palette well, add water to Winsor Violet (Dioxazine) and test it on scrap paper. Once you have your two colors mixed, use a 1½-inch (38mm) flat to wet the entire background with water. Start at the top of the paper and work quickly back and forth.

*Follow the technique demonstration on this page to add the background color. Once you have put in the background, remove the masking fluid, using your fingers to feel for any mask that remains.*

## TECHNIQUE DEMONSTRATION — *Creating the Background*

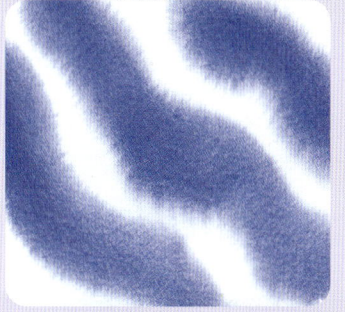

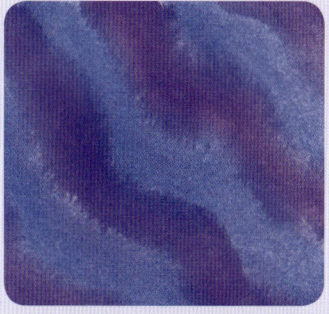

**1** When the sheen has disappeared, use a no. 8 round loaded with Cobalt Blue and start at the upper right-hand corner, painting wavy diagonal patterns and leaving wide unpainted spaces between each diagonal. Work quickly.

**2** Fill the empty spaces with diagonal waves of Winsor Violet (Dioxazine). Tilt your board from left to right to allow the colors to blend. With a dry brush, lift any pigment that pools in the nooks and crannies.

**4** Using a no. 1 round, mix Burnt Umber and Olive Green on your palette and shade the right side of the face, the neck, the hands and the feet. Wet the cheeks and charge in a bit of Cadmium Red, gently blending outward. Use the no. 1 round to paint the dress with Payne's Gray, leaving white highlights where the dress drapes and folds. When dry, paint between the wing veins with a medium mixture of Cobalt Turquoise Light and Chinese White. Next, paint the pale branches showing through the fairy's wings. Use a darker tint of Payne's Gray to shade the folds and creases of her dress.

🖌 *To create the branches, follow the technique demonstration on this page.*

🖌 *For the snowflakes, follow the technique demonstrations on pages 107 and 108.*

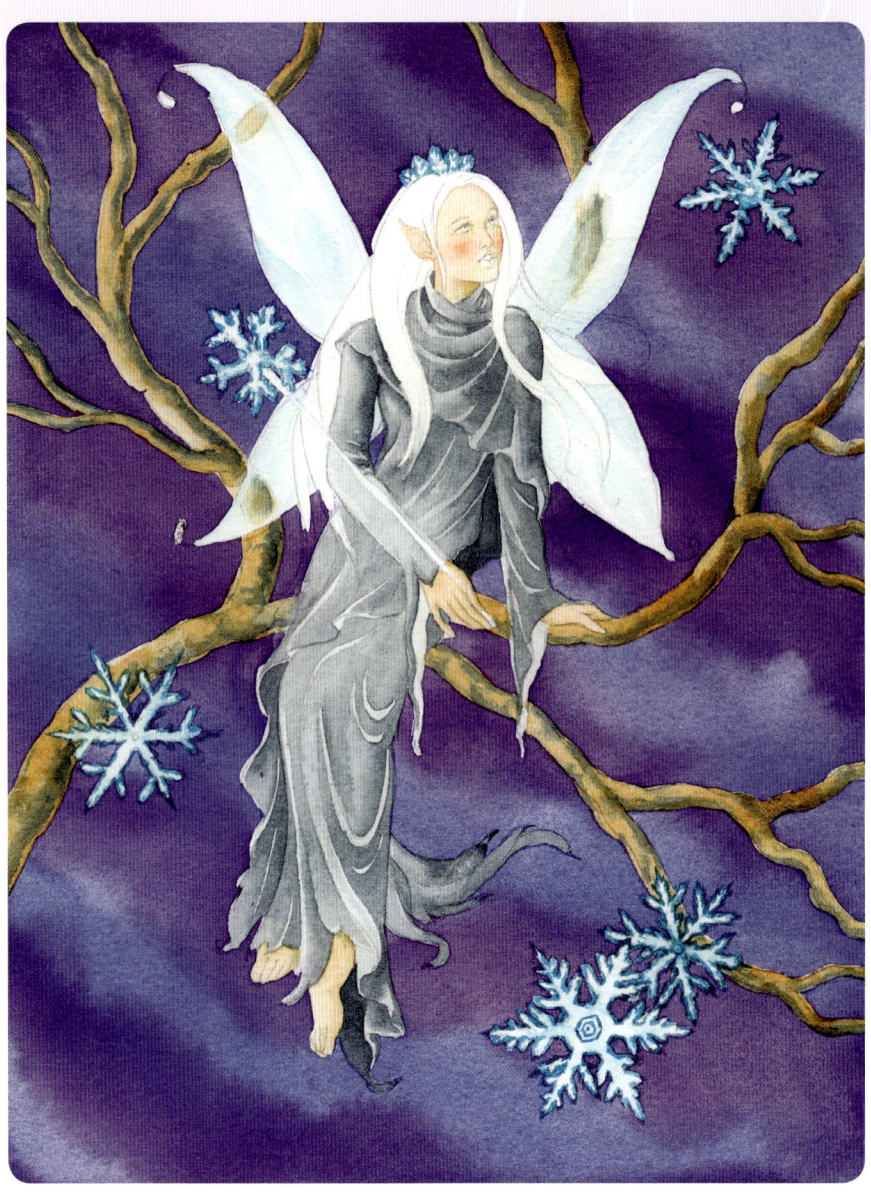

## TECHNIQUE DEMONSTRATION ~ *Painting Tree Branches*

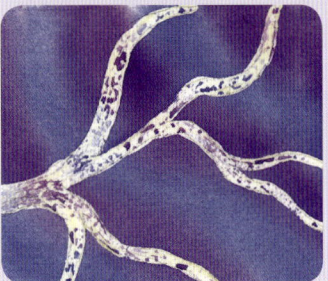

**1** When the background color has dried, remove the masking from the tree branches.

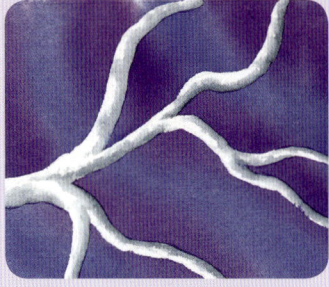

**2** With a no. 1 round, apply a medium-dark tint of Indigo to the right side of the branches, emphasizing the light source at the left.

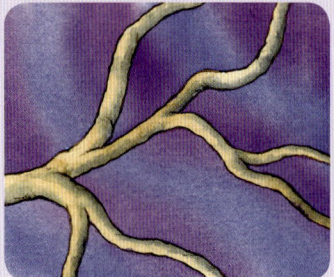

**3** When dry, use a no. 1 round loaded with Burnt Umber to paint the branches, leaving white highlights. Let dry. Next, use the same brush to apply a pale tint of a mixture of Burnt Umber and Chinese Orange over the branches. Finally, outline the branches with Sepia.

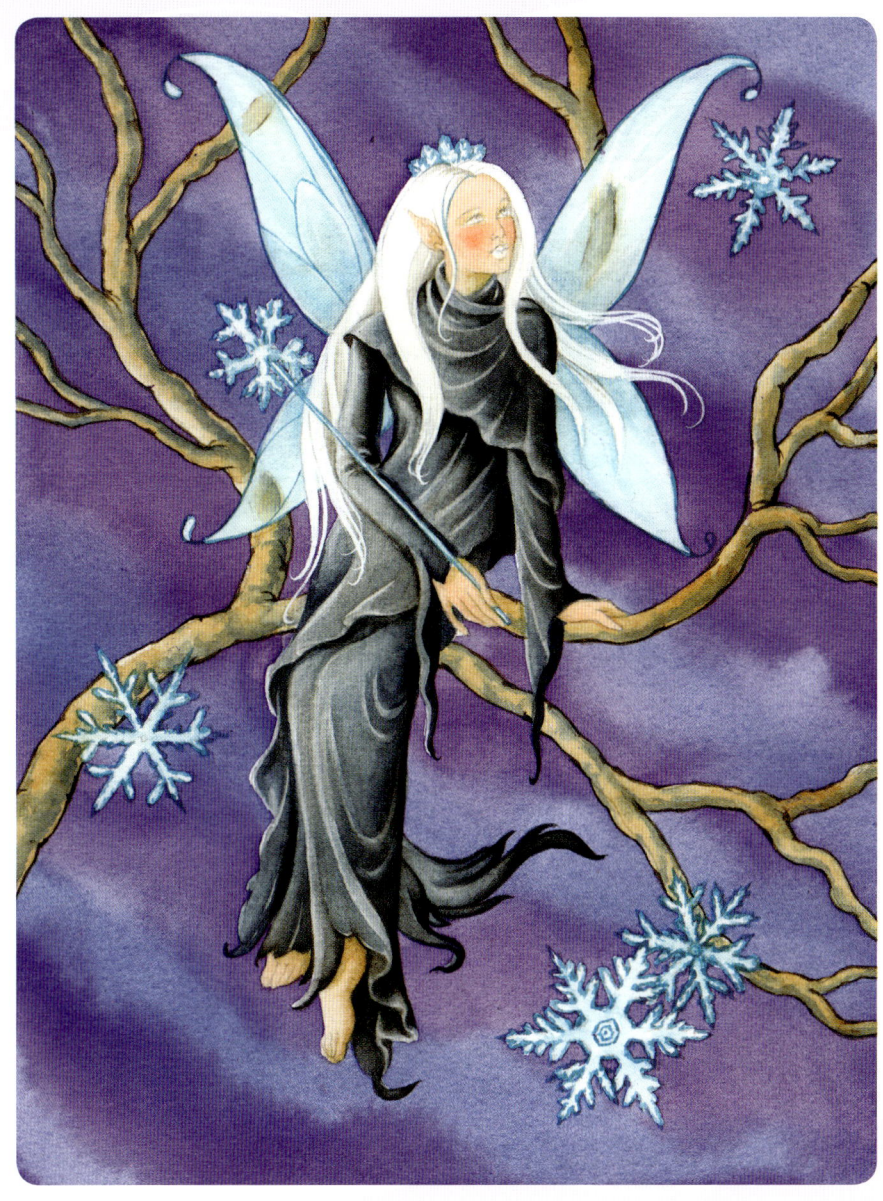

**5** With a no. 1 round loaded with a dark tint of Indigo, deepen the color in the folds of the fairy's dress. When dry, shade the darkest areas of the dress using Ivory Black. Let that dry, then apply clear water over the entire gown to set the colors. Define individual strands of the hair with a no. 000 round loaded with Ivory Black. Next, outline the wings with a mixture of Cobalt Turquoise Light and Ivory Black. Add Cobalt Turquoise Light to the inside edge of the wings. Shade the wings behind the fairy's hair using Payne's Gray. Use a no. 000 round and Chinese White to paint individual strands of the hair. Define the hair further by deepening the shadows with Cobalt Turquoise Light.

## TECHNIQUE DEMONSTRATION — *Creating Large Snowflakes*

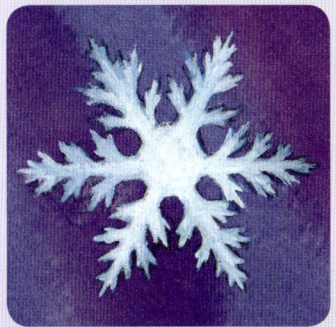

**1** With a no. 0 round loaded with Cobalt Turquoise Light, begin painting the snowflakes starting at the outer edges and blending inward with clear water.

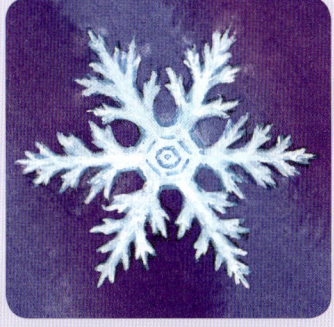

**2** To keep the snowflakes from looking rigid, paint Chinese White in a medium consistency over the edges of the Cobalt Turquoise Light. Let the Cobalt Turquoise Light show through the transparent white.

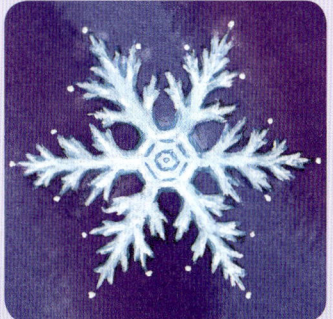

**3** Apply a mixture of Cobalt Turquoise Light and Indanthrene Blue to the outer edge of snowflakes and create the figure in the center of the snowflake with a no. 000 round. Rinse your brush, then add Chinese White dots to the tips of the snowflake.

## TECHNIQUE DEMONSTRATION — *Painting Small Snowflakes*

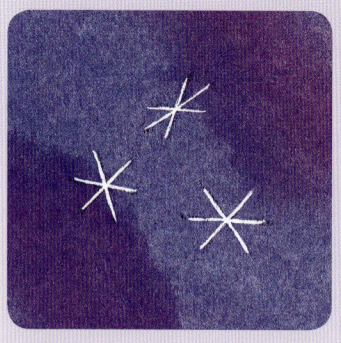

**1** With a no. 000 round dipped in Chinese White, paint the smaller snowflakes.

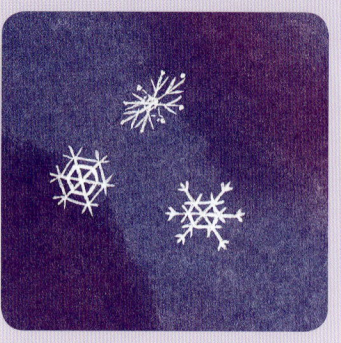

**2** To add interest, paint some of the snowflakes as if they were tilted.

## DETAIL DEMONSTRATION — *Winter Fairy's Tiara*

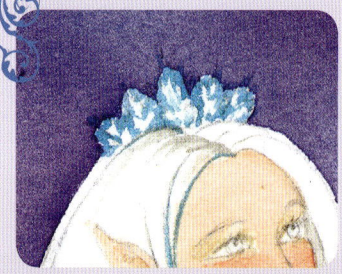

**1** Using the same technique as you used with the snowflakes, paint the tiara shape using a no. 000 round loaded with Cobalt Turquoise Light.

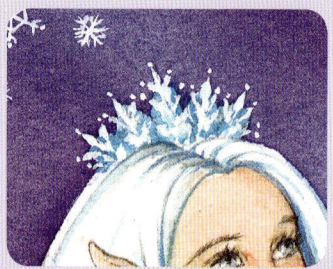

**2** In your palette well, mix a small amount of water and Chinese White. Using a no. 000 round, paint diagonal snowflake patterns on the tiara as shown. With the same brush, add Chinese White dots to the tips of the tiara.

**6** Using a no. 000 round, paint the fairy's irises with a mixture of Payne's Gray and Burnt Umber. Use Alizarin Crimson to paint her lips, leaving white paper for highlights. Add highlights to her eyes with Chinese White. Then, mix Burnt Umber, Chinese Orange and Cadmium Red to paint the shadows on her nose, under her lips, along her sleeves, fingers and the hem of her dress. Finally, use a no. 000 round loaded with Sepia to outline her eyes, ears, head, hands, feet and toes.

*To create the Winter Fairy's tiara, follow the detail demonstration on this page.*

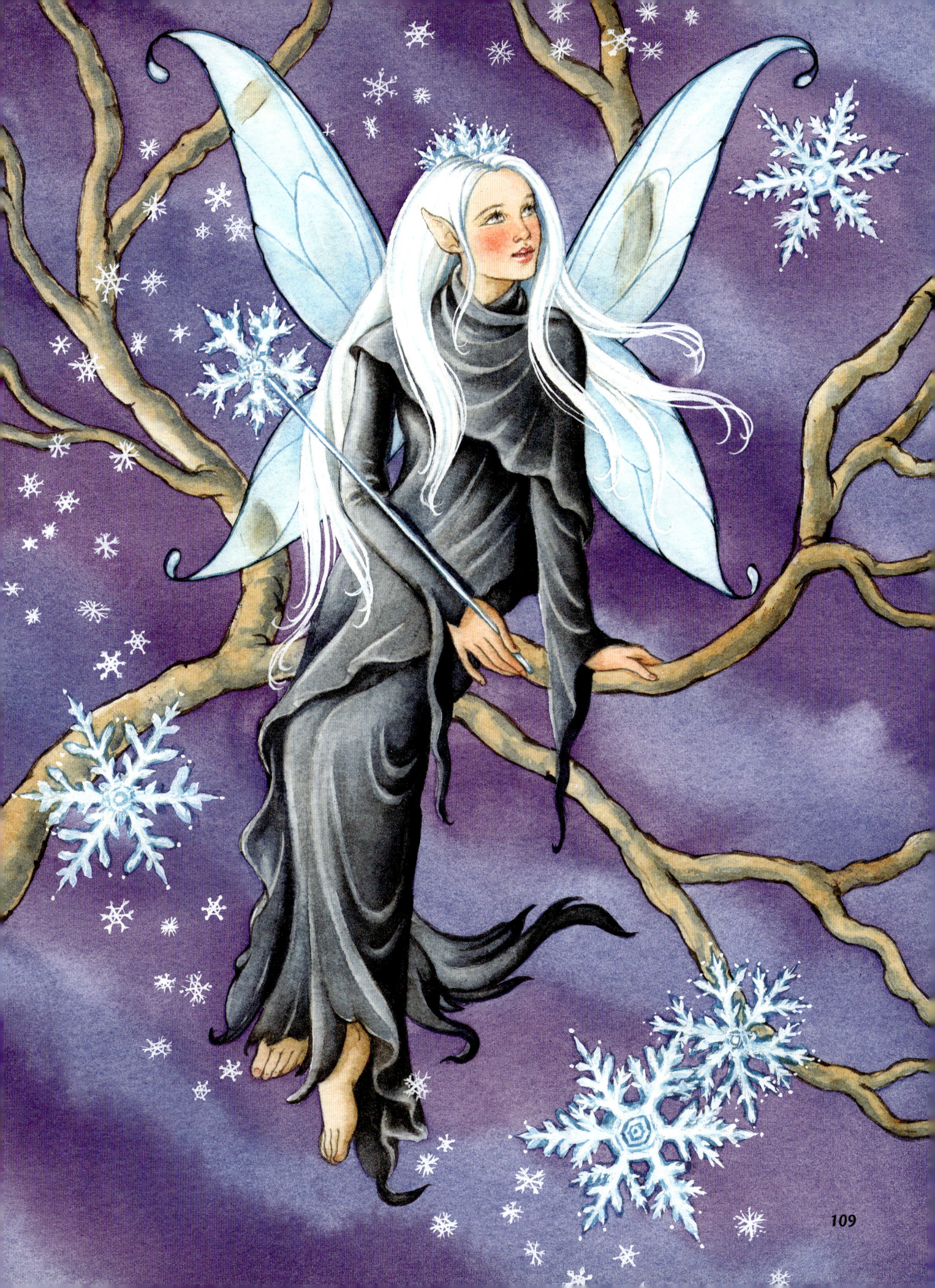

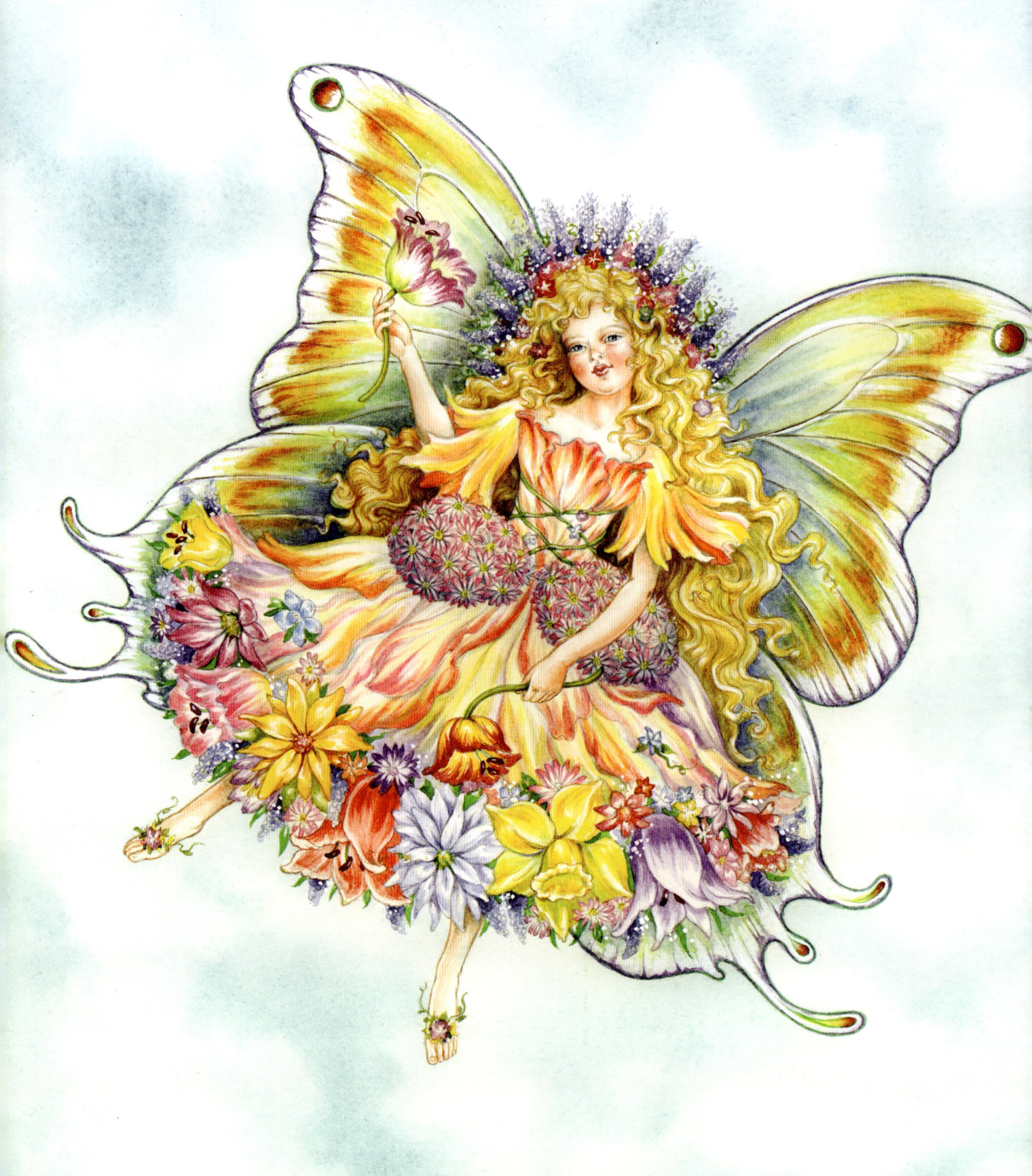

SECTION THREE

# THE REALM OF FAIRIES

For inspiration in imagining Fairy Scenes, get outdoors. Areas as small as window boxes offer far better opportunities to study lighting than what you'd find inside. The Internet can connect you to many fairy websites, on the other hand. Not only can you visit artists' sites but company sites that show fairy festivals, fairy costumes and ready-made fairy houses.

Flower catalogues show flowers in detail but not always their foliage, so visit parks, roadsides and backyards.

For the fairies who populate the scenes you imagine, ask friends and relatives to pose or have them take pictures of you posed as you'd like.

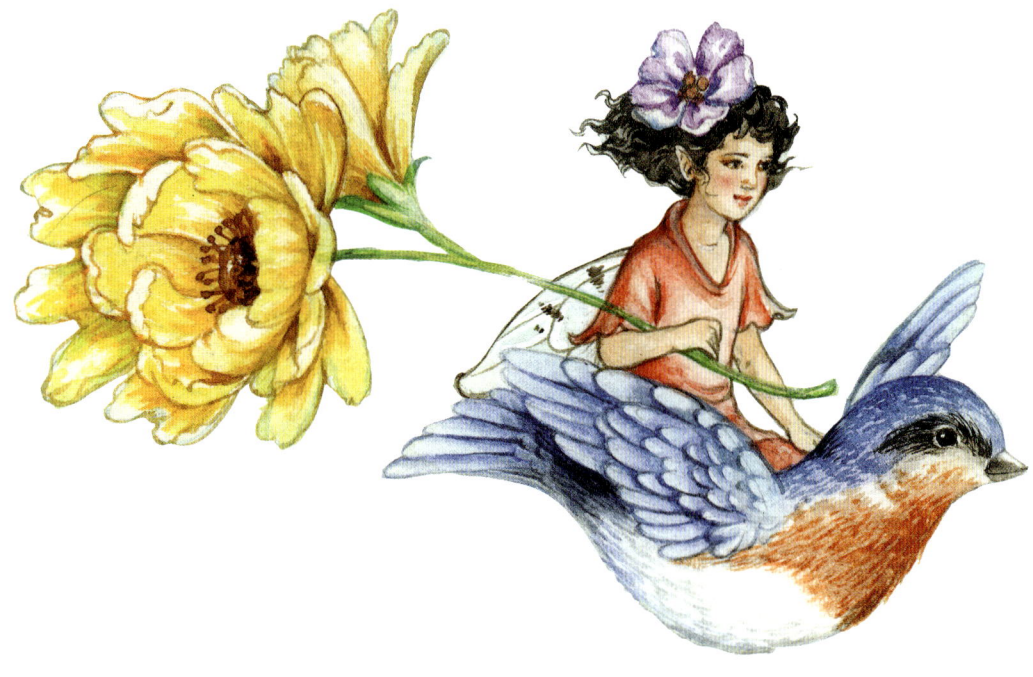

## DEMONSTRATION
# MOTHER AND BABY FAIRY

*Imagine walking through a garden and surprising fairies resting amidst the blossoms. That's the moment I tried to capture in this demonstration. Nasturtium leaves would be lovely to sit upon and the bright color of the blossoms would attract the eye before one noticed the fairies. To add some sparkle I've made the wings transparent and sprinkled with fairy dust. Substitute this technique for other fairy wings from throughout this book if they appeal more to you. After all, a little sparkle can add to the feeling of wonder you want your picture to have.*

### ~ YOU WILL NEED ~
#### MATERIALS
Bathroom tissue ~ blue Saral transfer paper ~ blue tape ~ hard-leaded pencil or ballpoint pen that has run out of ink ~ HB or 2B graphite pencil ~ kneaded eraser ~ no. 2 miniature round ~ nos. 000, 00, 0 and 1 round ~ stretched watercolor paper ~ tracing paper ~ workable fixative

#### PIGMENTS
Alizarin Crimson ~ Burnt Sienna ~ Cadmium Yellow ~ Chinese Orange ~ Chinese White ~ Cobalt Blue ~ Cobalt Turquoise Light ~ Hooker's Green ~ Indanthrene Blue ~ Indigo ~ Ivory Black ~ Permanent Mauve ~ New Gamboge ~ Olive Green ~ Opera ~ Oxide of Chromium ~ Permanent Sap Green ~ Quinacridone Red ~ Raw Sienna ~ Sepia ~ Ultramarine Blue (Green Shade) ~ Vermilion Hue ~ Viridian ~ Winsor Emerald ~ Winsor Violet (Dioxazine) ~ Yellow Ochre

**1** Stretch your watercolor paper and trace the image following the steps on pages 14 and 15.

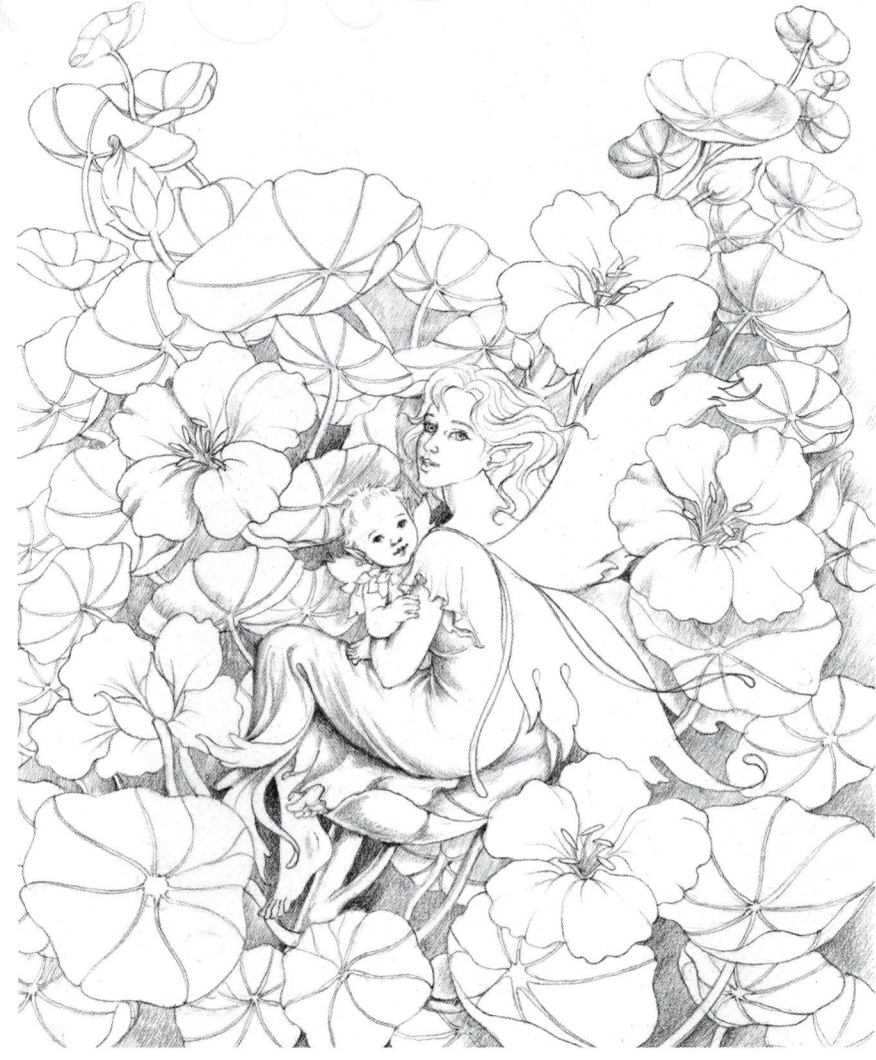

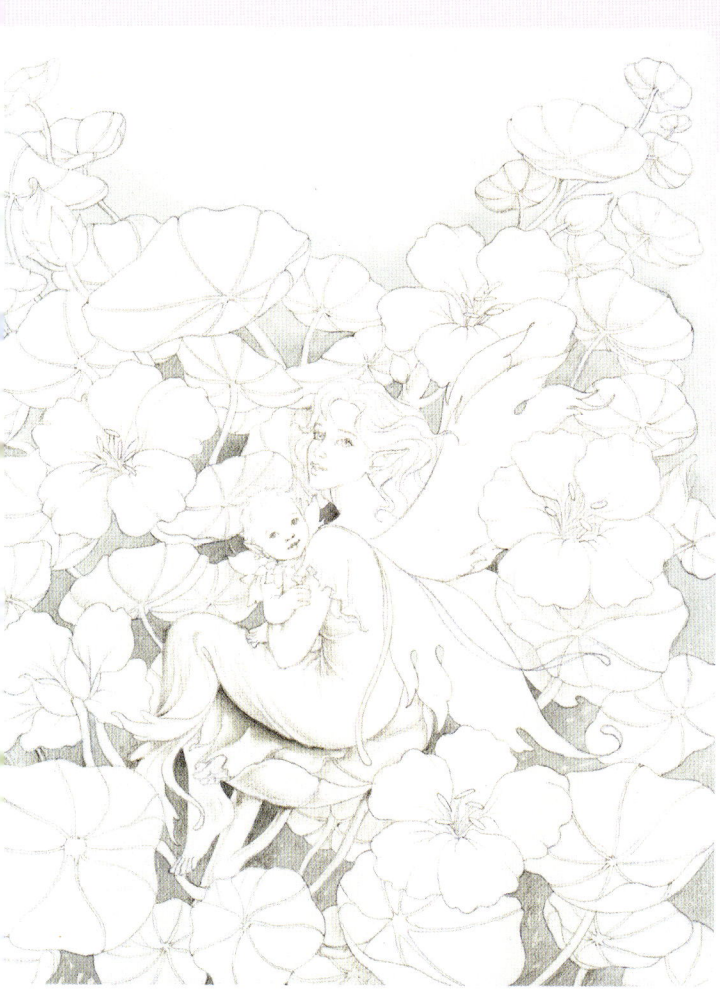

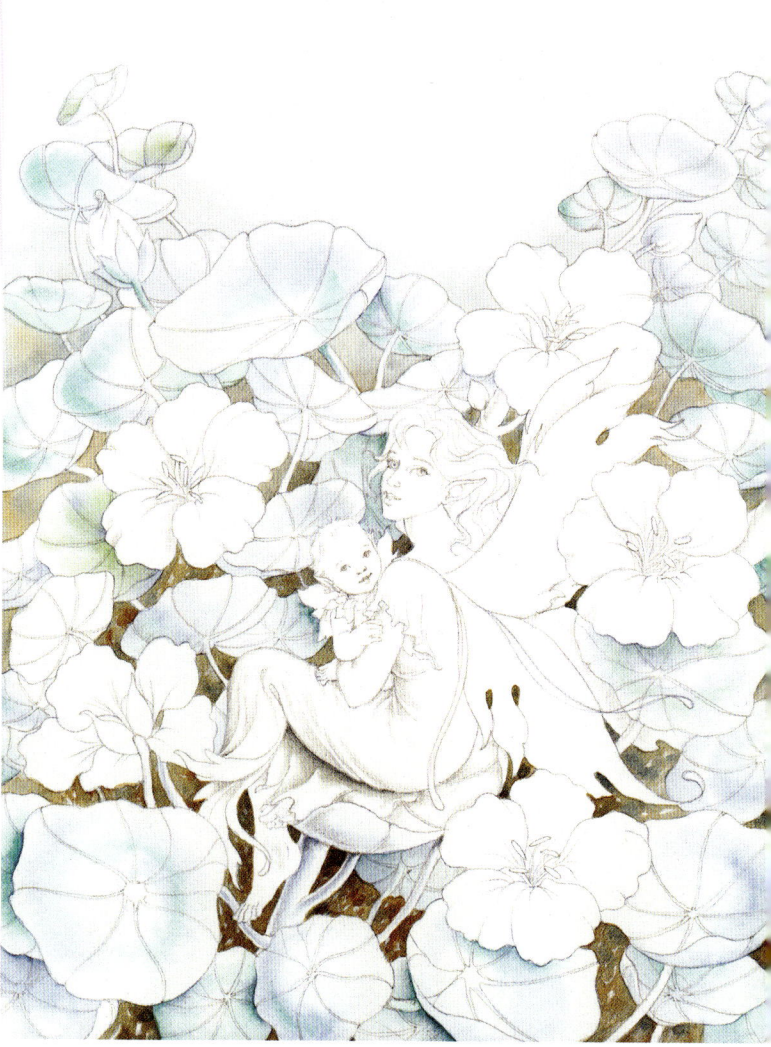

**2** Add a mixture of Indanthrene Blue and Sepia to the background areas between the stems and the leaves with a no. 1 round. While still wet, charge in a mixture of Burnt Umber and Chinese Orange into those places, keeping the tones in the center of the picture deeper than in the outer areas. Using a no. 1 round loaded with a medium tint of Indanthrene Blue, paint the contours of the leaves and stems. Keep in mind that the light source is at the upper right.

**3** With a no. 1 round loaded with a mixture of Indigo and Sepia, glaze the spaces between the stems and leaves. As you did in step 2, use paler shades in the outer areas of the picture and darker ones in the middle.

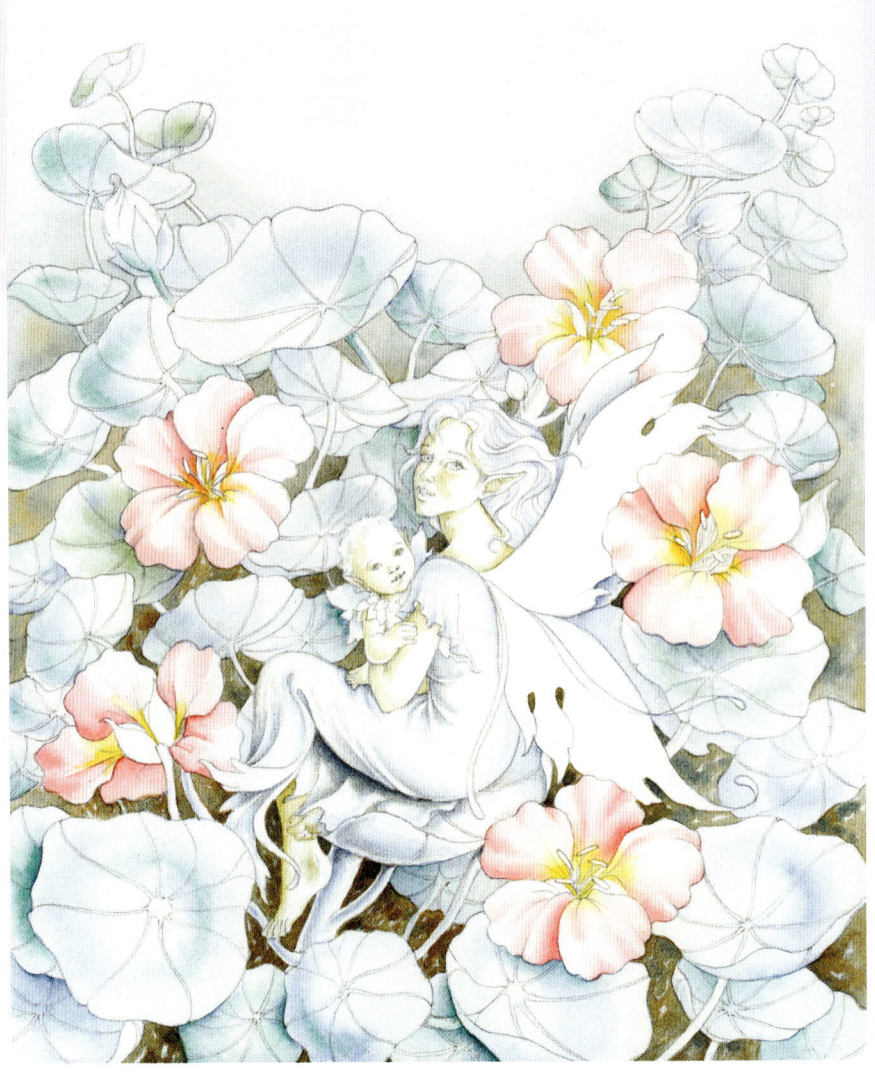

**4** Using a no. 1 round, wet one leaf at a time. Paint Indigo in the areas that turn from the light source that comes from the right. While still wet, add Viridian to the areas of deepest shade. Using a no. 1 round, begin shading around and beneath the Mother Fairy using Ultramarine Blue (Green Shade). With the same mixture and brush, add color to individual strands of her hair. With a mixture of Burnt Umber, Chinese Orange and Olive Green, paint the areas of both fairies' skin that are in shade.

 *To create the flower petals, follow the detail demonstration on this page.*

## DETAIL DEMONSTRATION — *Flower Petals*

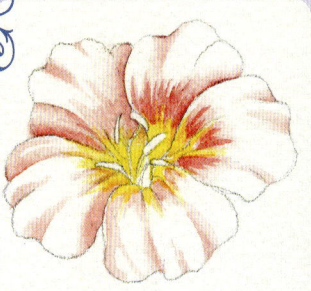 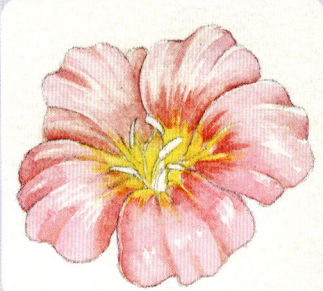 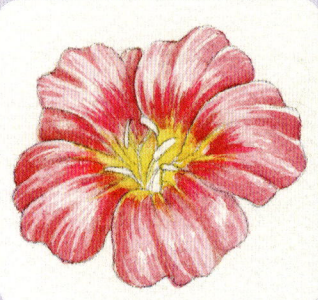

**1** Create the rippled effect on the petals by applying Alizarin Crimson along the ridge of the ripple using a no. 0 round, then blending outward with clear water. Let dry. Then, using a no. 0 round, apply a medium tint of Cadmium Yellow to the flower's center, blending upward with clear water.

**2** Using a no. 2 miniature loaded with a medium tint of Quinacridone Red, begin at the edge of the petals and stroke inward, lifting your brush at the end of each stroke. In the same manner, begin applying Quinacridone Red at the center of the flower and stroking outward. Blend the strokes with clear water.

**3** Using a no. 2 miniature, apply a deeper tint of Quinacridone Red at the center and outer edges of the petals. Let dry. Then, using the same brush, apply Opera to the flower's throat. Finally, outline the stamen using a no. 000 round loaded with a mix of Cadmium Yellow and Chinese Orange and add a medium dark tint of Alizarin Crimson where the petals overlap.

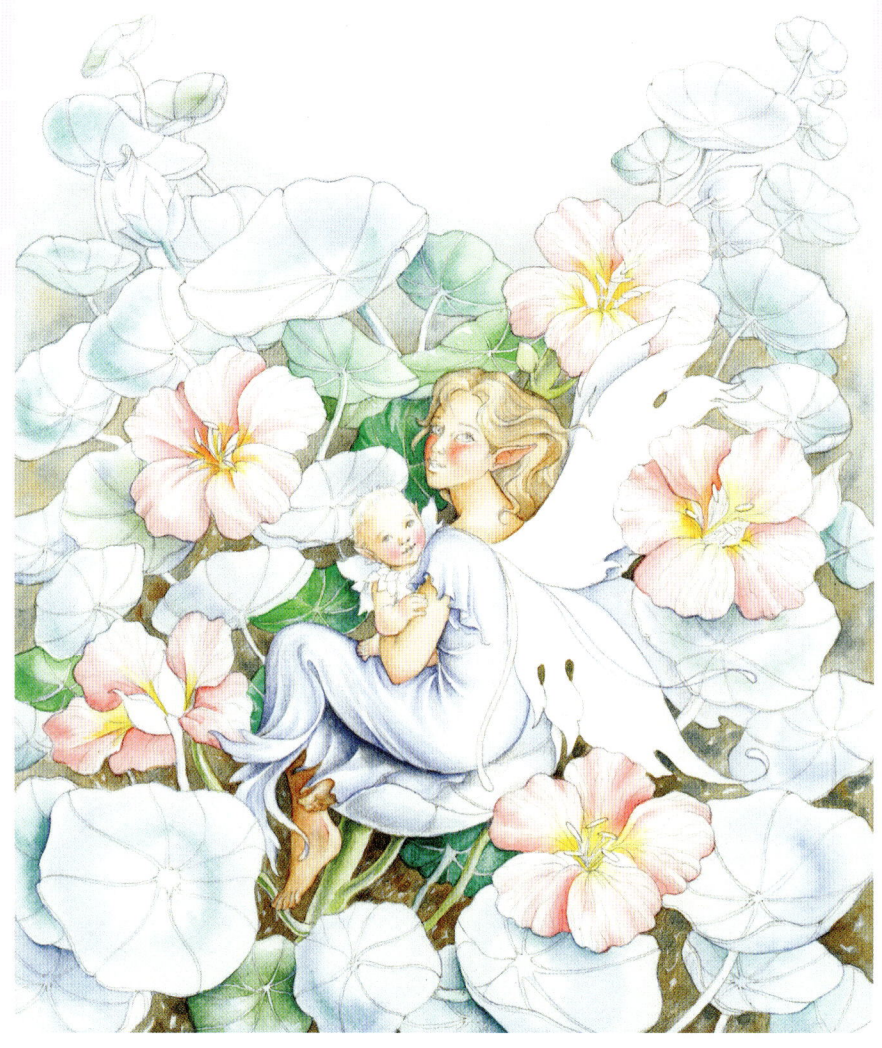

**5** Using a no. 00 round, apply a medium tint of Quinacridone Red to the cheeks of both the mother and the baby as well as the inner ears, elbows, ankle bone, toes and the baby's arm. With a mixture of Vermilion Hue, Burnt Umber and Chinese Orange, paint the skin of both fairies, using a more diluted mixture for the baby. Using a no. 1 round, paint individual strands of the Mother Fairy's hair with a medium tint of Burnt Umber. With a no. 0 round, apply a pale mixture of Yellow Ochre and Raw Sienna for the Baby Fairy's hair. Paint the folds and creases of the Mother Fairy's dress using a no. 1 round loaded with Indanthrene Blue.

*To paint the background leaves, follow the technique demonstration on this page.*

## TECHNIQUE DEMONSTRATION — *Painting the Background Leaves*

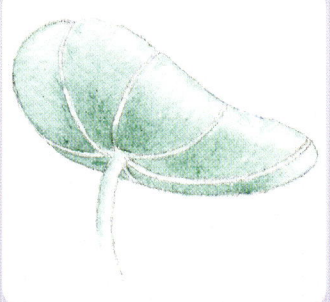

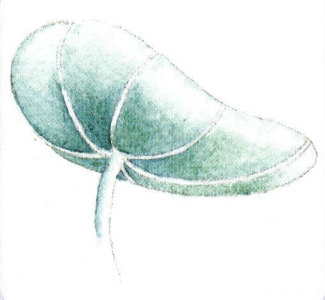

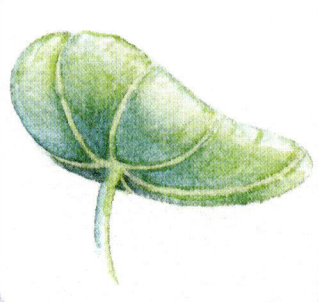

**1** On the background leaves, wet each wedge between the veins. Using a no. 1 round, charge Viridian into one wedge at a time, blending upward to a pale tint. Paint the edge of the leaf with a very pale tint of Viridian loaded on a no. 2 miniature.

**2** Wet one wedge at a time and then, using a no. 1 round, charge each wedge with Cobalt Blue. Apply Cobalt Turquoise Light to each wedge near the vein, blending towards the center.

**3** Wet one wedge at a time. With a no. 1 round, apply Oxide of Chromium to the leaf as it turns towards the light and along the top edge. Let dry and then apply clear water to set the colors.

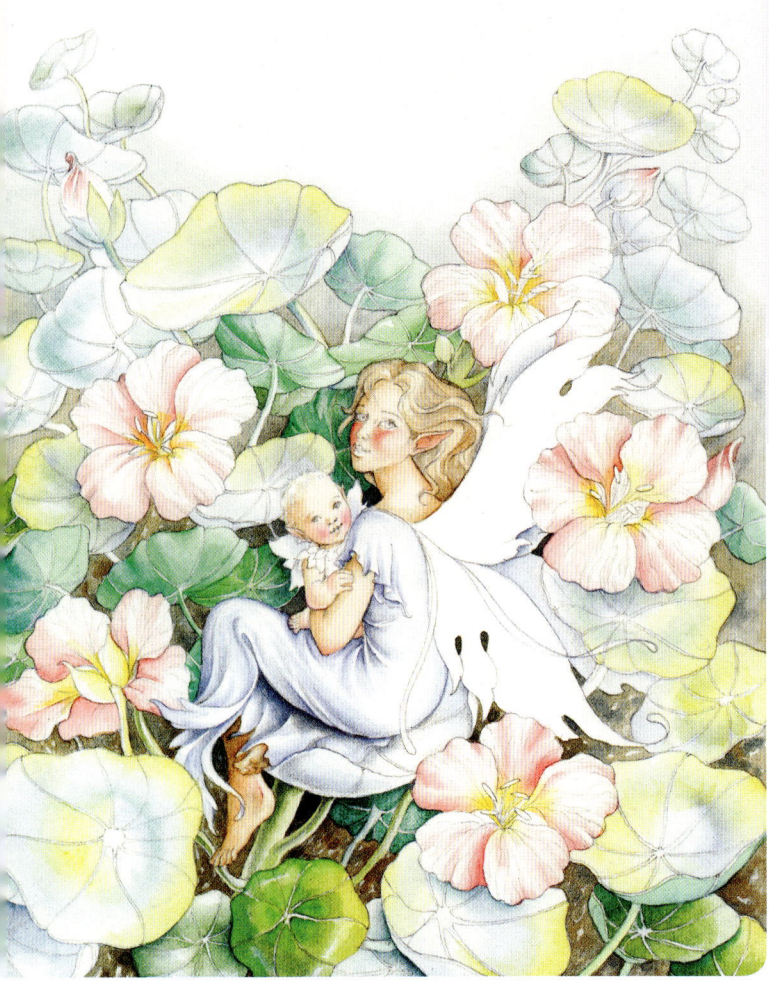

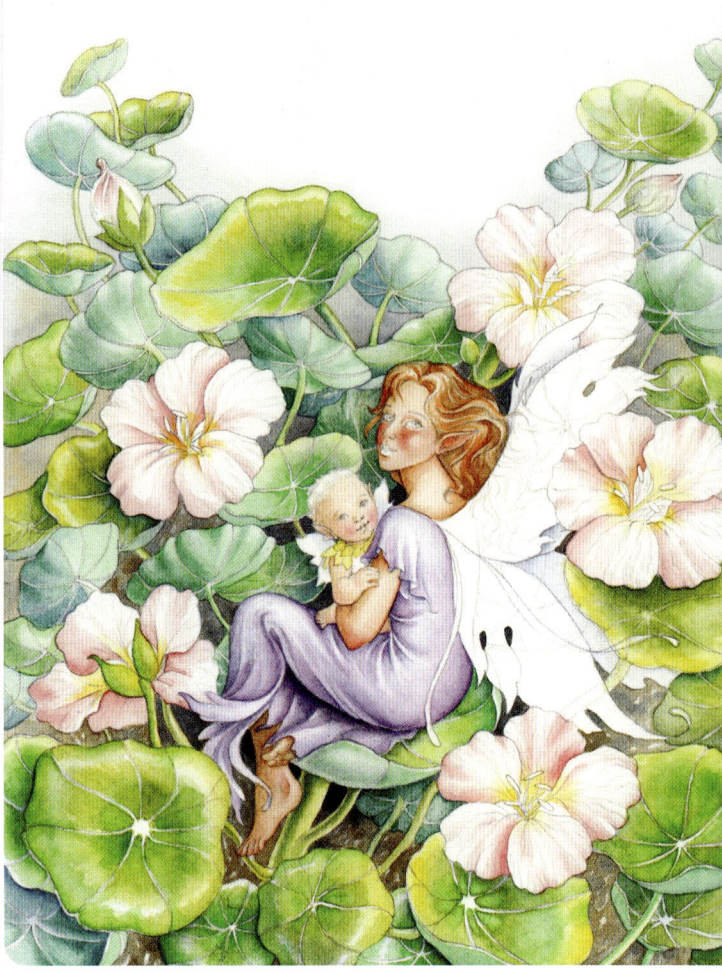

**6** Use a medium tint of New Gamboge loaded on a no. 1 round to paint the areas of the leaves that face the sun, usually around the outer edge of the leaves. Once dry, begin painting the leaves in the foreground using Olive Green over the layer of New Gamboge. Use Cobalt Blue on the shaded side of the large leaf on the extreme lower left. Paint the undersides of the leaves that turn up with a mixture of Winsor Emerald and Chinese White.

**7** Continue painting the leaves one at a time, charging the Olive Green foreground leaves with a mixture of Permanent Sap Green and Hooker's Green. For the background leaves, use a pale mixture of Winsor Emerald, Viridian and Cobalt Blue. Add Indigo to the areas around the fairies to help bring them forward. Continue to paint the undersides of the leaves with Winsor Emerald, charging with Viridian as in the technique demonstration on page 115.

Glaze the skin of both fairies with a mixture of Cadmium Yellow, Burnt Umber, Chinese Orange and Quinacridone Red. Add Winsor Violet (Dioxazine) to the dress, and New Gamboge to the baby's collar. Add a deeper mixture of Winsor Violet (Dioxazine) and Ultramarine Blue (Green Shade) to the folds of the dress. In pencil, add the details behind the wings of the Mother Fairy, thus taking the first step towards making the wings appear translucent.

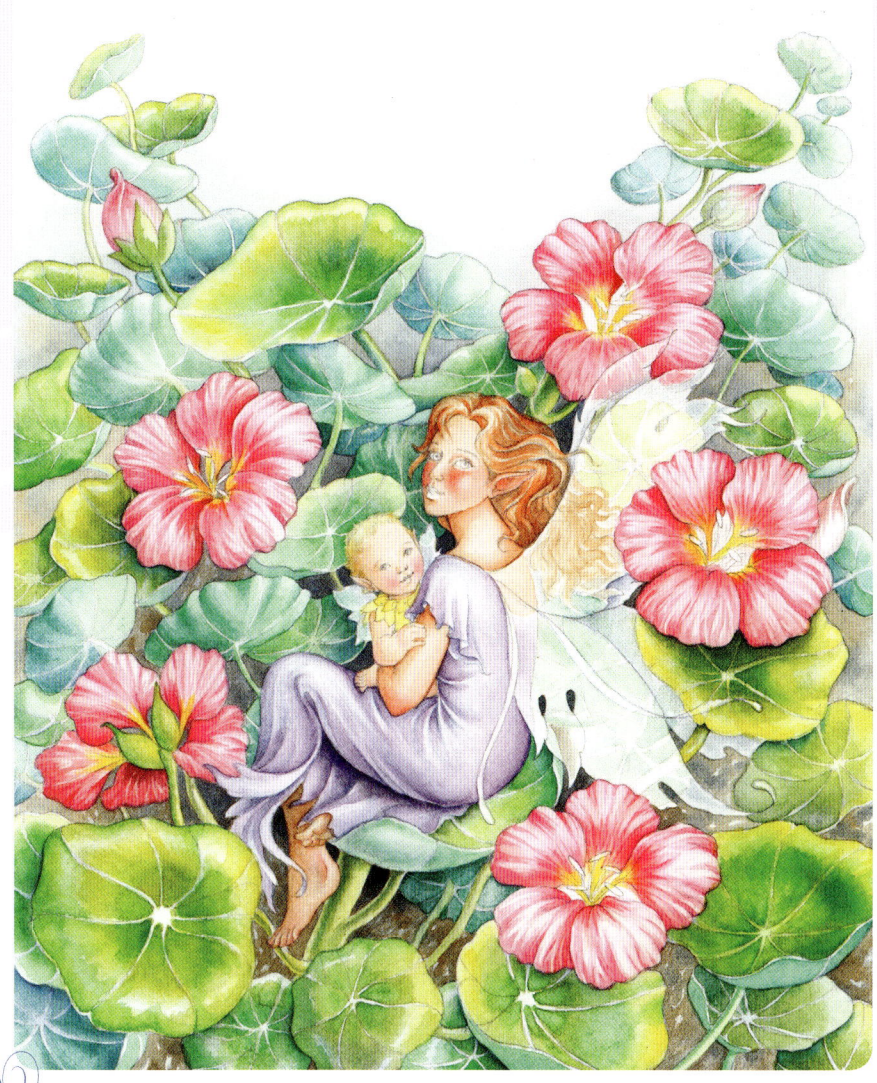

**8** When completely dry, erase any pencil lines that seem too harsh. Use Indigo to further define the spaces between the leaves, behind the flowers and under the figure.

*To create the elements behind the transparent wings, follow the detail demonstration on this page.*

## DETAIL DEMONSTRATION ~ *Creating Transparent Wings*

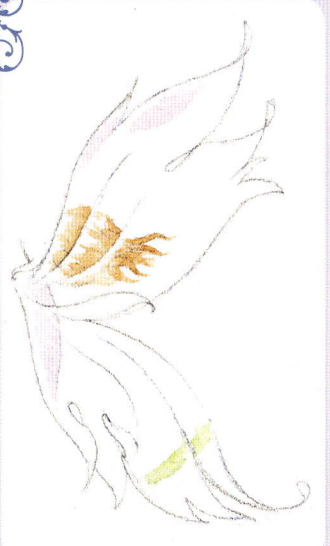

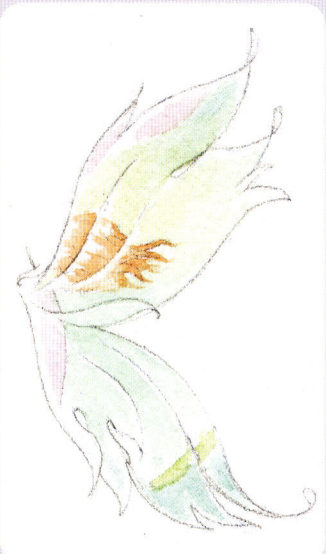

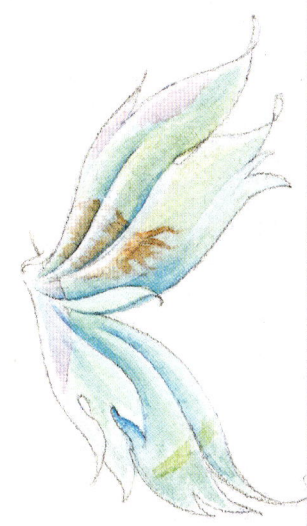

**1** With a no. 2 miniature, apply a mix of Burnt Umber and Chinese Orange to the hair and Permanent Mauve for the back of her dress. Suggest flowers and stems with Quinacridone Red and Olive Green.

**2** Using the same size brush, apply Olive Green on the top portion of the wing and Viridian to the rest of the wing.

**3** For the folds and creases in the wing, apply a medium mixture of Cobalt Turquoise Light and Chinese White. When dry, apply Chinese White to the ridges of the wing folds.

**9** Mix Cobalt Turquoise Light and Chinese White to paint the fairy wings, blending outward with clear water. Wet one petal at a time and glaze with Quinacridone Red, charging Opera into the flower centers. Add Hooker's Green, Olive Green and New Gamboge to the tops of the leaves, bringing them forward. Define the undersides of the leaves further using Viridian and Cobalt Turquoise Light.

*To complete the fairies' eyes, follow the detail demonstration on this page.*

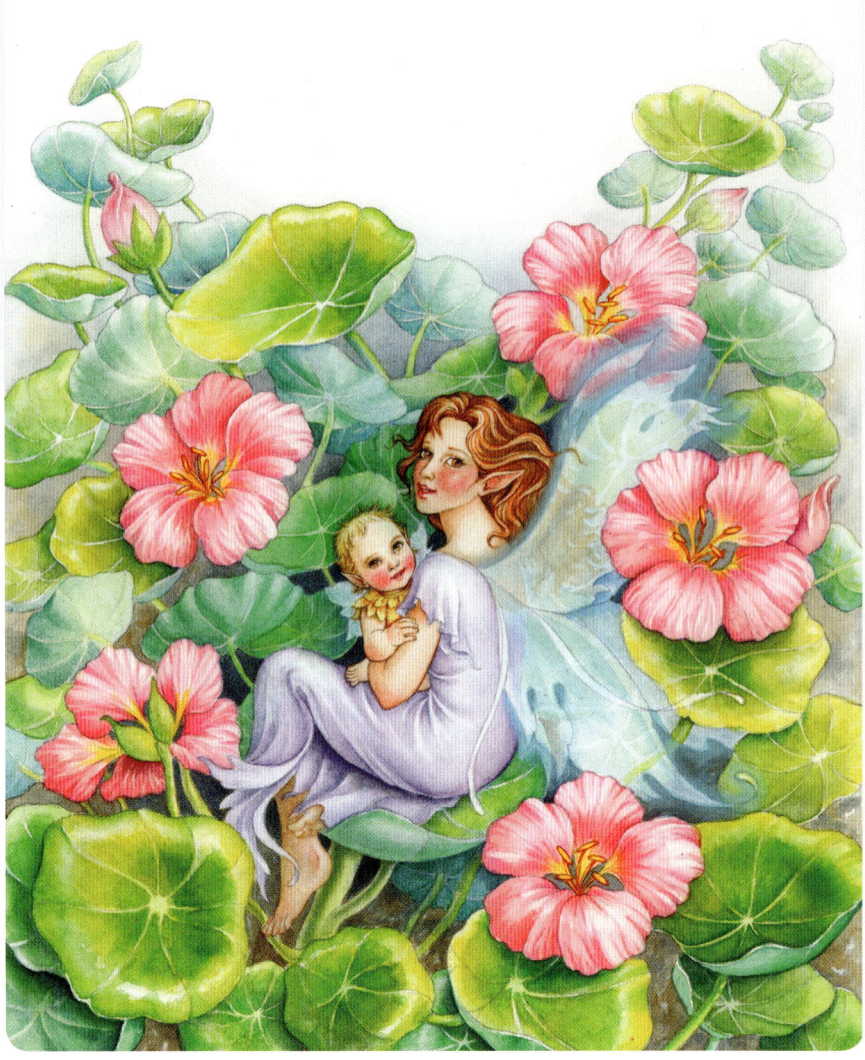

## DETAIL DEMONSTRATION ~ *Fairy Eyes*

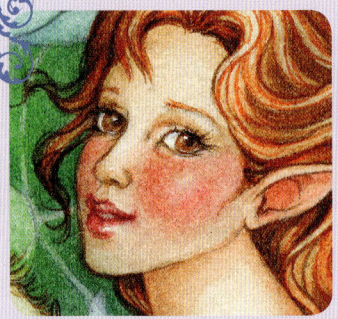
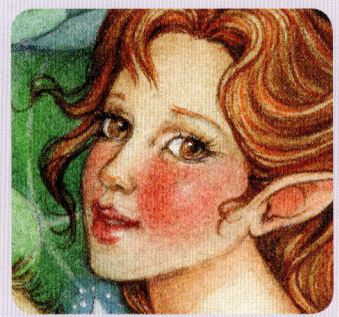

**1** Paint the Mother Fairy's irises with a mixture of Burnt Umber, Chinese Orange and Sepia. Paint the pupils with Ivory Black and add highlights with a dot of Chinese White.

**2** Use a mixture of Chinese White and Yellow Ochre to add highlights by painting tiny arcs. Finish the Baby Fairy's eyes in the same manner.

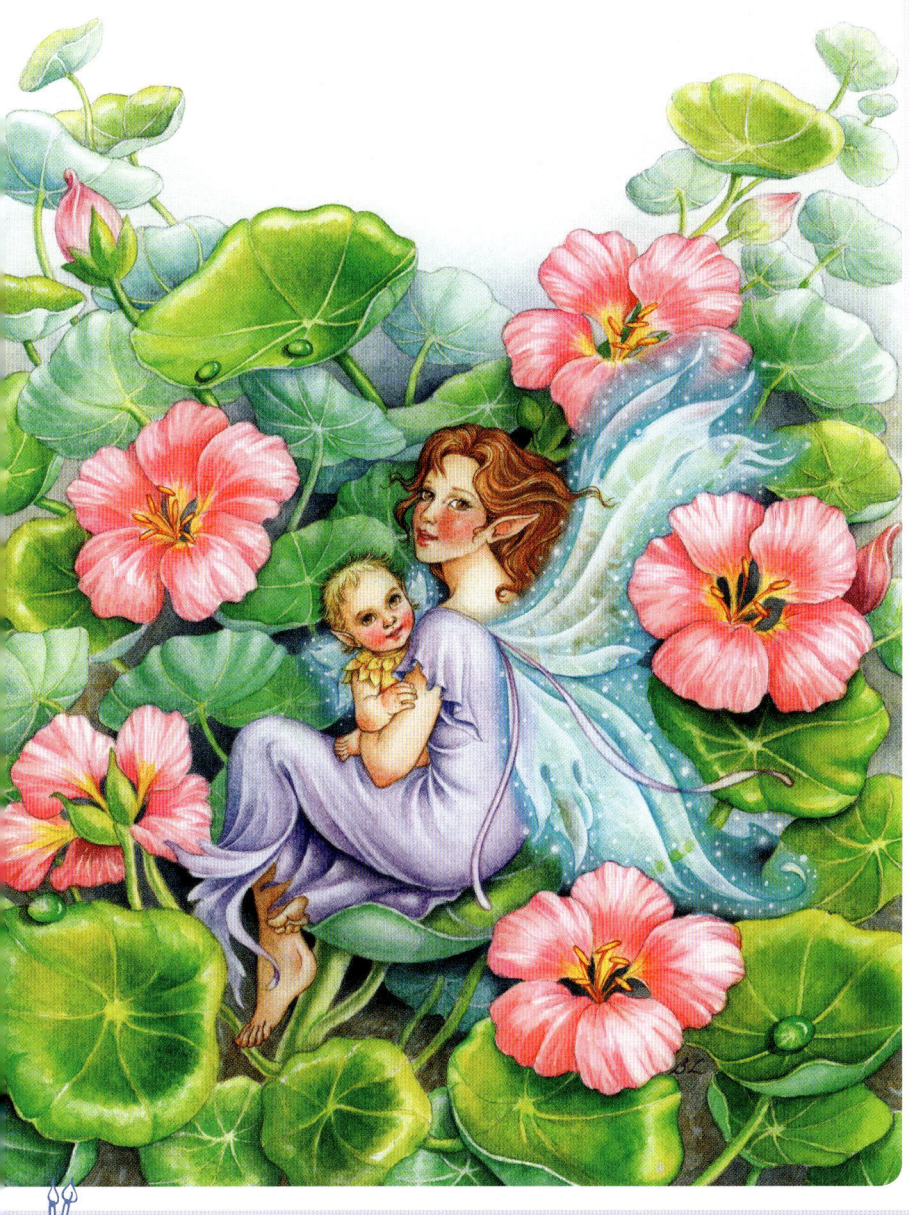

**10** With a no.1 round, apply clear water along the veins of the leaves and blot to remove any heavy color. Paint the veins of the leaves with New Gamboge loaded on a no. 00 round. Use Chinese White to highlight the edges and folds of the wings, then use diluted Cobalt Turquoise Light to define the back wing. Paint the fine wing strands with Permanent Mauve. Use Burnt Umber to suggest fine strands of hair for the Mother and Baby Fairy.

*To create the sparkling effects on the wing, follow the steps in the technique demonstration on this page.*

*Create the dewdrops using the method described in the Morning Fairy demonstration on page 50.*

## TECHNIQUE DEMONSTRATION — *Creating Fairy Dust*

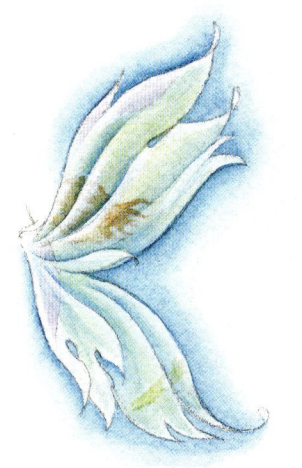

**1** Using a no. 1 round, apply a medium dark tint of Cobalt Turquoise Light along the outside edge of the wing. Let dry.

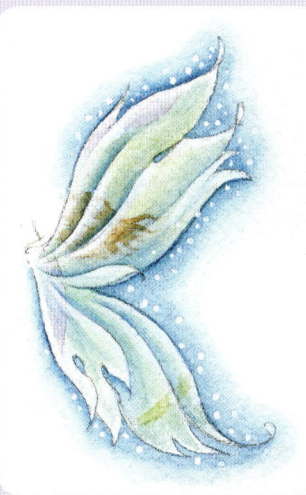

**2** With a no. 000 round, apply dots of Chinese White over the Cobalt Turquoise Light. Let dry.

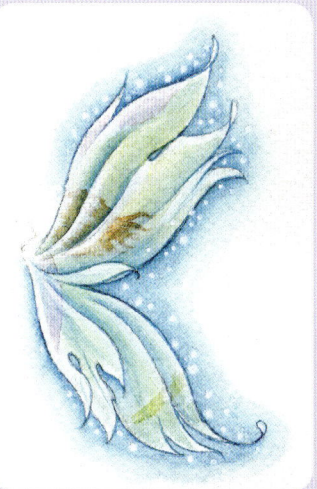

**3** With the same size brush, apply clear water around the white dots, blending the edges into the background.

DEMONSTRATION
# FAIRY DANCE

For this demonstration, I recommend using acrylics, which will help you achieve texture in the background and on the wings. When stippling, allow the pigment to dry a bit on the brush and keep the brush perpendicular to the paper. Practice on scrap paper until you have the hang of it to ensure consistency.

## ~YOU WILL NEED~
### MATERIALS
1½-inch (38mm) flat ~ ½-inch (12mm) stipple brush ~ blue tape ~ hard-leaded pencil or ballpoint pen that has run out of ink ~ HB or 2B graphite pencil ~ kneaded eraser ~ masking fluid ~ no. 1 acrylic brush ~ nos. 000, 0, 1, 2 and 6 rounds ~ square masking fluid pickup ~ stretched watercolor paper ~ tracing paper

### PIGMENTS
Burnt Umber ~ Carbon Black ~ Cerulean Blue Hue ~ Diarylide Yellow ~ Emerald Green ~ Indian Red ~ Nickel Azo Yellow ~ Olive Green ~ Phthalo Blue (Green Shade) ~ Phthalo Blue (Red Shade) ~ Process Cyan ~ Quinacridone/Nickel Azo Gold ~ Quinacridone Red ~ Quinacridone Violet ~ Raw Umber ~ Red Oxide ~ Sap Green ~ Ultramarine ~ Violet Oxide ~ Yellow Ochre

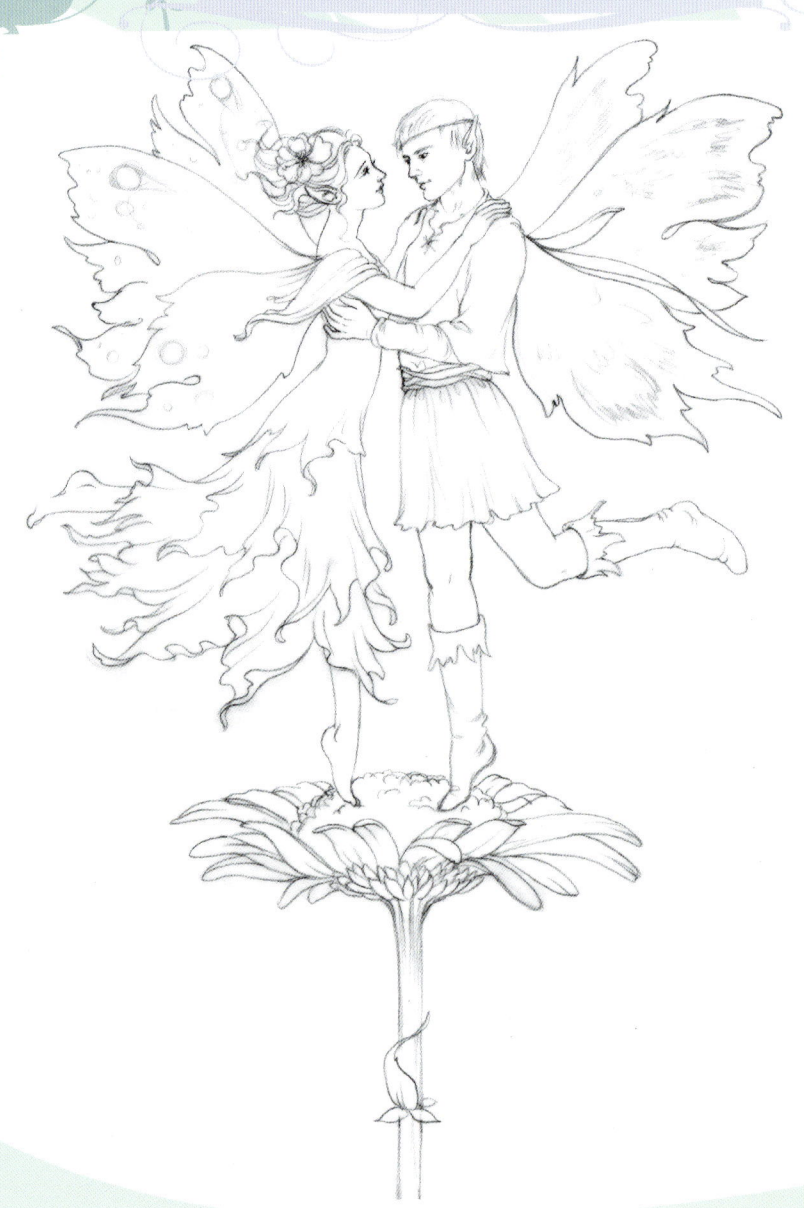

**1** Stretch your watercolor paper and trace the image following the steps on pages 14 and 15. Coat your brush with soap using a moistened bar and then load it with masking fluid. Cover all the areas in the foreground, including the fairies and the sunflower.

*Create the background by following the technique demonstration on page 121.*

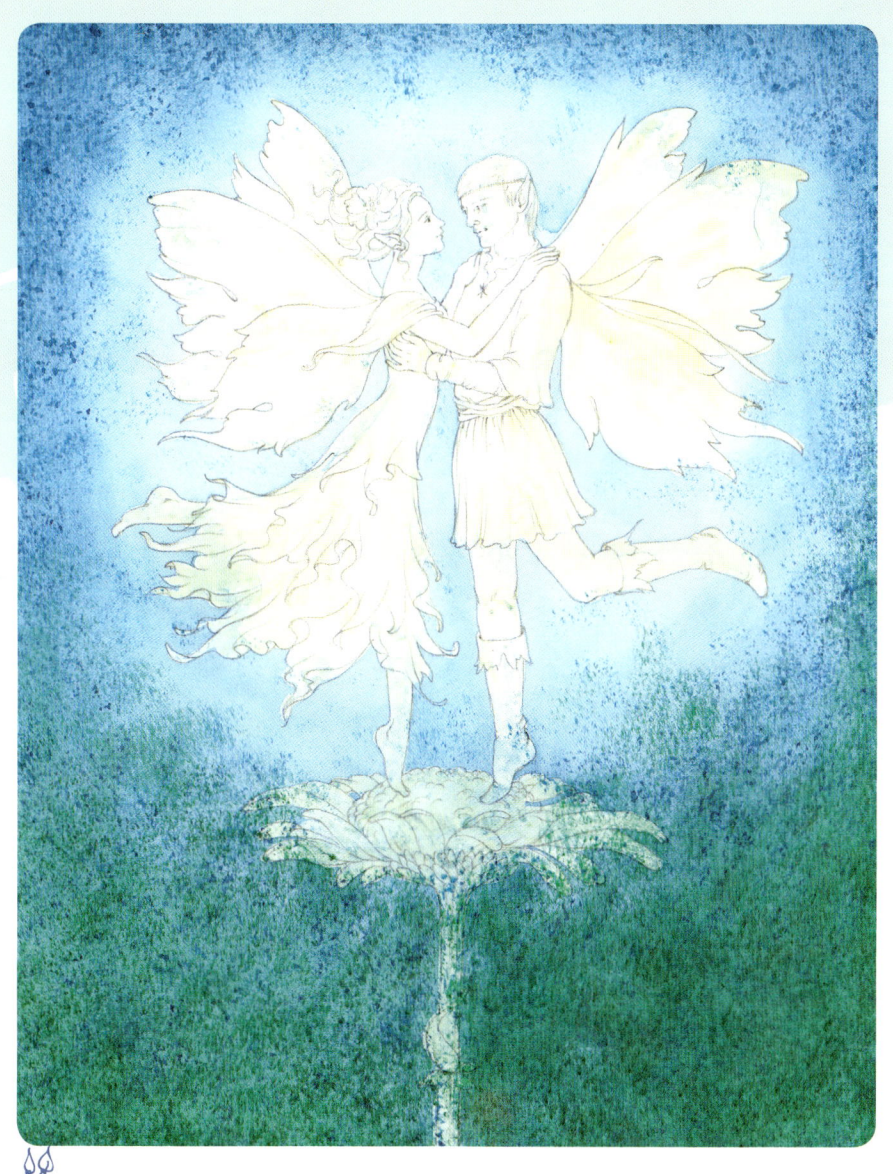

**2** When the background has dried, apply a somewhat dry mixture of Emerald Green on the bottom of the picture with the stipple brush. When that has dried thoroughly, wet the entire background again and, using the 1½ (38mm) flat, soften and blend the texture. This will create a more mottled effect.

Next, mix a medium tint of Cerulean Blue Hue and Phthalo Blue (Green Shade) and apply it to the upper three quarters of the painting using the flat brush. Using the same technique, add pure Emerald Green to the lower quarter of the paper.

## TECHNIQUE DEMONSTRATION — *Creating the Background*

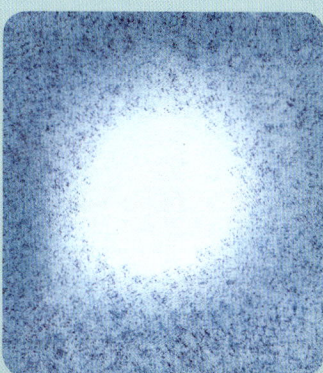

**1** Wet the entire background area using a 1½-inch (38mm) flat. When the surface shine has gone, use the same brush to apply a medium tint of Cerulean Blue Hue to the center of the background (behind the figures), guiding your brush outward in a circular motion.

**2** Using the 1½-inch (38mm) flat, overlap Phthalo Blue (Green Shade) on the outer edge of the Cerulean Blue Hue and repeat the circular motion, blending outward. Let dry.

**3** Using the 1½-inch (38mm) flat, re-wet the entire background. With the same brush, apply a pale tint of Phthalo Blue (Green Shade) to the center of the background and a darker tint to the outside. Let dry.

**4** Using the ½-inch (12mm) stipple brush, apply a somewhat dry mixture of Cerulean Blue Hue and Phthalo Blue (Green Shade) lightly to the area around the dancing fairies.

**3** Using a no. 1 round, begin painting the shadows of the fairies' skin with a mixture of Burnt Umber and Quinacridone Red. To paint the male fairy's boots, use a mixture of Red Oxide and Carbon Black to create a mottled effect by dabbing the color on with a no. 0 round, letting it dry and then applying clear water with a no. 1 round to soften the effect.

Next, paint the inner part of the female fairy's wing with Quinacridone Red and the inner part of the male fairy's wing with Indian Red. Use a dark tint of Carbon Black to paint his hair and shade hers with a tint of Raw Umber.

*To create the fairies' clothes, follow the detail demonstrations on page 123.*

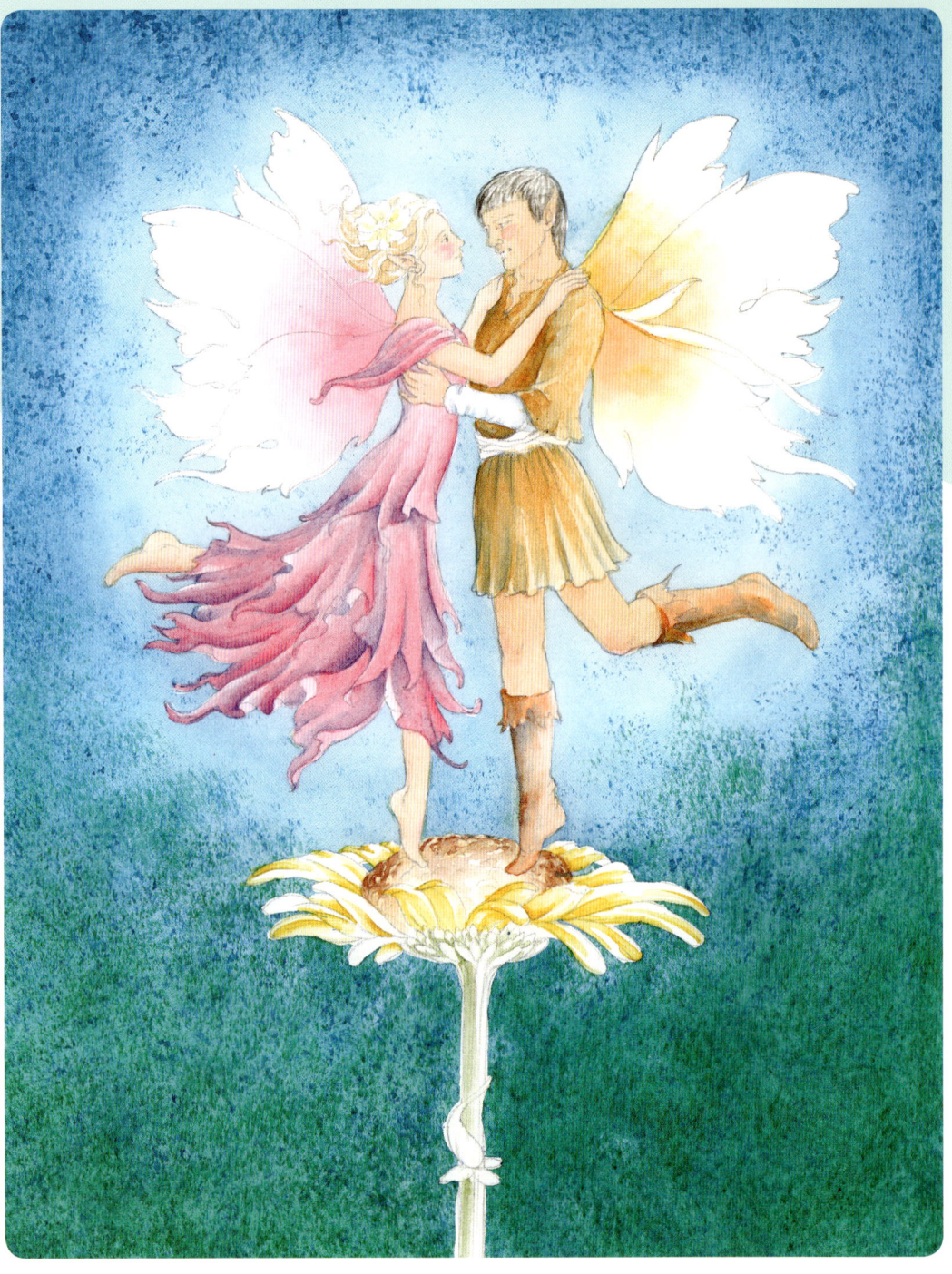

## DETAIL DEMONSTRATION — *Fairy Dress*

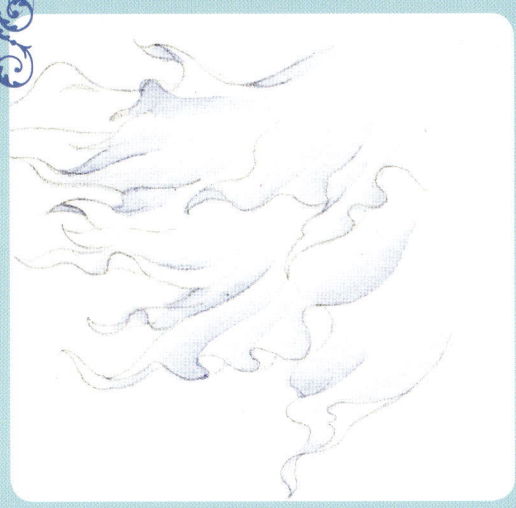 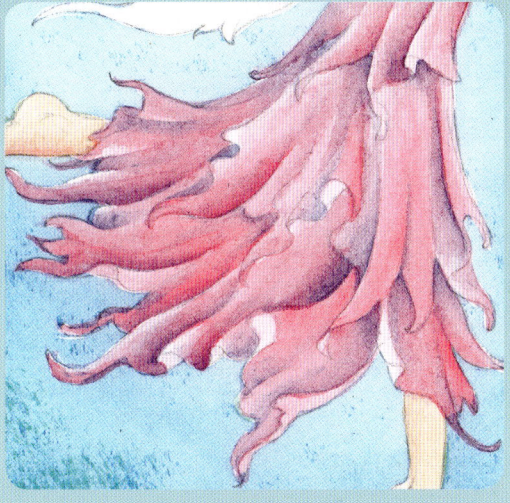

**1** Using a no. 0 round, apply Ultramarine to shade under the folds and creases of the female fairy's dress.

**2** With a no. 1 round, paint some of the outer folds of dress with Violet Oxide, concentrating the color at the tips of the hem and blending inward with clear water.

## DETAIL DEMONSTRATION — *Fairy Tunic*

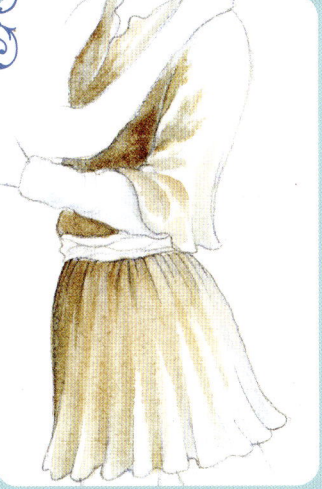 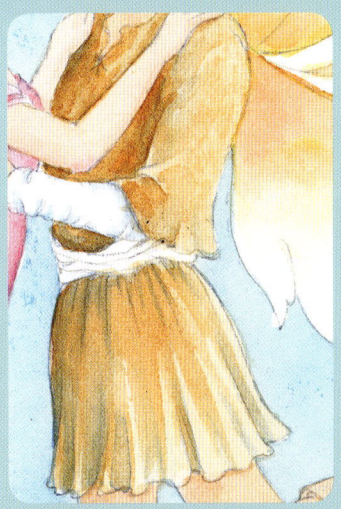

**1** Shade the folds and creases of the male fairy's tunic with a mixture of Burnt Umber and Phthalo Blue (Red Shade) loaded on a no. 1 round, keeping in mind that the light source is on the right.

**2** With the same size brush, paint the tunic with a pale mixture of Yellow Ochre and Red Oxide, using the same dabbing technique used for the boots in step 3. When dry, apply clear water over the tunic to soften the mottled effect.

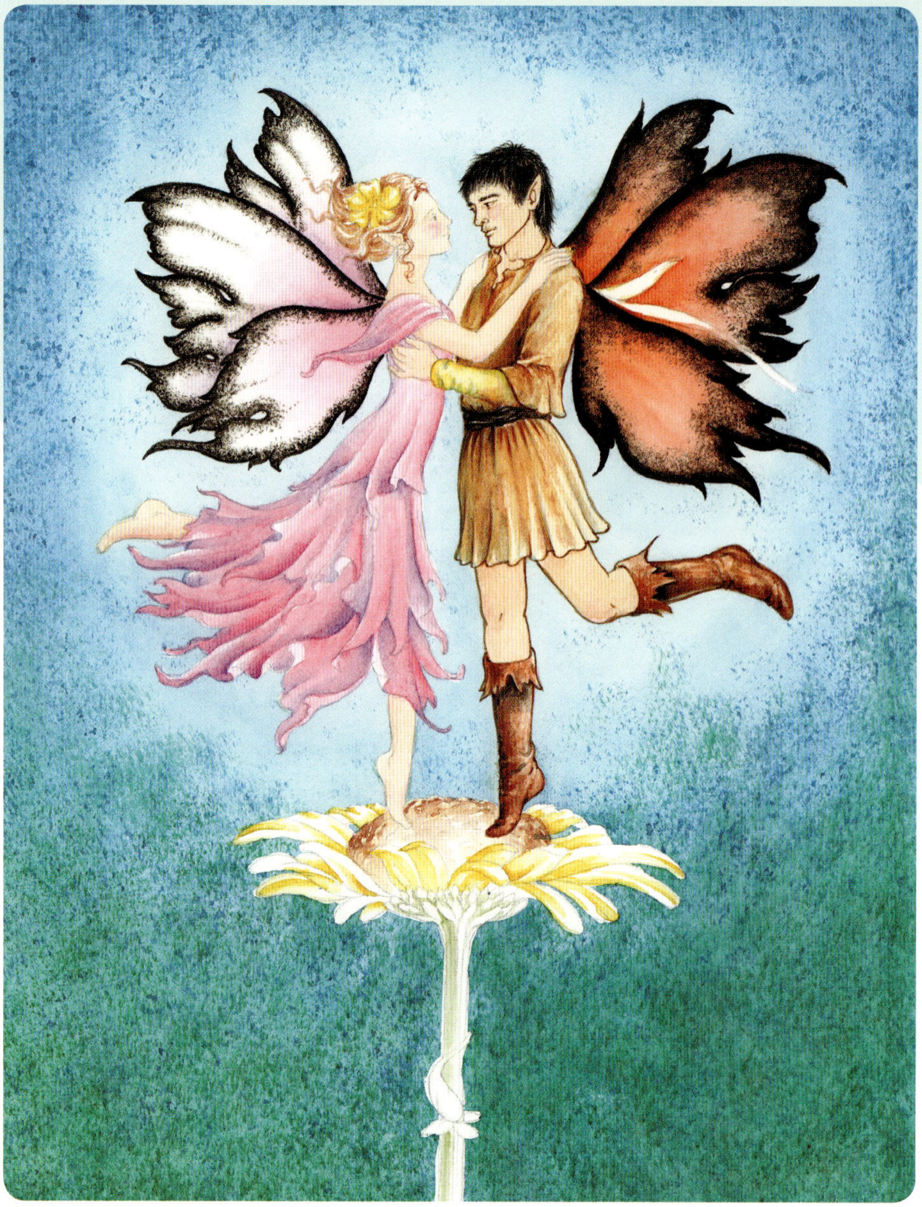

**4** Using a no. 0 round, paint a dark concentration of Carbon Black along the edge of the fairies' wings. Next, create a stipple brush by cutting off more than half of the bristle end of an old acrylic brush. Mix a very dark tint of Carbon Black, allowing it to dry for a minute, and then stipple along the inner edge of the wings using the stipple brush you made. Let dry. Apply clear water with a no. 2 round to the wings to blend the stippling. Begin outlining the figures with Burnt Umber and a no. 000 round then add Yellow Ochre to the male fairy's shirt sleeve and the female fairy's hair.

*To paint the sunflower, follow the detail demonstration on this page.*

## DETAIL DEMONSTRATION — *The Sunflower*

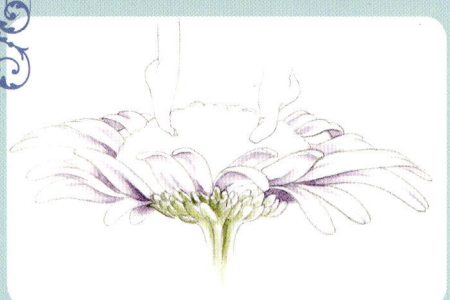

**1** Use Violet Oxide and a no. 0 round to shade underneath the petals. Add Olive Green to the base of the flower and the stem to add dimension.

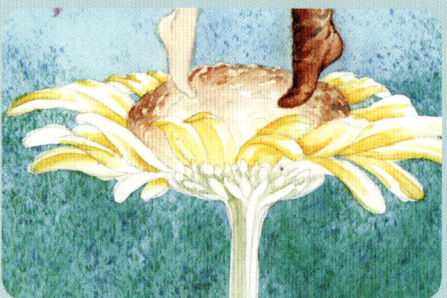

**2** With a no. 0 round, paint the petals with Yellow Ochre as they turn from the light. When almost dry, add Diarylide Yellow along the curves of the petals, blending the colors together with clear water. Paint the center part of the sunflower's seed center with a tint of Burnt Umber.

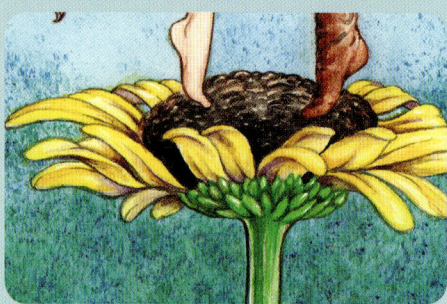

**3** Paint the outer edges of the flower's center with Carbon Black and a no. 0 round. When this is almost dry, create the seed shapes by outlining their curved forms with a mixture of Burnt Umber and Carbon Black. Add Violet Oxide at the base of the petals and, when dry, apply clear water to set the color.

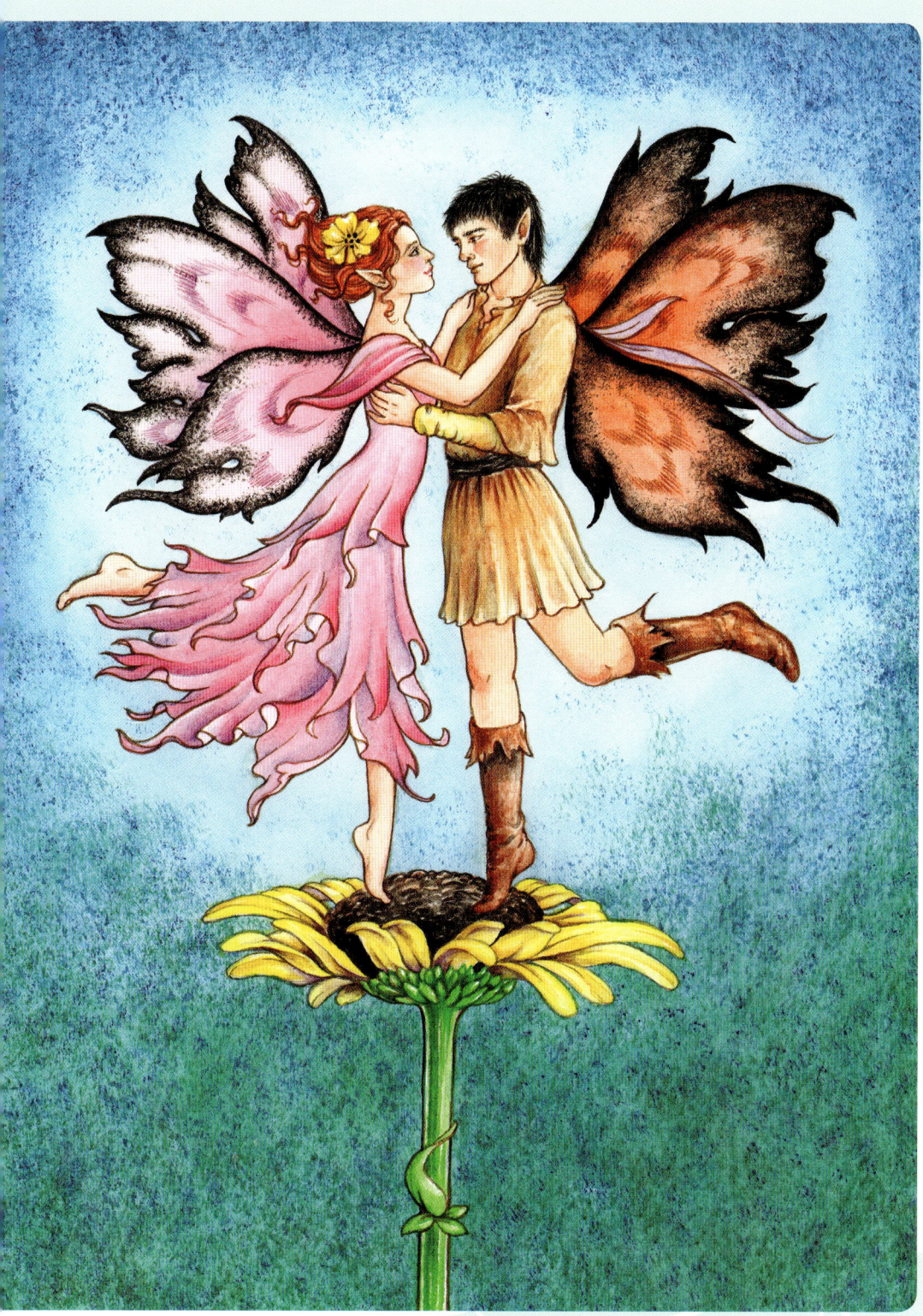

**5** With a no. 000 round, paint individual strands of the female fairy's hair with Indian Red and add detail to the male fairy's hair using short strokes of Carbon Black. Using a strong tint of a mixture of Quinacridone/Nickel Azo Gold and Nickel Azo Yellow loaded on a no. 000 round, add scallop shapes to his wings. Strengthen his wing outline with a mixture of Indian Red and Carbon Black. For the female fairy's wing pattern, mix Violet Oxide and Quinacridone Violet and apply in short, fine strokes. To the base of the sunflower and the stem, add Sap Green. Add a darker tint of Indian Red to strands of the female fairy's hair.

Add stippling to the bottom of painting using Process Cyan, decreasing the amount one third up. With a no. 000 round loaded with Burnt Umber and Carbon Black, outline the figures, wings and flower.

# Index

## A
Acrylic brushes, 21
Acrylic paints, 10–11, 13, 17, 20, 120–25
Acrylic palette, 10–11, 13

## B
Background, 10, 19, 121
   gradated, 65, 99
   night fairy, 62
   wind fairy, 72
   winter fairy, 105
   *See also* Washes
Bristle brushes, 11
Brushes, 10–11
Bubbles, 76, 80–81

## C
Cast shadows, 16
Charging color, 20, 40–41
Chroma, 12
Clothing, for fairies, 26–28, 90, 101, 123
   belt, 67
   *See also* Hats
Color, 12–13, 16–17
   experimenting with, 13, 36
   charging, 20, 40–41
Color harmony, 10–12
Color wheel, 12
Complementary colors, 12, 64
Composition, diagonal, 70
Contrast, 16, 46
Core shadows, 16

## D
Dewdrops, 50, 119
Drying time, speeding up, 14

## E
Elements (types of fairies associated with)
   earth, 64–69
   fire, 82–87
   water, 76–81
   wind, 70–75
Eyes, 34, 55, 118

## F
Fairies
   adolescent, 24–25, 27, 30, 36–39
   adult, 24–25, 28, 31, 40–43, 112–25
   baby, 24–26, 29, 32–35, 88–93, 112–19
   clothing for. *See* Clothing
   faces of, 23–25, 32, 68, 102
   cheeks, 29–30, 48, 63
   ears, 24–25
   eyes, 24–25, 34, 55, 118
   freckles, 39
   lips, 24–25, 56
   noses, 24–25
   figures, 26–31
   hair. *See* Hair
   Native American, 64–69
   wings. *See* Wing
   *See also* Elements; Seasons; Time of day
Fairy dance, 120–25
Fairy dust, 112, 119
Fairy jewelry, 60, 62, 67
Fan brushes, 10
Fire, 82–87
Flat brushes, 10, 14
Flower headdress, 60
Flower wreath, 49
Flowers, 19–20, 32–44, 111
   Chinese Lanterns, 98, 100
   crocus, 88–93
   dandelions, 70–75
   dewdrops, 50–51
   flower buds, 66
   flower hat, 41
   flower petals, 19, 33, 37, 40–41, 49, 90, 92, 114
   hydrangeas, 36–39
   moonflowers, 58–61
   morning glories, 46–49, 51
   nasturtiums, 112–19
   roses, 94–97
   wild, 32–35
   small, 20, 54
   summer garden, 94–97
   sunflowers, 52–57, 120–25
   windflowers, 40–43
Form shadow, 16
Frisket squares, 11, 21

## G
Glazing, 20
Gray, neutral, 12

## H
Hair, 31, 43, 54, 61, 69, 85, 107
Hair dryer, 14
Hard-edged shadows, 16
Hats, 33, 41. *See also* Flower wreath; Headdress; Tiara
Headdress, 60, 68
Highlight, 16
Hue. *See* Color

## I
Image transfer, 15

## J
Jewels, 60, 62, 67

## K
Key color, 13

## L
Layering, 20
Leaves (plant), 47, 72
   nasturtium, 115–16
   rose, 96
Light, 16, 20
   reflected, 16, 19
Light source, 16, 32

## M
Masking fluid, 11, 21
Materials, 10–11
Mermaid scales, 80
Miniature brushes, 10
Mushrooms, 98, 101, 103

## N
Neutral gray, 13
Night background, 62

## P
Paint rags, 11
Paints. *See* Acrylic paints; Watercolor paints
Palette, selection of colors for, 13
Palettes, 10–11
Paper
   selection of, 11

stretching, 14
   watercolor, 14–15
Pearls, 60, 62, 81
Pencils, 11
Petals. *See* Flowers
Pigments, 13
Primary colors, 12
Proportions, 26–28

## R
Reflected light, 19

## S
Sable brushes, 10
Scales, mermaid, 80
Seagrass, 79
Seasons (types of fairies associated with)
   autumn, 98–103
   spring, 88–93
   summer, 94–97
   winter, 104–9
Secondary colors, 12
Shades, 12, 17
Shadows, 16, 30
   blending, 20
Skin tone, 28, 40–41, 53, 59
Smoke, 86
Snowflakes, 107–8
Soft-edged shadows, 16
Stems (plant), 72. *See also* Flowers
Stipple brush, 10
Stippling, 10, 120–21, 124–25
Stretching watercolor paper, 14
Summer garden, 94–97

## T
Tail, mermaid (fin), 78
Temperature, of color, 12, 17
Tertiary colors, 12
Texture, 10–11, 120
Tiara, 108
Time of day, 16
   types of fairies associated with
      morning, 45–51
      night, 45, 58–63
      noon, 45, 52–57
Tints, 12, 17
Torch, 84
Tracing an image, 15, 21, 29
Transfer paper, 15
Tree branches, 106

## V
Value, of color, 12, 17

## W
Wash brushes, 14
Washes, 10, 18–19
   acrylic, 18
   gradated, 65, 99
   watercolor, 18
   *See also* Background
Water, painting, 76–81
   *See also* Bubbles; Dewdrops
Watercolor paints, 10–11, 13, 20
Watercolor palette, 10–11, 13
Waves, painting, 77
Wet-into-wet method, 19
Wings, 23, 26–31, 34, 38–39, 40–43, 50, 61, 66, 78, 96, 102, 112, 116–17
Wreath, flower, 49

# Learn From the Pros With North Light!

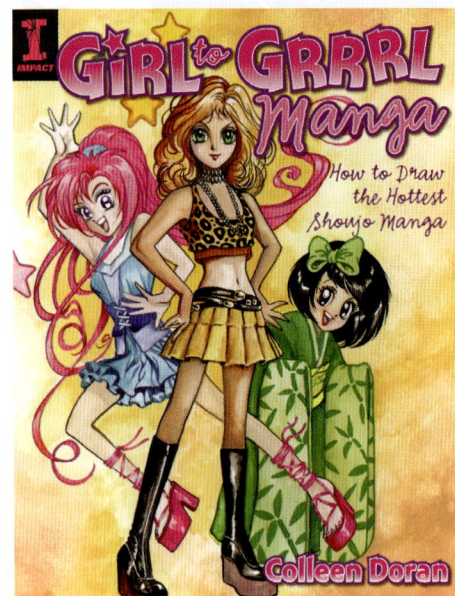

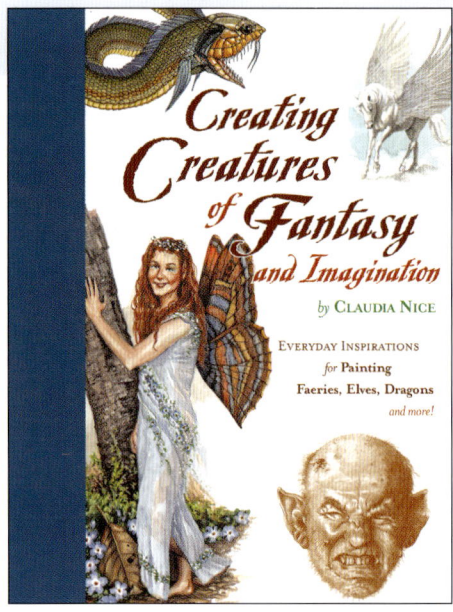

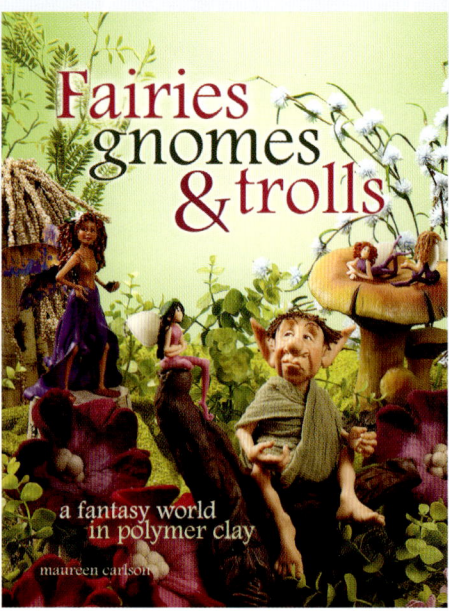

*Girl to Grrrl Manga* is your invitation to the drama, high romance and dreamlike settings of shoujo manga! Page after page of step-by-step instruction lets you get right to it as you learn the simple tricks to drawing different shoujo looks... Beautiful, glamorous girls in funky costumes. Gorgeous guys with smoldering, direct gazes and tortured storylines. You'll see how the smallest details, like extra-long eyelashes or a highlight on the lips, can make the biggest difference!

**ISBN-13: 978-1-58180-809-4;
ISBN-10: 1-58180-809-7;
Paperback; 128 pages; #33487**

Learn to create realistic-looking fantasy artwork with this latest book by Claudia Nice, one of the foremost pen & ink, watercolor artists and teachers. With Nice's characteristic friendly instruction you'll learn ways to create everything from unicorns to pixies and centaurs to dragons, as well as easy methods to add accessories, homes and vibrant backgrounds.

**ISBN-13: 978-1-58180-618-2;
ISBN-10: 1-58180618-3;
Hardcover; 128 pages; #33189**

Open the secret door into the fantastical world of fairies, gnomes and trolls when you create the magical figurines in this whimsical polymer clay book. Author Maureen Carlson gives step-by-step instruction for creating each fairyland creature in the book. A wide array of variations provides inspiration for making your own imaginary world.

**ISBN-13: 978-1-58180-820-9;
ISBN-10: 1-58180-820-8;
Paperback; 128 pages, # 33502**

*Fast & Fun Flowers in Acrylics* gives you all you need to create great looking paintings right away. Featuring more than 50 step-by-steps in subjects ranging from garden flowers to wildflowers that can be completed in 8 steps or less, you'll discover a simplified approach to painting beautiful flowers. Plus, a bonus section on embellishments such as butterflies, ladybugs, dragonflies and dewdrops, plus 6 complete paintings created from the flowers shown in the book.

**ISBN-13: 978-1-58180-827-8;
ISBN-10: 1-58180-827-5;
Enclosed wire-o; 128 pages; #33503**

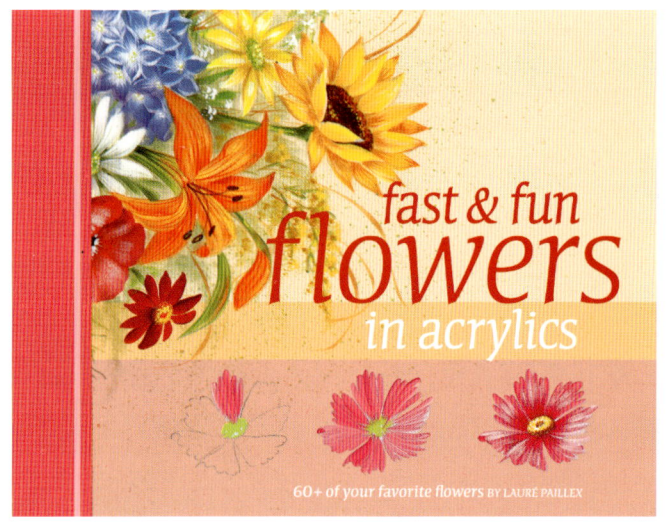

**THESE BOOKS AND OTHER FINE NORTH LIGHT TITLES ARE AVAILABLE AT YOUR LOCAL FINE ART RETAILER OR BOOKSTORE OR FROM ONLINE SUPPLIERS.**